21075

MODERN REFORM EXAMINED;

E
449
.S86

OR,

THE UNION OF NORTH AND SOUTH

ON THE

SUBJECT OF SLAVERY.

BY JOSEPH C. STILES.

PHILADELPHIA:
J. B. LIPPINCOTT & CO., PUBLISHERS,
NOS. 22 & 24 NORTH FOURTH STREET.
1857.

Entered, according to Act of Congress, in the year 1857, by

JOSEPH C. STILES,

in the Clerk's Office of the District Court of the United States for the Southern District of New-York.

INTRODUCTION.

Years have passed since I dwelt on the territory of the Third Presbytery of the City of New-York, of which I am a member. I have consequently been denied the privilege of attending many of its sessions during that period. I especially regret my absence from its last five meetings, devoted as they were mainly to the discussion of the late movement of the American Home Missionary Society respecting slaveholding churches. That movement of my brethren of the Society I do not approve. Since, therefore, my Presbytery deemed it proper to send to the General Assembly a strong vote in its support, I rejoice in that moderation which finally declined to pass the commendatory resolutions so elaborately discussed.

Indeed, so deep has been my interest in that great question which agitates all society in our day—which lies at the foundation of diversities, Denominational as well as Presbyterial—and which has so recently once more divided our unhappy Church—that I do respectfully solicit of my brethren of the Presbytery and of my Christian brethren and countrymen at large, the privilege of laying before them some general views upon this subject.

I am alive to all the uncomfortableness of this step—the seeming forwardness yet painful publicity—the apparent voluntary contribution to the controversy—the necessity of decided disapproval of sentiments so warmly espoused by many excellent men—nor would I forget the possibility, that the grand error, after all, may be rather with myself than with my brethren.

Notwithstanding all this, strong conviction, and the hope of serving the cause of God and man, prompt me to commend myself to our common Master, and proceed at once to the discharge of the duty undertaken.

The *title* of the Book needs a word of explanation. The phrase, "*Modern Reform*," is a little abstract; but it suggests the *exceptionable* character of the *Reformation spirit* of our day, and avoids the unwelcome synonym—"*Abolitionism.*"

The phrase, "*Union of North and South*," may seem a little high-sounding. The reader will relieve himself by interpreting it, not as asserting an achievement, but suggesting a principle. And yet the reader will be deceived if he looks for a logical argument direct to the point of *union.* I have but little experience, but venture to presume that books are not often written to fit titles. He who would unite the North and the South should address himself to a three-fold work—examine and refute extreme Anti-Slavery views—set back liberty and slavery to their just and proper bounds in the public mind—and press the grounds of conciliatory appeal. This is a tolerably fair representation of the topics discussed—but they have not been evolved by the prosecution of a preconcerted plan to conciliate dissensions. The two last topics, just views of liberty and slavery, and political and Christian union, spring up rather in the way of natural suggestions or impromptu improvement by a mind—*set to work to examine extreme Anti-Slavery views.* (*Italics, in quotations, are often my own.*)

CONTENTS.

CHAPTER I.

CHAPTER II.

CHAPTER IX.

APPENDIX.

CHAPTER I.

PRELIMINARY OBSERVATIONS.

THE universe holds only one free Being—God over all! *Subordination* is the grand law of all created mind. In subjection to authority, lies the only escape from the evils of anarchy—confusion, crime, and calamity: the only passport to the welfare of the community—virtue, order, and salvation.

Human society presents four grades of rectitude in the authority exercised by man over his fellow-men. There are relations involving authority—right in their nature, though sometimes wrong in their circumstances—relations wrong in their nature, which may yet be right in their circumstances—relations wrong in their nature, and only tolerable under peculiar circumstances—and relations so utterly vicious in their nature, as never to be tolerated under any circumstances.

The first class consists of four species. Such as have their foundation in divine institution—as, Pastor and People; in human structure—as, Parent and

Child; in human structure and divine ordinance—as, Husband and Wife; and in social necessity and divine institution—as, Magistrate and People. These constitute the only natural and permanent sources of authority in the family of man.

The second class finds a specimen in the relation of Master and Servant. In general this is a condition of human society which, in its origin, all must acknowledge a most heinous offense in the sight of God and man; but its perpetuation, under certain circumstances, constitutes the only discharge of the great duty incumbent on the one party—the only protection of the great right possessed by the other. The relation of master and servant has its origin and its apology in man's fall, and will be swept away in the progress of the Gospel.

The third class is represented by Polygamy — a relation never right, either in its nature or its circumstances. All that can be said in its behalf is this—time was when God tolerated it. This relation does not belong to the second class, though always located in this category. There are three things decisively peculiar to polygamy. God never so far arranged for its introduction amongst a people, as to direct where a man should go to find his many wives. This God did do touching the master and his slaves. Again: God never drew up a code of laws regulating the duties of the one husband to his many wives, on the one hand, nor of the many wives to the one husband, on the other. This God has done in the case of master and slave. Finally: God substantially pronounces Polygamy a sin, both in the Old Testament and in the New, and dismisses it forthwith from the world. This God has not done in regard to slavery, either in the Old Testament or in the New.

The fourth class consists of connections instituted by bad men for the sole purpose of perpetrating iniquity. Such as Slave-making, Piracy, etc. Under all circumstances, all such relations are insufferable.

Humanity has four grand states. The last two lie in the future—judgment and retribution. The first two have been developed in time—the original constitution of things and man's fall from it. Our views of slavery, I judge, should vary, as we place our stand-point in the first temporal condition of things or the second. Man's Author, structure, relations, and end, proclaim this truth—God made every man the proprietor of the same rights, and subject to the same duties.

Under the original constitution of things, be the circumstances what they may, the existence of slavery would seem to us as inconceivable as the sin of slavery would be insufferable. The moment man fell two changes take place. The first palpable change is this: slavery, inconceivable in the first condition of things, comes into existence very naturally in the second. Man will introduce it. He now seeks himself supremely, and hating labor, in his superior strength, will force the weaker to work for him. God will introduce it. If to express his displeasure with sinning man he introduces earthquake, tempest, pestilence, famine, and war, it is perfectly natural that he should employ this unnatural institution, and many other similar evils, for the same purpose.* The second palpable change is this: slavery, so necessarily sinful in the first condition of humanity, may be entirely free from sin in the second. The sinful conduct of man may justify bondage both temporary and permanent. It is ascertained with absolute certainty, that the captain and his crew have plotted to put every passenger to death, take possession of the ship, and become pirates on the high sea. Nay, they have commenced their work of murder. The passengers rise, subdue their enemies, put them in irons, sternly compel them to navigate the ship into port, and then give them up to the laws of the country, whereby they are condemned to involuntary hard labor for life. Who doubts for one moment, that God's law of love to your neighbor either justifies the temporary captivity of these fellow-men at first, or their subsequent slavery for life? In like manner, the utter incapacity of the subject, in the view of wisdom and benevolence, may justify his continuance in a state of involuntary servitude.

Why is it that all men do not instantly discern and acknowledge these plain truths? Why is it that, on this and other subjects, our fellow-men do sometimes

* Does he not employ it to evangelize the heathen? Gen. 17:12, 13.

seem to exhibit a singular and incurable perverseness? Is not man's mind as subject to epidemics as his body? Corrupt the atmosphere, and a multitude of physical constitutions shall imbibe the poison, and exhibit the fact by the most unquestionable marks. In the bosom of valuable truth throw out some captivating error, and there shall spring up in society an unwholesome spirit, marked by a class of symptoms as well defined as those of the measles or the small-pox. Like physical epidemics, mental distemper outworks conservative forces, works strongest in elements most akin to itself, and always works its likeness upon the subject of its operation.

One of the boldest encroachments upon a sound public mind in our day, is the REFORM SPIRIT, or SPIRIT OF PROGRESS, so called.

This *Reform* temper first fastens upon some prevalent evil in society, and then fires itself with such an extreme horror of its sins and mischiefs, as can not endure the slow process of legitimate means, and would therefore hurry its victim to destruction by the most vigorous and violent powers it can command. The moral character of this agent is mixed. Ordinarily, it is right in its object and its energy, but wrong in its temper and its measures. It carries upon its face philanthropy, intrepidity, vigor; but is often embittered by a heart of willfulness, intolerance, and violence. Many are unaffected by it, as many are controlled by it; while the greater number, severally, exhibit every degree of its influence intermediate between these extremes. The principle and the peace of Church and State are sufficiently involved by the prevalence and direction of this mighty agent, to demand its moral analysis.

I shall ask your attention to its most prominent demonstration in the EXTREME ANTI-SLAVERY MOVEMENT of the day.

Before I embark upon this discussion, I beg leave to record a few explanations. Let it be understood, that from commencement to conclusion, I am confining myself to the examination of the *extremest* class of Anti-Slavery sentiment prevalent in the country at this day.—Let it be remembered, also, that I do not question for a moment the high degree of personal piety exhibited by many of those who entertain these sentiments, especially such as have enjoyed no opportunities of personal observation, but have been perpetually plied with all the extravagances which such a spirit must enlist.—I may be condemned for an inadequate censure of the obliquities of the South, and perhaps justly. I solicit, however, the kind remembrance of this fact: while the faults of the South are not my subject, indirectly its better qualities are. I purpose to discuss the excesses of a Northern party. The range of the discussion calls for a favorable view of the South, since the wrongdoings of the North can be justly and strongly presented only in view of the claims of the opposite section.—In the ardor of mental operation upon such a subject, I shall often express myself so decidedly and strongly, as to start in my own mind an inclination to pause and explain. Now, let this thought comprise a part of every strong adverse opinion or expression I may utter. At the very moment when I am expressing the most decided condemnation of what I deem pernicious error, I acknowledge my obligation to cherish the very heartiest sympathy with every good thing in the character of him whom I oppose, and as my fellow-creature, to hold his soul to mine by all the chords of the truest fraternity; and the more so, as I am compelled to differ from him so decidedly. I do not say that I shall adhere strictly to this line of duty. But this I do say, just as far as I depart from it—before my injured fellow-man and our glorious Christianity, I offend.

CHAPTER II.

ARROGANT.

YOU will permit me to remind you that this *Anti-Slavery* spirit assumes the office of—a REFORMER. It charges a high immorality, and essays to correct the evil.

If I mistake not, *our Modern Reform defines itself, by taking ground in the teeth of the five capital qualifications of the true reformer.*

The very first motion of accused mind is, to put upon trial the superiority assumed by him who steps forward to correct it. So far as facts permit it to question the preëminence so invidiously asserted, just so far they generate a feeling of self-righteousness impregnable to conviction, and the accused will be sure to fling back the charge in the face of the accuser: "Physician! heal thyself." The primary qualification of a reformer, therefore, is rectitude—the undeniable possession of that personal superiority in virtue practically assumed by an attempt to reclaim another from sin.

Were a candid mind summoned to pronounce the primary property of the *Progress spirit* of our times, he would be apt to respond, it is—

ARROGANT.

The Reformer assumes superiority—

I. In *Character.*—No language can speak the profundity of his self-righteousness in this connection. He never imagines for an instant any kind of comparison of himself with a slaveholder. He never doubts that rectitude is with himself, depravity with his neighbor. It ever lies in his mind, without a question, that he, as it were, is the civilized man, the other the savage; he, the puritan, the other the publican; he, the philanthropist, the other the man-stealer. Should a slaveholder, hard pressed by his vehement denunciations, undertake some sort of defense, he would very probably provoke the ancient retort of outraged phariseeism: "Thou wast altogether born in sin, and dost thou" deign to compare thyself with me. "Stand by, I am holier than thou."

What shall we say of these enormous pretensions to comparative personal rectitude? That there are very many excellent persons amongst those who hold extreme views on this subject, we renewedly and cheerfully acknowledge; but beyond a doubt very many slaveholders, judged by every law which God has addressed to the hearts and consciences of men, are far holier persons than multitudes of those most forward in their condemnation. There are a few masters, 'tis true, who deserve the deepest reprehension for ill-treatment of their slaves; but there are many, very many others who do exhibit the soundest friendship toward those committed to their care, and this, simply as one demonstration of a beautiful Christian character in some, and a symmetrical natural character in others. Our Reformer, on the contrary, while it will be conceded that he practically confers very few blessings upon the slave, certainly does exhibit toward the master such a hard and bitter spirit, and does carry out, in his general deportment, such arrogant and degrading assumptions, as may well start the inquiry whether the slave would not be greatly the loser, in many cases, if the Reformer himself were substituted for the party he so violently toils to improve.

But our more decisive inquiry on this head respects—

II. *Doctrine.*—The great reforming proposition is this:

Slaveholding, or such a state of society as is common at the South, in the very nature of the relation, is sinful in the sight of God. Compulsory servitude—is sin in itself; and therefore never was right at any time—never can be right under any circumstances.

No language can express the supreme confidence of the Reformer in the truth of his principle. Let it be remembered if slaveholding under any circumstances ever was, is, or can be justifiable, then the dogma of the Reformer is overthrown. I can but glance at the impregnable array of adverse evidence.

1. Does not the *law of love* lift up its voice

against this doctrine? Behold the masters and servants of the South! Upon the face of the earth never were two races of men thrown together more diametrically opposed to each other in complexion, condition, capacity, cultivation, connection, and history. Their present coëxistence for good, in any other relation, is an exact impossibility. See how the Free States themselves legislatively fight off the introduction of even a few of the most enlightened of them. Listen to the recent language of Col. John Prince, a member of the Canadian Parliament: "It has been my misfortune, and the misfortune of my family, to live among these blacks (and they have lived upon us) for twenty-four years. I have employed hundreds of them, and, with the exception of Richard Hunter, not one has ever done for us a week's honest labor. I have taken them into my service, have fed and clothed them year after year on their arrival from the States, and in return have generally found them rogues and thieves, and a graceless, worthless, thriftless, lying set of vagabonds. This description of them as a body will be indorsed by all the western white men, with very few exceptions."

At a blow destroy the existing relations of the white and colored population at the South: By an edict of instantaneous and universal emancipation place the parties upon a perfect equality: The sure result will be the rapid and wretched extermination of the inferior. But if the relation of master and servant is sinful in itself, it must be instantly abandoned. Tell me, What kind of love is that which deliberately or furiously plunges a nation of dependents into so dark and bloody a destiny? God's venerable servant in the city of New-York is not the only man who would prefer to go to God's bar and answer for the present bondage of the slaves of the South, rather than for their immediate and universal liberation. Compare, too, the slaves of the South, in all important to man, with their normal condition in their native country, and who can fail to see that from the depths of savage slavery in the black bosom of Africa, since the day that Providence cast them upon our shores, they have been rising, if slowly, yet steadily and soundly, toward civilization, Christianity, and freedom? Should they even fare no better in the future than they have done in the past, what kind of guardian love is that which would cut down at a blow a nation's prospects of rising from the darkest curses to the brightest blessings of humanity?

2. Does not the very law of *human rights* itself discard the doctrine? Whenever a human being by reason of youth, insanity, incapacity, or any other cause, possesses no present power of self-government, under the cover of the great primary law of love to your neighbor, that human being has a right to demand of those upon whom he depends, that they qualify him for freedom. Admit, then, that the slave holds a clear right to be conducted by his master through that process which shall educate him for ultimate

liberty. This very fact proves that the master holds as perfect a right to command the slave with the full, unabridged power of a master's authority. For it is a clear impossibility, in nine cases out of ten, to accomplish the work without it. That very law of human rights, therefore, which gives ultimate freedom to the slave, gives present authority to the master. Carry out your *sin per se* doctrine. It is a *felo de se:* for the slave never gets his liberty.

3. The *word of God* condemns it.

The doctrine is *discountenanced*—

(1.) By the whole face of the Bible. Idolatry, adultery, fornication, falsehood, theft, robbery, drunkenness, violence, murder, and a multitude of smaller offenses, are never mentioned in the Scriptures without decided condemnation; and yet not one word of censure is pronounced upon master and servant, though this relation is brought up frequently and discussed abundantly in the Old Testament and the New.

(2.) By the face of every code of universal and permanent obligation laid down in the book of God. There are three recorded systems of divine legislation whose obligation is commensurate with the extent of the human family, and the duration of time—the covenant with Abraham, the ten commandments, and the gospel of Jesus Christ. Now it is a remarkable fact that each of these august codes, codes of the very highest morality under heaven, contemplate master and servant as an existing state of human society, and lay down regulations for the conduct of the parties, but never pronounce a syllable of distrust of its legality.

(3.) By the whole face of God's treatment both of masters and servants, both in the old world and in the new. By God's authority, masters were members of the Church in good standing under the old dispensation, and members of the Church in good standing under the new dispensation. The only slave reported by the early Scriptures to have abandoned the service of her master, was divinely ordered to return to her duty; the only servant reported by later Scriptures as a fugitive from his master's service, an apostle himself restored to his owner. He whom God selected as the standard man of his race in the great Church covenant, even the father of the faithful, was a great slaveholder. He who in ancient times was pronounced by God the best man on earth, and through all time shall stand the pattern of patience to the race, was a great slaveholder; and he whom Jesus commended as the best man he had seen in his day, whom he seated beside Abraham, Isaac, and Jacob in the kingdom of heaven, was made known to Jesus only through his ownership of a slave, and in the very face of Jesus boldly asserted that ownership, and said: "A man under authority, I say to my servant, Do this, and he doeth it."

The doctrine is *disproved*—

(1.) By God's direction to the Jews, at a time when

they were not slaveholders,* concerning the manner in which, at a future day, they should form the relation of master and servant. Leviticus 25 : 44. Say! can God direct his creature in the formation of a relation which is sinful in itself?

(2.) By God's directions to the Jews concerning what they were to do when they became the owners of slaves. See the slave laws of Moses. Say! can God direct a man to do many things as a master habitually, if to be a master for one moment is sinful in itself? Can the being a master be sinful, if acting as a master is not?

(3.) By God's most explicit and reïterated recognition of the whole sum and substance of the relation in a word. "Ye shall buy bondmen." "They shall be your possession." "He is his money." "Ye shall take them as an inheritance for your children after you." "They shall be your bondmen for ever."

(4.) By God's express recognition in both Testaments of the master's claim to control, correction, service,

* Two things would seem to be true. First,—at this time the Israelites had no slaves. The language indicates this fact. It looks to the future. Thy bondmen, which thou *shalt* have, "*shall* be of the heathen;" "of them *shall* ye buy bondmen." History corroborates it, negatively, for we hear of no slaves among them at this time, nor for the space of forty years; and positively, for they themselves had just been emancipated from the bitterest bondage. Second, God's language on this subject may therefore be termed—divine legislation preparatory to the future introduction of slaves among the Hebrews.

honor, and love. Tell me! can God acknowledge the rights of a relation that is wrong in itself?

(5.) By the commands which God addresses to the Christian masters of the New Testament Church. Tell me! if these masters act in accordance with divine injunctions, can it be sin to do what God commands? If it is sin, can God instruct men how to commit it?

(6.) By the whole catalogue of commands addressed to masters in the word of God. They all pre-suppose the formation and imply the continuance of the relation. Ex.: "Ye masters, forbear threatening." If the relation had not been formed, the command could not have been given! If the relation did not continuc, the command could not be obeyed. Can the ground a man stands on—be sin, when God's commands imply his continued occupancy of it?

(7.) By the explicit teaching of Christ and his apostles on the precise point of the master's authority. I shall assume what the scholar will not deny, that the term "*servant*" in our proof-texts is employed to mean—*slave.*

It will not be denied that God successively and explicitly commands wives, children, and servants to obey their husbands, parents, and masters. What is the import of the command to the servant in this connection? Is it not that he, in his place, is to obey his superior, as the preceding parties, in their respective relations, are to obey theirs? Brethren say that master and slave are not to be placed in the same category with husbands and wives, parents and children. What do they mean? That there are conceivable differences between these relations? To say this, is to say nothing. What two things exist between which there is no specific difference? The argument is not evaded by the existence of a specific difference between these relations, but is established by the existence of a generic resemblance on the point in hand. There is a rightful authority in the husband over his wife, and a rightful authority in the parent over his child. Mark now, the words of Scripture in this very connection speak out an authority in the master over his servant, and speak nothing else. In the face of this simple, unmistakable Scripture teaching, will any man deny the authority of the master? Every rule of interpretation fixes the fact immovably. The first great rule establishes it. Words are to be understood in their most known and usual signification. Scripture words in their plain sense seal the authority of the master and the duty of the slave. A second great rule confirms it. Words are always to be understood with reference to what was previously known of the subject about which they are employed. It was known before that husbands exercised a gentle authority over their wives—that parents exercised a stronger authority over their children—and that masters wielded a still sterner authority over their slaves. Now when Scripture comes along and commands wives to obey their husbands, and children to obey their parents, and slaves to obey their masters, does Scripture teach men that wives are indeed to respect the authority of their husbands, and children are to respect the authority of their parents; but when in this connection it commands slaves to obey their masters, are we to understand by this language that God's word means to revolutionize society, and repeal for ever the master's authority! It is not enough to say that such interpretation is perfectly preposterous—it destroys the Bible! Rather, in accordance with what was previously known upon this subject, Scripture hereby establishes the master's authority. There is a third very similar rule of interpretation just as clearly in point. Words are always to be understood in the sense in which the speaker knows that the party addressed will understand them; or, in other words, in view of the usages and customs prevalent in the community where the language is employed. Who are the speakers? Christ and his Apostles. What are the usages and customs of society on the point in hand? Both the parties speaking and addressed live in a slaveholding community. The moment, therefore, the words master and servant are pronounced, in the minds of the parties addressed, instantly, powerfully, unavoidably, the authority exerted by masters over servants all around them is brought up to view. Now if language explicitly calling up and enforcing the very ideas that have always dwelt in the mind, and are carried out in the every day customs of surrounding society, is to be interpreted to eradicate those ideas and establish an opposite state of society, then I affirm, we have not only no Bible, but *no language* on earth.

Let it be understood, we do not pretend to say that the argument, at which we have only glanced, proves that slavery is a *good institution;* that philanthropy and Christianity have no work to do in this field; that there are no sympathies to be cherished, no conscience to be cultivated, no plans to be formed, no energies exerted, no laws rectified, no expenditures incurred; on the contrary, we affirm that there is a great work to be done by masters at the South, and their neighbors at the North, through following generations. Nay, we shall be recreant to every high principle, and sin against God and man, if we do not heartily labor to bring up our colored fellow-men, both in America and in Africa, steadily toward that summit-level of human rights and blessings spread out by God's most glorious law: "Thou shalt love thy neighbor as thyself."

But this we do say: this argument proves, and proves conclusively, that the grand *position* of our modern Reformer is *false;* that it is *not true*, as he affirms, that to hold a slave is a *sin* against God. For if God's law of love often forbids us to free the slave, and the true doctrine of human rights as often commands us to hold the slave for the present; if the Bible amply discusses this relation without condemning it, and every irrepealable code of heaven's law embraces this relation without a hint of its illegality;

if God has always acknowledged slaveholders as irreproachable members of his family, pronounced slaveholders the best patterns of humanity, and conferred upon slaveholders the very highest honors the race ever received from his hand; nay, if God himself made arrangements for the introduction of the relation of master and servant, ordained the respective duties of the parties, affirmed the rights of the master, and returned the slave who practically disputed those rights; if the master's authority God places side by side with the authority of the husband and of the parent, expresses that authority by the very same terms, and reveals that authority in the very same manner; in a word, if the Scripture can not be broken, and, of old, the slave was his master's *money;* and if God's commands are law, and to do his will is *no sin;* then so surely the fundamental principle upon which the Reformer sets out to reclaim his neighbor is an enormous error.

The first property of a reformer, we repeat, is *rectitude.* He seeks to reclaim, and must, therefore, instruct by *truth*—from sin, and must therefore influence by *virtue.* He should possess, therefore, *superior rectitude*, both of character and of sentiment. While the possession of this superiority should be undeniable, its exhibition should be modest.

Our Modern Reformer makes a most unhappy commencement of his work. He *proudly arrogates* to himself *superiority* both of character and of doctrine, while in point of fact we have seen that he is *deficient* in both.

CHAPTER III.

MALIGNANT.

THE second qualification of a reformer is *benevolence.* The *object* of reformation is the good of the transgressor. Nothing but benevolence will seek this. The *method* of reformation is by conviction; an operation almost sure to make the sinner perverse. Nothing but benevolence will bear this. The *work* of reformation is never finished until the transgressor renounces his sins. Nothing but benevolence is likely to influence him to this.

Were a candid mind called to judge the second property of our Reform spirit, he would probably pronounce it—

MALIGNANT.

That the testimony of conscience should be recorded against sin is due alike to heaven and earth; but heaven and earth have a right to require that the temper of the witness should be modified by the relations of the parties and the circumstances of the case.

Our Modern Reformer arraigns for sin. He publicly, solemnly arraigns his fellow-men, his countrymen, his Christian brethren, for deadly sin before God. Such an accusation plants an afflicting touch upon character, happiness, and influence. If guilty, the sinner must be destroyed, if not reclaimed; if innocent, the charge must yet dishonor, harass, and tempt. Feeble is that man's claim to philanthropy who can deliberately prosecute such a charge without pain.

It is some evidence of malice that there exists no proof of crime. An accuser's work is every way so uncomfortable, that a benevolent man would hardly undertake it without conclusive evidence of criminality. The presumption of malice is augmented when the party accusing does not seem to have been called to table the charge; when, for example, the accused dwells at a distance. His conduct of course must be better known to others, and all competent tribunals are nearer at hand. We gather additional indication of malice when the accuser records a charge of profound criminality against a vast body of persons indiscriminately, very many of whom are known to be as consistently pious as are any members of the Church of God. That these marks describe the Reformer's charge of slaveholding against the South, will not be questioned.

Our conviction of malice is greatly increased when the voluntary accuser, in all his spirit and temper, exhibits an utter incapacity to appreciate the imperative proprieties of the case. Whether this principle has not equal application we shall be instructed by pertinent history.

Our own Northern fathers were themselves slave-holders. They were slave-traders also. They transported the miserable captives from Africa, sold them at the South, and were well paid for their work. Some of them were aggravated slave-dealers. When emancipation laws forbade the prolongation of slavery at the North, there are living witnesses who saw the crowds of negroes assembled along the shores of New-England and the Middle States, to be shipped to latitudes where their bondage could be perpetuated. Their posterity toil to-day in the fields of the Southern planter. At the close of the war, when the memorable Convention assembled in Philadelphia to form the Constitution, the subject of Slavery was referred to two committees, successively. The *majority* of the first were *Northern* men. They reported a recommendation that the slave-trade should be legalized perpetually. The majority of the second were *Southern* men. They recommended that the slave-trade should *not* be extended beyond the year 1800.* Nor let it be forgotten that the constitutional provision on this head would never have prolonged this infamous traffic to the year 1808, and consequently, all the slaves introduced into our country during the last eight years of the trade, and all their posterity, would never have been numbered amongst the bond-

* Appendix A.

men of this land,—never if either Massachusetts, or New-Hampshire, or Connecticut, had stood by Delaware and Virginia in that crisis of the country, and like them, voted *against* the extension. This right of importation! Why was it extended from 1800 to 1808? The answer to this question lays its hand precisely upon the foundations of our government. The property of the South lay in her slaves, of the North in her ships. Government is not wanted, if it does not shelter rights. The South refused—firmly refused—to enter into confederation with the North, unless her property in her slaves was constitutionally protected. The North felt equally unwilling to confederate with the South, unless a Navigation Act secured the profit of her ships. The South constitutionally accorded to the North all that was necessary to a Navigation Act. The North constitutionally accorded to the South the protection of her slave property. Just here—here, in this great original compromise, lies the basis, the very basis of the government of this country. Mark, now! The North, largely by the unobstructed enjoyment of her Navigation Act, has become rich; while the South, largely through the failure of the North to carry out efficiently the true spirit and intent of the constitutional provision in her behalf, has been subjected to constant and serious pecuniary loss, disquietude, and peril.

I hasten to acknowledge that all this does not touch the moral character of slavery; that all this should not work the very slightest change in our views of the institution. But I affirm that it does decidedly affect the spirit and manner in which the North should table this charge of slaveholding against the South. If I must present an ignominious charge against my neighbor, which all the world knows lies just as strongly against my own father—if I must charge a crime, into which all the world knows the accused was betrayed by the complicity of my own father—if conscience compels me to table an accusation known by the whole world to be intimately connected with an incalculable loss and mischief which the accused has suffered largely through my own and my father's unfaithfulness to covenant in the premises—and thus I seem to be the very last man on earth fitted to personate the accuser—then, for my father's sake, my own sake, the sake of the accused, and of all morality, Heaven forbid that I should bear down upon the abused man with a hard, self-righteous, and vindictive temper. But tell me! Has the heart of our Modern Reformer the very slightest acquaintance with this tender, humble spirit? No, indeed! No more, we fear, than if these histories had never transpired! No more than if man's soul had never been constructed capable of just and generous sensibility! Oh! what is it that in one direction can steel the heart, beautified with sympathies in every other, against all the appeals of modesty, honor, and justice? What is it that can tread down without a thought all those sweet and beautiful charities which would spring to respond to the call of equity and honor? It is malignity! nothing but malignity! She has fixed her stern eye so intently and so long upon the imagined crime of her victim, that she can look now on nothing else; and has thus effectually shut off from her vision all those pertinent facts which else had kept the heart alive to the proprieties of the case.

The evidence of malice rises higher still, when the criminal charge is virulently held up before the public through long, long years. It is true, intrepid conscience may testify for God through a long period. When it does, we give the testimony cheerful record amongst the noblest deeds of earth. But where there is piety there is justice, and justice will see to it that this reïteration is not infliction without foundation. Where there is piety there is wisdom, and wisdom will see to it that unnecessary repetition shall not work implantation instead of extirpation. Above all! where there is piety there is benevolence, and benevolence will be full of anxiety concerning the cause of God and the soul of the sinner; sometimes fearing lest prolonged reïteration may pang the heart without cause; lest unskillful reïteration may breed only irritation and reäction; or lest the slightest reiteration should prevent reformation. Most assuredly, therefore, where there is no malignity the testimonies will be intermitted or modified, as prudence prompts; always held up in an unprovoking manner, and often with the most considerate kindness.

If you say we should not expect perfection in man, I ask whether our Modern Reformer exhibits any approximation to such a spirit as this? I am ashamed to be compelled to ask whether, on the contrary, his whole spirit, in all this unintermitted crimination of the South, does not exhibit such a naked hardness, such an entire absence of all doubt of himself, allowance for his brother, or wise concern for our great cause, as must start the peradventure whether, on this point, (be his general goodness what it may,) he has not been left to exchange the love of Christianity for the hate of fanaticism?

The proof of malice is perfect when this solemn charge is renewed at all times, in all places, on all occasions, through all channels; in private and in public, in Church and State; and prevailingly with the most extravagant and unrelenting bitterness. Is not this too near a faithful history of the manner in which a portion of the North, in our day, do press this accusation against the South? You need not go to Anti-Slavery meetings, nor search Anti-Slavery records; you need not call up here and there the most violent words or acts of which you may have read or heard. Go to any meetings in the country —religious, political, literary, or miscellaneous; go to any journals of the land—daily, weekly, monthly, or quarterly; go into any coach, car, ship, or steamer; go anywhere, everywhere; is it not true that, wherever you find the language or conduct of man, *there* you too often find the bold, obtrusive spirit of our Reformer? Survey now the grand mass of mental exhibitions thus assembled, and tell me what is the moral temper of the man they represent? On the one hand, while I forbear to affirm the impossible coëxistence of a principle of piety with all this wrong—nay! while I cheerfully avow my strongest assurance of the intermixture of many an honest conviction, many an upright principle, many a pure and noble aspiration—on the other hand, is there not some reason to question whether more enormous outrages of reason, oversight of facts, breaches of charity, or breathings of hate, ever found record, than are brought to view in the history of this Reform? Who can doubt the deep-toned malignity of this formidable spirit of our day? Why, our Reformer! He hates the master more than he loves the slave. Why is it that he can rarely be persuaded to advance a farthing toward the redemption of a captive at the South? Is it not because the money must go into the hands of the *master?* Why is it that he is so reluctant to contribute a dollar to colored evangelization at the South? Is it not because the agents of the operation are deemed to fraternize with the *master?* Why does he fight against Colonization?—the angel which conducts that captive to the only liberty for him on earth? Is it not because this enterprise gives up a part of the ground taken against the *master?* Why does he build up barriers of law, and forbid the captive a refuge in the latitude of his own dwelling? Is it not that he would have these *masters* keep their negroes to themselves? Nay! if all the prodigious energy of this Anti-Slavery Reform finds its fountain in pure love of the slave, why is it, when this unhappy wanderer reaches his own boasted region of liberty, that he must be content to dwell so far below the level of freedom, and share so sparingly the sympathies of the free?

Ah! who can doubt the malice of the Reformer? Look at his black portraits of slavery and of the man-stealer! Hark to his fierce imprecations upon the head of the sinner! Mark his reckless measures for the overthrow of the curse! Calculate the immense interest he is willing to sacrifice to accomplish the work! Above all! tremble as you mark that demoniac frown upon every great and holy thing upon earth which dares for an instant to stand in the way of his deadly wrath.

George Washinton! * He held a slave, and is "a scoundrel." The Constitution of the country! It stands in the way — crush it under foot. The Church of God! If it tenders not its coöperation— it is a hypocrite! The Bible! If it tolerate slavery for an instant—away with it! And God himself! If he sanctions this hell-born monster—even He is unworthy of respect!! Oh! how opposite to the spirit of the Gospel! This is gentle and peaceable, and easy to be entreated, and full of mercy and of good fruits: that is stern, warlike, implacable, vindictive, destructive. This would give the cloak also

* Appendix B.

to him who would take the coat. That is the very temper which would first smite you upon the right cheek, and then upon the left; first take your coat, and then your cloak also.

If the strength of a cause may be judged by the energies it can employ, the perils it can dare, the sacrifices it can make, and the resistances it can overcome, then must the strength of Anti-Slavery malice be stupendous. What a multitude of restraining relations, histories, and truths it overbears in its impetuous tide; to what amazing heights and depths of adverse excitement, to what bold extremes of position and measure it rushes in its course; and if unarrested, what sacred interests of earth, what holy principles of Heaven, are doomed to be overwhelmed in its issue.

The second attribute of a true reformer is benevolence. The sinner loves his sins, and therefore hates the truth. Nothing but love can allure him to look at the light; nothing but love win him to leave his darkness.

The second essay of our Reformer is as unfortunate as the first. He had approached the slaveholder claiming a superior rectitude which he did not possess. And now, instead of securing influence by conciliation, he bears down upon him with a temper as malignant as it is arrogant. Ah! this may drive man into sin, but will never, never draw him from it.

CHAPTER IV.

BELLIGERENT.

THE third qualification of a true reformer is *intelligence.* The means are not more necessary to the end than instruction is to reformation. Without truth, reformation is impossible. But through the truth which the instructor presents, the mind may apprehend sin and renounce it, appreciate righteousness and appropriate it.

Were a sagacious man called to speak out the third property of the Reform movement, he would probably exclaim, it is—

BELLIGERENT.

The two great powers that work in this world may be termed suasion and force. Suasion works upon mind, by instruction. Force, upon mind and body, by compulsion. When employed as instruments of reformation, they ordinarily differ from each other in each of the three parts proper to an act —motive, means, and end. The motive of suasion is friendship; its means, truth; its end, reformation.

In the nature of things, truth is fitted to sanctify; the legitimate use of suasion, therefore, implies kindness both in the motive and in the aim. On the contrary, when force is enlisted in the work of reformation, ordinarily its motive is selfishness; its means, will; its end, the accomplishment of some purpose of its own. Force embodies no light, consequently can not reform. When the work to be done, therefore, is reformation, he who employs force justifies the apprehension that he is animated by some motive and object of self-gratification, since the welfare of his antagonist can hardly be his aim. The established temper of the movement we discuss, casts light upon this analysis. If the spirit of this Reformation is malignant, it can not be employing suasion for the sanctification of an enemy, but may very naturally be using force for a different purpose.

God forbid that one man should do injustice to another. Let me hasten to explain. Although the ultra Anti-Slavery mind of this day, I do verily believe, is fairly chargeable with the malignity imputed to it, still I am well assured that compassion for the slave, and not hostility to the master, was the feeling which started this enterprise. When the emancipation of their own slaves had removed the beam from the eyes of our Northern fathers, they then began to look upon this relation as philanthropists. At this time to fly into a rage with the master, for his unrighteous imposition upon his weaker fellow-man, was precisely impossible. They themselves had been too recently and largely involved in the very same condemnation. But it was at this precise epoch in the history of the country that three causes were set in operation, which combined to work all that has since transpired, and especially to produce the present Anti-Slavery sentiment of the North! 1. *Abstractly*, the *Northern* mind, through its separation from slavery, becomes progressively more enlightened than the Southern, touching the unnatural condition of the slave, and the entire unwholesomeness of the relation. 2. *Practically*, the *Southern* mind, from its now extensive and growing involvement with the institution, experiences more clearly than the Northern the impracticability of any present remedial movement commensurate with the evil. 3. *Naturally*, the sons of the original actors at the South are coming upon the stage, and feel their comparative innocence, since they were the inheritors, not the originators of the institution; and the sons of the original actors at the North are in turn taking the place of their fathers, and acquiring a far stronger Anti-Slavery feeling than their ancestors could have transmitted to them. Farther removed, both from personal complicity in the matter on the one hand, and from experimental acquaintance with the nature of the relation and the difficulties of its management on the other, they are of course less capable of making the allowances or exercising the forbearance which their fathers displayed. What then? Why, growingly displeased at the neglect of the South to sympathize with their views of philanthropy, and restive under a sense of their inability to bring their Southern neighbors to any practical movement for the liberation of the slave, they felt that something should be done! For the honor of the country, and the claims of suffering humanity, they accordingly resolved to do all in their power to rouse a public sentiment which should secure some redeeming movement in the premises. An active spirit forthwith sprang up among the people, and the most intrepid and vehement men in the land took the field. And what a topic! What an instrument to stir the blood of men was in their hands—Slavery! And mark! Slavery, apart from its circumstances! (For these are never clearly seen, never duly weighed by distant spectators.) Think! Slavery in the abstract! What heart does not instantly swell in vision of its glaring unrighteousness! Slavery in its excesses! What soul is not roused by their narration! Suffice it to say, Anti-Slavery men betook themselves vigorously to the work. They dragged forth the most blood-stirring details which the history of the South and the tongue of rumor could supply, and wrought up the most horrid descriptions which fired fancy could start into life. They threw out these moving elements vehemently upon the people all over the land, through their presses, pictures, lectures, and sermons, until the hearts of the multitude sprang up in violent sympathy with the clank of the chain, the crack of the lash, and the blood and the moan of the captive, and the tears and the woes of parted kindred, and all the shocking enormities so powerfully depicted. Love of liberty and morbid conscience took the lead; ere long political preferment, party power, journalism, literature, and almost every strong thing in human society, one after another, naturally fell into the ranks, and worked to impress the burning appeal upon the imaginations and impulses of men. Remember, too, the South was not present! Her voice was not heard! Nay, those calm and pertinent facts and truths, destined one day to take down this unreasonable excitement, could not be heard while such a tempest was howling through the country.

But the results! the results of this powerful movement! What are they? A mighty change in the excitement! In its direction—from the slave to the master. In its spirit—from philanthropy to misanthropy. In its means—from persuasion to compulsion. How could it be otherwise? For five and twenty years never were a people exposed to a stronger temptation, peradventure, since God made the earth. Think of the constitution of man. There lies the truth! hate and rage are infinitely stronger elements than consideration and compassion, and, equally addressed, will always and utterly overthrow them in the conflict. Think of the cast and bearing of the appeal. There is the record! far less calculated to breed just consideration for the master, and gentle compassion for the slave, than to rouse a heaving, indignant swell that must work wildly to sweep away from the earth the entire relation. Tell me! what, what could prevent the very issue which has transpired? If He who reigns over the affairs of men wrought not a constant restraining miracle through all these years, most assuredly consideration and compassion must have given way before the gigantic growth and triumph of hate and râge, and the whole character of the movement must have been turned to the right about from the persuasive to the belligerent.

Should any man question the truth of the philosophy, he certainly will admit the justice of the verdict, whether he decides the case by testimony or analysis.

Except the party on trial—the ultra Abolitionist—call up every man in the land to the witness-stand, and the grand mass would speak out a prompt and hearty conviction, that the character of the movement has been palpably belligerent.

Examine the elements of the operation, and the result will be powerfully confirmed. There are three prominent methods whereby the ends of the party are sought to be accomplished.

1. *Agitation.*—The *material* of agitation consists of any such fact, argument, appeal, or agency, as is deemed effective to overthrow what the Reformer terms the *Pro-Slavery,* position in the country. Its *channels* are societies, meetings, papers, lectures, sermons, resolutions, memorials, protests, legislation, private discussion, public address, in a word, every

conceivable method, in Church or State, whereby appeal may be made to mind. The prevailing *object* is not to teach, not to reform mind by instruction. This, the agent thinks he has tried. He has no hope in it; he has no patience with it. Its uncertainty does not suit his determination; its demand of deliberation and respect does not suit his temper; while the material he naturally employs, is ill-adapted to this work. What then is his object? Why, he means, largely through the vigorous and obstinate perpetuation of this agitating process, to bring the offender to his terms, by getting up a public sentiment which shall harass, disgrace, or appall him into an ultimate surrender of his principles. Now I affirm that all such agitation is a flagrant violation of the natural rights of man.

(1.) It violates my right of *private judgment.* My neighbor should certainly be permitted to lay before my mind his views of truth and duty. If I do not assent to their correctness on the first presentation, he has a right to a second, a third, and a fourth, and to any and all reasonable opportunities of placing his views of our common Master's directions before my judgment and conscience. Let it be that he has already made repeated essays to convince me, and all in vain; if some change in my circumstances, or any general occurrence of providence, or the acquisition of any new light, or the unusual presence of a spiritual power; in a word, if any conceivable influence leads him to hope that I might now be brought to receive his sentiments—surely, surely, he has a perfect right to place himself before me again, and I am bound to give him, from beginning to end, the kindest and most teachable attention. For I must never forget, that naturally we are all fallible and prejudiced; that the interest at stake—mine, man's, and God's—is incalculable. But when my neighbor has tried all possible methods, with all possible facilities, through all reasonable periods, to bring me to his views, until it is a fact that he himself entertains not the slightest hope to change my mind by suasion—if he still throws himself before me, and insists upon throwing out upon me all such utterances as he may choose to employ with a view to subdue me into coïncidence with his views—I solemnly demand, Is he not a wrong-doer? I respectfully inquire, Does not this man practically affirm that I have no right to think for myself? Does he not make my very soul his slave? For, see! he insists that my mind shall get out of existence, that his mind shall be my mind, and that I shall bow down and go by it. Such agitation as this!—clearly it is not suasion, but force; from beginning to end, out and out belligerent.

(2.) It violates my *right of personal happiness.* Surely, I have a right to live in peace in the dominions of the God of love, so far as he himself does not move to abridge it. I was wonderfully made, and am richly supplied for this very purpose. Now if my neighbor, after failing (in the full use of all his rights in the premises) to convince me of the rectitude of his views, will insist upon ringing his empty arguments in my ears, upon rattling his annoying shafts upon my shield, and this, that by pure dint of unceasing disturbance he may bring me to his opinions, I put it to you, is not that man a tyrant? Does he not unjustifiably take away my natural right of enjoyment? Does he not practically say to me, You shall never be happy until you submit to me? Such agitation as this, is not discussion, but compulsion; a process out and out belligerent.

(3.) He robs me of my *right of character*. My Maker gave me a law, and a right to respect from every creature proportioned to my obedience of it. When therefore I have done no wrong, but obeyed God's law, and thereby entitled myself to his respect, the man who, to force me to his views, constantly dishonors me—nay, whose daily treatment of me involves the affirmation, that even here on the territory of the God of justice, so vile a creature am I, that I have a right to no mind but his, to no peace but his, and who insists upon the unlimited repetition of this outrage—may I not pronounce that man a daring robber? He violently, degradingly divests me of the most precious right my Maker gave me, a right to sincere respect from all minds, proportioned to my conformity to his law. Now, an agitation that would drive me to another's mental position by disfranchising me of my choicest natural rights, does not reason with me as a man, but forces me as a brute, and clearly presses a belligerent movement upon me.

This system of accomplishing violent party ends by unrelenting public agitation, a system which the Progress spirit of our day has introduced to make the world move faster than God's agencies can be made to conduct it, I wonder whether the men of our time have not long felt that there is something deeply wrong about it? I wonder whether they have not *felt* its chafing against the great rights which God has planted in the depths of the soul? its violation of all the sweet charities of the Gospel?

This Progress spirit! This boasted friend of liberty! what an economist of freedom! It seeks to secure liberty to a few men outwardly, by a principle which makes slaves of all men inwardly! This high-souled philanthropic guardian of human equality! What a display it makes of love and equity! It brings down a force upon my soul which would crush out the very likeness of God, by insisting upon the surrender of my mind, my heart, and my conscience, simply to his tyrant will. Oh! if there is an overthrow of freedom upon earth, it is that which modern agitation demands! If there is a bullying belligerence on earth, it is that which modern agitation employs!

2. A second means of Modern Reform is *testimony.* In its nature testimony is a solemn attestation to some specific sin, usually pronounced by an ecclesiastical body. Essentially testimony is well adapted to work in the reformation of the world, and practically has often been employed with great ad-

vantage. It is, nevertheless, a most delicate and sacred instrumentality—so much so, that nothing short of all human purity, benignity, and wisdom, should dare to handle it. As for testimony, in our day, while we are assured that some of the best men on earth are implicated in the judgment expressed, we must still aver our apprehension that, (innocently to many, perhaps in some sense undesigned by all,) testimony is made to work as a party engine, whose more stringent utterance from year to year seems well calculated to bring down an augmenting odium upon the offender, until he is made to bow to the mandate of morbid conscience.

Were a Christian to come to me and say: "I am sorry, my brother, that you hold such doctrines, that you indulge in such practices. I know it will wound your feelings, and distress your family and your friends. I know it will irritate your pride, and bring down public dishonor upon your character. I do feel very sorry to be compelled to be the minister of such disquietude and degradation; very sorry, indeed! But, my brother, I profess to be a man of God: I feel that your ways are a serious damage to God's cause, and peril to your soul. For the kingdom's sake, therefore, and for yours, I must bear testimony before heaven and earth, that your principles and practices, in my judgment, *are sin against God.*" Such a testimony must do good; and in a spirit of reluctance, anxiety, and prayer, deepening with every successive repetition, may well be employed more than once. Such a testimony seems to be the offspring of conscience, kindness, and wisdom. It will be sure to select its times and its terms so as to show that it watches and embraces every providential, every spiritual suggestion to withhold, renew, or modify its witness precisely as a conscientious regard to the best good of all shall dictate. But a testimony which does not seem to be the child of holy conscience in communion with God, so much as of an epidemic fanaticism in the public mind; which makes you feel its purpose to conquer you more than its heart to love you; which does not touch you by its generous, judicious planning for your salvation, but awes you by its wild, stern sympathy with its own ends; in a word, a testimony which is a prominent element of that system of Modern Reform, whose every breath seems to cry: "We are determined to agitate, and agitate, and agitate! To testify, and testify, and testify, until we break you down and accomplish our purpose!" Surely, such address as this is not *suasion*—it is *will!* It is not *argument*—it is *force!* and out and out belligerent.

3. The language, fruits, and measures of the Reform, place its belligerent temper beyond all question.

In *language* no element ever flung out more defiance of authority, contempt of religion, or malignity to man. The Reform movement has long been accustomed to express its most descriptive instincts, by passing formal Resolutions to break the arm of the Southern despot, and bid the captive go free, though to do the work it must crush out the government with one foot, and the Church with the other.* As to *agency*, no element on earth has broken up more friendships and families, more societies and parties, more churches and denominations. And if it divide not the nation, it shall be because the belligerence of Abolitionism shall be made acquainted with one power at least superior to itself. As to *measures!* what spirit of man ever stood up on earth with a bolder front, or wielded fiercer weapons? Stirring harangues! Stern resolutions! Fretful memorials! Angry protests! Incendiary pamphlets at the South! Hostile legislation at the North! Underground Railroads at the West! Resistance to the Constitution! Division of the Union! Military contributions! Sharp's rifles! Higher law! If this is not belligerence enough, Mohammed's work and the old Crusades were an appeal to argument, not to arms!

The spirit of Modern Reform! Does it not do its work as a belligerent? What says *philosophy?* By the law of cause and effect, its address could engender nothing but belligerence. What says *experience?* We have *felt* its force on every hand bending us to its will. What says *history?* This Reform has been walking through the earth, rupturing organizations in Church and State, frowning upon the powers that be, in heaven and earth, and shouting as from its inmost soul: "If I live, I shall live by inhaling the expirings of my dying victim."

* See Resolutions at late Anniversary in New-York.

The third *agency* of a reformer is *instruction*. Clear truth must reach the calm mind through kindness, or there is no reformation.

The third step of our Reformer is as much misplaced as were the two that preceded it. Arrogating a rectitude which he did not possess, and advancing with a malignity which closed the heart against him, he now, forsooth, puts the sword to the flesh, to renew the spirit. Ah! Belligerence may kill the world, but it can not reform it.

CHAPTER V.

IMPRACTICABLE.

The fourth attribute of a reformer, is *teachableness.* The first ray of truth which falls upon a misled mind, will not complete its reformation. On the contrary, that dark mind must work its way out to light, by throwing back upon its teacher a multitude of half-way honest counter-suggestions, started by the action of truth. When all these shall have been severally met by the reformer, and answered, the work is done. Now, if the reformer does not fairly weigh, and duly appreciate all that the pupil addresses to him, without one thought of the process, he will act out this result instantly: "That man does not take truth; it is not truth that he gives. Truth from me, he will not receive; but to statement from him, I must succumb. Away with his teachings!" On the contrary, let the reformer be perfectly teachable; nay, let him not only do ample justice to every scintillation of truth projected by his *protégé*, but let him even look out for it, that he may exhibit his appreciating spirit.

And without one thought of the process, as if by lightning, the party addressed will reach this result: "That man knows truth, loves truth, yields to the reign of truth; that must be truth which he sends, as well as that which he receives. This fellow-man respects me, is honest with me, and seeks to do me good. He understands my case surprisingly better than I do myself. I am safe in the hands of that man; kindly, reverently, I will take his teachings." Yes! teachableness is indispensable to the reformer's influence over the mind he would reclaim.

The fourth attribute of *Modern Reform*, a sagacious man will promptly pronounce—

IMPRACTICABILITY.

All mind may be diseased; especially that which is constitutionally impulsive and unbalanced. The ordinary indication of disease lies in one fact: On some given subject the faculties and the feelings do not act as they do on all others. There is a loss of equable movement. The mind does not weigh truth, nor the heart feel objects as by the laws of reason they should, as on all other subjects they do. There is an oversight of some things that never can be seen; a false impression by others which never can be corrected. The machine is evidently a little out of gear; nor can you make it work right. Try it as you may, you will find the perversion just as incorrigible as it is palpable. One of the most common forms of diseased mind, is *fanaticism*. This is that impracticable condition which an over-earnest and unbalanced mind often contracts when it is fiercely set upon the belief of some false dogma, or the accomplishment of some unreasonable purpose. It is—

Incurably *self-reliant.* Fanaticism has no faults, and makes no mistakes. So infatuated is its impression of the rectitude of its own position, that it amounts to practical infallibility. The adverse judgment of the universe would not start it in the least. Try to shake the solidity of our Reformer's conviction of the justice of his feelings on the subject of slavery: Remind him that to err is human; that his mind may not have worked with perfect accuracy, and the case may not be altogether as bad as he supposes: You will find him perfectly impracticable, because perfectly self-reliant.

Incurably *contracted.* Fanaticism fixes its eye tenaciously upon those features or imaginings of the object which feed the disease of the soul, and there it ever keeps it. It can never, never be sufficiently withdrawn for an instant, to weigh duly either its adjacent parts, governing connections, or ultimate bearings. Try to confute this man's *sin per se* sentiment on the subject of slavery. Draw off his thoughts from his peculiar view. Tell him that, philosophically, circumstances are a part of the subject; that you never compass the case until you have embraced the circumstances; that the character, complexion, shape of the entire thing is derived in part from its circumstances; that, clearly, he has but a partial view of the object, who does not embrace them. Try as you may, you will find him perfectly impracticable, because incurably contracted.

Incurably *intolerant.* Fanaticism is so fixed and fiery in all its purposes and instincts, that it condemns, and hates, and strikes instantly every thing which comes between itself and its object. No matter how wise the approach, how benign the spirit, how conclusive the argument, the moment you commence to assume an adverse position, this is enough; it will not, it can not brook the very slightest opposition, and you are scorned in the very depths of his soul. Enlist all your tact, stretch all your courtesies to the utmost, and strive to remove our Reformer one hair's breadth towards the charity which believeth all things, hopeth all things, endureth all things—the moment his soul realizes your so-called Pro-Slaveryism, the game is at an end. He is perfectly impracticable, because incurably intolerant.

Incurably *reckless.* If the truth which undertakes to break the grasp of fanaticism, were the truth that saves the world, fanaticism will destroy that truth, and the world with it, sooner than let go its hold. I do not say it will *intend* to do it, but there is no safety-valve, no redeeming spirit in fanaticism, and do it, it will. The fact is, fanaticism is not the mind which God created to weigh argument, and follow truth; but the mind which disease has set to storm the redoubt, or die in the ditch. You may spread out before him all the mad results of his doctrine—he will fling them all off, and stand furiously unmoved, and shout:

"Fiat justitia, ruat cœlum." He is perfectly impracticable, because incurably reckless.

Let us illustrate a little more at large the nature and the bearing of this capital feature of fanaticism, as exhibited in that formidable Anti-Slavery movement which shakes Church and State to their foundations in our day.

1. The Anti-Slavery Reformer demands of the slaveholder, that in view of the *crying sin* of the relation, he shall *free his slaves instanter.*

To this, the Southern man responds: You call upon me to *do wrong.* Say nothing of the massive interests of the frame-work of society, fearfully imperiled by the universal adoption of your principle—in general such a deed would not only destroy the present support and happiness of the slave, but ultimately murder his liberty and the hopes of his posterity for ever. I must hold him under my authority, and by God's help strive to do a better part by him. You call upon me *to do what you will not do yourself.* If slavery, essentially, is such monstrous unrighteousness, then you have a part to do as well as I. Your fathers and our fathers, and you and I, are all concerned in this sin. We have received that slave-part of the mutual transaction which your fathers brought to our fathers, and you have received that money-part which our fathers paid to yours. If now by the laws of right and wrong you demand that we give up our part of the unrighteous mammon—our slaves—do you, then, disgorge your part of the unrighteous gain—their proceeds in your hands, with interest from the date of sale. Until you do this, you call upon us to act upon a principle you yourself dishonor. You call upon us *to do what half of you do not believe to be right.* Analyze your own consciousness closely, and you will find this to be true. To heaven and earth you have cried out so loudly of those *chains!* and *lashes!* and *groans!* and *blood!* and all the other horrid cruelties of slavery! You have stirred up every sensibility of your nature, and to their highest capacity stretched all the powers of your soul so long to take in the full power of all this rhapsody, that the echo of your own piercing outcries moans in the bottom of your soul to this day, and for your life you can not break away from the dark, superstitious foreboding that there must be something deeply wrong in any such relation between man and man. But bring the matter boldly to the test of your own reason. Where the destruction of the relation would destroy every ground of hope for the good of the slave; where there is no motive of gain, and no lack of conscience; you know that there is no sin in the simple act of holding a slave for his own advantage. That poor weakling, who has never yet learned to walk alone; who has not strength enough to stand on his own feet for an instant; whom you have been holding up ever since he was born, with your own hands; what! take off your hands and let him go—when you know that he will fall to the ground and bruise himself, and keep falling and hurting both himself and others, until he dies? You know in all your soul that this would be sheer cruelty. You know that justice and humanity demand that you continue still to hold him up, and try to strengthen and train him along, as best you can, until he shall be able to take care of himself. Such are substantially the views of many Southern minds. All men see and feel that there is some force, some truth, in these responses. What says our Reformer! He makes nothing, nothing of them. He himself has always been true to principle on this subject; but as for the slaveholder, he has not performed the first act, nor advanced the first word that mitigates the entire unrighteousness of his conduct. If you would reform the Southern man, say, if you please, that his explanations do not entirely satisfy you; but say something of them; give them some regard, some weight. For he knows, and so do you, that his views and feelings are such as an intelligent and honest man may well entertain.

2. The general demand of the Reformer presses upon the slaveholder the charge of *violating the natural liberty* of the negro.

In connection with explanatory views already presented, the slaveholder advances one fact in mitigation of this charge. In the way of restoring slaves to their liberty, he avers that the South has surrendered more than one hundred millions of money*—a sum, to say the least of it, more than twice as large as the whole

* Appendix C.

United States have paid for the saving of the world. Is not this a fact worthy of some consideration? What similar testimony of their philanthropy have Northern men furnished in late years? They answer: "The slaves were yours; are found in your hands. You are the proper party to make the surrender." "Ah! if the negroes are ours, why do you intermeddle with our business? Why do you not leave us to manage our own affairs as we please?" The Reformer responds: "You do wrong; you oppress our fellow-men; we feel for their affliction, and would plead their cause." Very well; you thereby identify yourself with the work of seeing them restored to their natural rights. You lay yourself under obligation to do what you can to accomplish this end. We call upon you, therefore, for the practical evidence of your sincerity. You see the *proof* we advance of our desire to promote the liberty of the slaves. Where is yours? How much money have you advanced in this cause? Now the Southern man feels that there is a voice in these facts of extensive emancipation; they speak out to the point in hand; if not all rectitude in view of the charge, they are at least pertinent truth. But you will observe, they make not the slightest impression on the mind of the Reformer. They do not furnish him the very feeblest ground either of acknowledgment on his own part, or of allowance on the part of his neighbor. How can the Southern man escape this conviction: "The Reformer does not weigh truth; does not do justice. That mind never, never can conduct me to virtue."

3. But our Reformer has a far more serious count in this indictment to read out against the slaveholder. He accuses him of insufferable outrage upon the *spiritual liberties* of the slave. He has taken from him the book of God. He will not allow him to read the Bible.

Observe, if you please, this charge commits the Reformer to the work of contending for the Christian rights of the man of color. He assumes the obligation of doing all in his power to bring back to the slave the debarred privileges of the Christian religion. To this charge, the Southern man thus responds: "If we have kept the Bible from the slave, then you are our witness that the slave, of himself, did not go to the Bible for any Christianity he may possess. We aver now, that in our day, hundreds of thousands of our slaves have been hopefully converted to Christ."* How will you account for this fact? You are our witness that we, the *masters*, have carried Christianity to our slaves; carried it by word of mouth; carried it by a Christian life and spirit; carried it by Christian prayer, and all manner of Christian effort and influence.

What now have you done for their Christian privileges? for their conversion to God? There are various institutions within your reach which employ

* Appendix C.

missionaries who labor exclusively for the slaves of the South, some of whom have been intrusted by the American Board, to carry the same Gospel to the heathen. Pray, what have you done to send Christianity to those maltreated slaves, through these institutions? Have you ever made a solitary contribution to their treasury? Your neglect to take part with your brethren in sending the Gospel to the poor you profess so deeply to pity, is not all of which we complain. Have you not been for years laboriously struggling to cut them off from a Gospel supply which they had long possessed? The messengers of the American Home Missionary Society, had long been accustomed to wend their way to the home of the captive, and to bear to him the glad tidings of salvation. Why is it, that among her thousand heralds annually commissioned to go forth and carry the glorious Gospel of the blessed God to the poor and destitute of the United States—if we except the State of Missouri, why is it that this day there hangs over this country the dark peradventure that its very strongest Home Missionary organization may never send another messenger to a solitary captive of the 3,000,000 who live within the limits of her missionary field? Is it not because your spirit and principle which started an organization many years ago, and confined your Home Missionary operations entirely to the North, from that day have never suffered the American Home Missionary Society to rest, but have pressed your point with unfailing vigor, until you have now, to all intents and purposes, constrained that body to pursue such a course as will assuredly cut off the South from her missionary patronage, perhaps for ever?

How stands the case in this connection? If censurable Southern laws, which none had so great influence in enacting as yourselves, did place the bondman under an inhibition of the letter of God's word, the slaveholder affirms that he himself did yet so carry the substance and spirit of the Gospel into the very region of this prohibition, that a very great multitude of souls have been brought to the hope of the Gospel. We repeat the inquiry: In the very matter of your own charge, what have you done? You yourself never did preach or send the Gospel to the slave, though always declaiming about his rights and wrongs in the premises. The little that others did, you sternly opposed from year to year, and today, with the world's strongest Home Missionary arm under your control, and the world's loudest note of philanthropy to the American slave upon your lip, for aught we can see, in solid phalanx their millions must go to perdition if left to the spirit or letter of any gospel you shall send them. Now the Southern man says: Here are facts which all the world must see do bear and bear strongly upon the point charged. Admit that they do not acquit of all blame, yet they certainly should have *some* weight. But our Reformer remains perfectly unaffected by all this. Nothing advanced operates to convince him in the matter of religious duty to the slave, that either he himself is chargeable with the slightest short-coming, or that the master is to be accredited for the smallest fidelity. By the very nature of mind, and its reformation, how can such an impracticable, unreasonable temper hope to work any improvement in Southern morality?

4. Irritated by what he deems the unprincipled sluggishness of the slaveholder under all his discipline, he presses the general charge in a more stirring form. You admit that slavery is a great evil. Why then do you not take ground against it? From generation to generation the poor down-trodden slave is crushed into the earth as though he were a very clod. And nothing is done! In verification of your sincerity, why do *you not lift up a standard* against this horrid oppression, and start some bold remedial movement, and *begin your work at once?*

The slaveholder responds, Come, brethren! just practise your own principle, and show us how to do this thing! You will not say that we have all the sin of the earth. You will not deny that you have great sins as well as your neighbors. Brethren! *Covetousness!* Is it not a sin? Is it not a great sin? Lay it side by side with slavery, and whatever you may think of their relative turpitude, what does God say? Can you show me one clear word, in all the Bible, through which God plants his frown upon the holding of a slave and calls it—sin! What a standard, on the contrary, God has lifted up against covetousness! God commands: "Thou shalt not covet." God affirms—that covetousness is idolatry, the root of all evil, not to be named amongst saints, and worthy of death; that covetousness brings temptations, snares, defilement, sorrows, mourning, destruction, and perdition; that he abhors it, is wroth with it, curses it and will smite it. Finally, he assures all men that he will no more permit a covetous man to enter into his kingdom than extortioners, idolaters, adulterers, fornicators, whoremongers, drunkards, murderers, or blasphemers. Say, my brethren of the North, have you no covetousness among you? None amongst the merchants of your great cities? None amongst the manufacturers of your towns and villages? Call over the catalogue of your church members confessedly worth their hundreds upon hundreds of thousands, and some of them million after million of dollars! These disciples of Him who had not where to lay his head, what do they with all this silver and gold of the Lord in their hands? I acknowledge when Jesus says, "He of you, whosoever he be, that forsaketh not all that he hath can not be my disciple," he does not teach that the rich man is to cast his wealth into the sea; nor that, reserving food and raiment, he is forthwith to scatter the residue for the good of the kingdom. But this he does mean: As "ye are not your own," and "no man liveth unto himself," so "the silver and the gold are the Lord's," as well as body, soul, and influence. The Christian, therefore, should so use this money as both to feel in his heart and show by his life that he does not hold it as a worldling, but as a steward. Appropriating an all-sufficiency in every reasonable sense for himself and family, he is religiously to account the residue as the Lord's, and to make such use of the same as, in the exercise of an honest Christian discretion, he believes will best promote his kingdom. It may not be wise to place even the greater part of it out of his hands; but this he should not forget, he robs God and strikes a blow upon the Church, if he permits valuable Christian objects around him to perish, struggle, or fail to be established, because he holds his wealth more as his own than as his Master's. But do all the rich men of the Northern churches hold and handle their wealth on this principle? Having food and raiment, so far as they and theirs are concerned, are they content therewith; and do they conscientiously employ the residue of the Lord's money for the Lord's glory? As far as they are rich, are they just so far strong to spread the Bible, scatter tracts, build churches, and preach the Gospel at home and abroad? Tell me, I beseech you, is all this mighty wealth of the member—holiness to the Master? Sacred to the kingdom? Look, my dear brethren, look! O the nations, the nations of the earth! O the myriads of our own countrymen, bond and free, who sit in the region and shadow of death, and no light springs up to them! And why! why do they perish for the lack of vision? Is not one reason clearly *this?* Because so much of God's money is locked up in man's coffers, and held under a heart-tenure that would not be called to find a new use for one solitary dollar of it, if the cause of God were this moment struck out of existence. Oh! bring a Christian heart into the Church of Christ! Let the salvation of this world rise up before the mind in its proper, infinite preëminence above all the carnal ends of the nations combined. Let all the dead money of the Lord be brought out from the clutches of a covetous heart. Let it set to work, just as far as they can be well spared from secular duty, all the good men and women in the world who have capacity to serve God's cause. In a word, all this hoarded wealth, which now only gives a worldly eminence to a Christian man without lifting a finger for the Christian cause, let it set up and sustain all such enterprises of benevolence and religion as Christian wisdom may devise, and would there not be a change in the earth in a day! Observe! I do not now ask any such entire consecration of church wealth. But one point, one distinct point, you must permit me to press upon your Christian judgment and conscience. In the just exercise of the authority which our great Head has committed to the Church militant for the saving of the world, command that all the millionaires, all the greatly wealthy in the Northern churches from this day revolutionize their habits of using God's money. Command that annually they shall hereafter lay up for themselves what they have been heretofore accustomed to contribute to the kingdom; and hereafter contribute to the kingdom what they have been heretofore accustomed to lay up for themselves. Mark! this does not abstract one dollar from their huge fortunes, not a dollar! Just do this, and would not this incipient disgorging of the covetousness of the Church start up every good cause under heaven, and make the entire kingdom move along before the world? Would it not fling into the eyes of men a light from heaven, a conviction of the reality of religion which, from this hour shall almost double the power of every line of Scripture, and every sentence from the desk? Now, my dear brethren of the North, so opposed to slavery, look around you upon the self-consecrated masses of God's money in the hands of church members, and if God's description of covetousness is no error, oh! the *sin*, the *sin* that lies at the door of the Northern Church! And its mischief, who can speak it? Before the whole world what a death-blow does this covetousness daily strike upon that weighty word of heaven: "No man liveth unto himself." What a death-blow daily upon that great command of Christ: "Seek ye *first* the kingdom." What blows it insidiously, effectively, perpetually deals upon the power of all the saving truth of God! Retort not, my brother, that this charge lies as heavily against the South as against the North. Were the allegation true, the argument is false, for your neighbor's sin does not diminish your own one whit. But it is not true that the North and the South stand upon the same level in this matter.

Proper Christian example in the right use of the Lord's money, the North stands under paramount obligations to display, for two reasons. The North has been intrusted by the Lord with a more signal opportunity of speaking out to the world on this subject, since he has placed more than twice as much of the property of the North in the hands of the Northern Church as of the property of the South in the hands of the Southern Church. Again, the North has received from the Lord far clearer knowledge of the example which the Church of Christ should give to the world respecting this precise point of Christian morality. For the world knows, as to the proper use of his silver and gold, the Lord has given to the Northern Church ten times the teaching and the training which, in his providence, he has been pleased to allot to the Southern Church.

But be all this as it may, you admit, my brother, that Northern Church covetousness is a great evil. Why, then, do you not take ground against it? From generation to generation, before heaven and earth, this monster sin leaves God's cause to suffer and decay in every land, while it prostitutes God's property to foster the spirit, power, and fame of the world. In verification of the sincerity of your confession of sin, why do you not lift up a standard against this mighty mischief? Why do you not start some bold remedial movement, and begin your work at once? You respond: "We do preach against it." *Preach* against it! Why, if we had such *texts,* such *divine words*, against slavery as you have against covetousness, we should indeed stand exposed to your rebuke for the toleration of outrageous sin. *Preach* against it! If *preaching* does not break down such palpable, shameful sin, why do you not *arraign* it, and *condemn* it, and apply the *knife* of the Church to it? Why do you not treat your own Scripture sin as you eternally insist upon treating our sin that can not be found in the Scriptures?

How stands our case on this head? Our Northern brother says that slaveholding is a great sin, of long standing, guiltily tolerated; and the Northern Church will never be satisfied until the Southern Church takes some bold, decided stand against it. The slaveholder responds, Northern Church covetousness is a great sin, of long standing, guiltily tolerated; that the Southern Church will never be satisfied until the Northern Church takes some bold, decided stand against it. Pray, what ground of obligation do you make out against the South, which we do not make out against the North? "Thou that teachest another, teachest thou not thyself?" No, indeed! our Northern brother is perfectly unteachable. What every other mind on earth must see, his diseased mind never discovers. Tell me! must not the slaveholder cease to be an ordinary man if he does not indignantly feel and say, that man will not heed the truth—I will have nothing to do with him?

5. No language can speak the confidence with which the Reformer presses the last head of the gen-

eral charge upon the slaveholder. In your superior strength you have forced a most unrighteous relation upon a feeble fellow-man. You have crushed out all his natural liberty, robbed him of the word of God, and while you admit that all this is a great evil, it is not only true that you will do nothing, but the fact is, you will *hear* nothing. *You resist all light.*

By all his attitude, feelings, and language, the Reformer avows himself every way willing to encounter all truth upon this subject. So far from being disposed to evade or to wrest truth, he feels in all his soul that he is ever looking it directly in the face, and desires to do nothing else. No! It is he that doeth evil who hateth the light. It is the miserable slaveholder, blinded by his education, corrupted by his associates, and prejudiced by his enormous stake in the question; it is he—who is unteachable,—he who will not come to the light. The Gospel, the very Gospel itself, can not be preached where he dwells. That minister would be forthwith expelled who should dare to preach the truth of God to the slaveholder or to the slave. The master knows well that the holy light of the Gospel would give him no quarter; that if he himself did not instantly break the chains of the slave and let the captive go free, that light of liberty would be sure to stir up such an insurrection in the land as would instantly and terribly settle the question. Yes, there is no language which can express the honesty of the Reformer's conviction that he himself is perfectly open to all the light of heaven on this subject, but that the slaveholder as studiously and stubbornly spurns and perverts it.

But does not this charge belong where it was born? It is not the South, but the North, the accusing, ultra Anti-Slavery North, which is inaccessible to the truth. It is the Reformer, the accuser himself, who can not stand God's Gospel of master and servant.

Pray what is the Gospel? Is it any thing other than the word of God? What God says—is not this the Gospel? Are we allowed to go to any point under heaven for the Gospel, but to the Bible? Are not the very words of the Bible—the Gospel? What God himself in the Bible tells the master, is not this the Gospel? May we not preach these very words to the master, and say, we preach the Gospel to that master? Are not the very words which God addresses to the slave—the Gospel; and may we not preach these very same words to the slave, and say, we have preached the Gospel to that slave? Let that man deny this who dare! Many, many years ago, said that man of God, Dr. Leonard Woods, of Andover, to his brethren in the ministry: "Come, and let us get up a Society that shall send Gospel ministers to preach the glad tidings to the slaves of the South, and promote their present and eternal happiness. And when they asked me," says the good man, "what I would have such ministers preach, I have replied—*just what the Lord Jesus aud his apostles preached, and so far as possible, in the same manner*." Take then the words which God speaks to the master and the slave in their plain and obvious import. Yes, take this, God's Gospel, and begin at Mason and Dixon's line, and preach it in its palpable sense, to every church, and every family, and every man, woman, and child—down to the Gulf, and to the Rio Grande, and far away to the Rocky Mountains; and, peradventure, not a solitary tongue of the ten millions of the people of the South shall lift a syllable of opposition to the proclamation. Is this so? What do our brethren mean, then, when they tell us that the South is inaccessible to the Gospel? Ah! see! see! It is not *God's* Gospel that the South objects to—but *theirs!* It is something they would add to, or take from, the plain meaning of God's words. Something they would connect with, or substitute for, the clear simple teaching of holy writ. It is this, the humanism of the doctrine, and nothing else, which the South objects to! No! It is not the South, it is *New-England* and the North that are inaccessible to inspired truth, that can not stand God's Gospel of master and servant. Begin at the remotest point in the State of Maine and go through all the Northern States, and in every church where the sentiments of this Reform are entertained, when the preacher shall have laid down the *master's duty* in the use of every enjoining word of Holy Writ, compel that preacher to go on and deliver this further message to his people: "It is God's command that the slave shall 'obey' his master. It is God's command that the slave shall 'honor' his master." But our masters, say they,

4

are "froward." Still it is God's command: Froward though they be, ye slaves, "be subject to your masters with all fear." Tell me, will the North stand this Gospel? Will she? Mark! While this, God's gospel both to master and to servant, is preached through all the South without opposition, I venture to affirm that this Gospel preached plainly and decidedly in this latitude will rend every church or expel every minister where the prevalent sentiment concerning master and servant approaches no nearer to divine teaching than do those of our Reformer.

How stands the charge on this head? With a self-righteous, uncourteous, belligerent air, our Reformer looks upon the slaveholder and exclaims: "Like other sinners, you skulk from the truth, you will not, you can not stand the light." The slaveholder moves up to the words of Holy Writ, speaking precisely on the point in hand, and avows his readiness to take them in their plain, unwrested, necessary import. He retorts the charge, and avers that it is the accuser himself who will not come to the light, but is perpetually dodging from its resistless force behind his own inferences, drawn from human instincts, or providential development, or from more distant and general Scriptural teaching. This statement is undeniably true; but the Reformer, as usual, is impervious to conviction, and only increases the assurance of the slaveholder that his mind, however free from conscious insincerity, neither receives nor emits light on this subject, and therefore can render him no assistance in seeking the moral attitude which shall be well pleasing in the sight of God.

We beg leave to explain, touching the argument on this general head of—impracticability. We do not affirm that our responses to the several points of the general charge of slaveholding entirely justify the defendant. We simply say they do break the force of the assault. We insist, therefore, that the perfect clearness of this fact, compared with the perverse refusal of our Northern friend to accord to it the very slightest consideration, establishes his fanaticism, seals the utter impracticability of his mind, and consequently his perfect disqualification to officiate as a reformer.

We have seen that the fourth qualification of a reformer is, teachableness. The process of reclaiming another's mind lies largely in such a prompt reception and ample admission of all the truth which the party to be reformed mixes up with his countless essays at self-defense, as will assure him that you honor and love truth, and that all you desire is to persuade him to adopt it.

The fourth step of the Reformer is as precisely unfortunate as are the three preceding. Assuming, malignant, and belligerent, he completes his disqualification to reform, by an impracticability which refuses to appreciate the truth or justice of a single word addressed to him by the party whom he expects to bow instantly to all he advances.

CHAPTER VI.

DESTRUCTIVE.

OUR last requirement of the reformer is, that he shall do his work and reclaim the transgressor, or at least work reasonably toward this end; in a word, that he shall do good.

Were any candid man called to express his judgment concerning the fifth and last quality of our Modern Reformer, I think he would pronounce it—

DESTRUCTIVE.

The work of a cause depends upon its nature. What but mischief could reason expect from such an agency as we have discussed? The actor sets out to *reform.* Four things are essential to this work—purity, kindness, instruction, and candor. That the reformer may command the *conscience* of the apostate, he should possess *rectitude.* In the place of modest rectitude, our Reformer brings *arrogant assumption.* That he may conciliate the *heart* of the transgressor, the reformer should possess *kindness.* Destitute of benevolence, our Reformer sets to work *malignantly.*

That he may reach the end, the reformer should use the means, and *teach*. Indisposed to the patience of instruction, our Reformer applies *force*. That he may finish the work and secure the lodgment of reforming truth, the reformer should himself be *teachable*. Incurably perverse, our Reformer will do justice to nothing the transgressor may advance. If four virtuous influences are necessary to secure a certain good result, what must be the character of that work which is wrought by four agencies precisely opposite?

The work of a cause is often indicated by its first palpable effects. Look over the face of this nation. Call up the most obvious fruits of this Reform. Does it not seem as if under your very vision this mighty agent pervades the entire organization of society, tearing its elements to atoms, setting on fire the course of nature. Church or State! Nothing escapes it. Nowhere pure, nor peaceable, nor gentle, nor easily entreated, nor full of mercy and good fruits; everywhere forward, scowling, uncompromising, and fierce; breaking peace, order, structure, at every step; crushing with its foot what will not bow to its will; defying government, despising the Church, dividing the country, and striking Heaven itself if it dares to obstruct its progress; purifying, pacifying, promising nothing; but marking its entire pathway by disquiet, schism, and ruin. Would it not be strange indeed, if, under-lying such a surface, we should find the developments of truth, virtue, and blessing?

Let us subject the working of this agent to a more systematic investigation of its bearings upon the great interests of society. What is its influence upon—

1. NATIONAL UNION? What a country! Did the sun ever shine upon its like? The soil of the earth! The histories of time! Can they tell us of its equal? Oh! it is right to love one's country! With an exultant and grateful heart it is right to survey her strong, bright, broad glories, and all their high and holy promise. Come, then, ere the sacrilegious hand of some destroyer shall mutilate our fair heritage; come and let us luxuriate for a moment in the vision.

Look at the vast extent of the nation, territorially; the amazing augmentation of the nation, numerically; the extending wealth of the nation, commercially; the rising glory of the nation, politically. Behold this nation, the only perfect model of free institutions to man; the great granary of half the adjacent nations of the earth; the producer of the raw material of more than half the work-shops of the civilized world. Mark her own factories, throwing out, annually, increasing quantities of wares, ornamental and useful, unsurpassed by the skill of man; her schools, colleges, universities; her churches, societies, and all sorts of humane institutions of excellent and improving regimen, and so multiplied as to be accessible to all parts of her broad population; her almost interminable lines of telegraphic, railway, canal, and river communication, connecting and girding all sections of our glorious Union. Oh! look at the swelling magnificence of her great commercial marts; her cities, towns, and villages, multiplying and brightening through all parts of our older settlements; and the seeds of states and nations springing up all over our boundless Western domain. When she sails out upon the ocean, mark ye well her ships and steamers of surpassing speed and splendor. When she marches forth to meet an enemy, hearken to the echo of her military prowess as it comes back to us from every quarter in the high praises of the nations of the earth. But why expatiate! In rapid advancement in the entire circle of social improvement—religious, educational, agricultural, commercial, manufactural, political, martial, what nation on earth, what page of history can furnish a parallel? The gravest sages, the warmest patriots of the only people under heaven whom providence has placed in competition with the United States of America, have been overheard in their soliloquies to apprehend that gray hairs are coming upon the head of Old England; that she must arise and shake herself from the slumber of the past, and work up to a far more vigorous and enterprising figure, or the gigantic strides of her wonderful offspring shall ere long leave her far in the distance.

At such a point of the world's history, with such a relation of the grand sections of humanity to Christianity and to herself—that such a nation, so highly endowed to bless, should be scattered to fragments! A nation, too, bound by such a three-fold bond! By that great wall of waters which threw us together and apart from that Old World, the birth-place and home of our forefathers—By that sacred blood of the Revolution our fathers shed when they laid the foundations of those glorious institutions which lift us so high above all the nations of the earth—By that holy mission to liberalize and evangelize the world, conferred by the God of love when he placed us in possession of a liberty and a religion which not only compose the two great blessings most necessary to the happy progress of man, but each of which in its very nature pants for universal radiation. That such a nation—so sacredly bound, so built to bless, so prosperous in the past, should now be ruptured! And by such an agent! An element without dignity, without benevolence, without wisdom, without candor! An agent distinguished alone by its power to disturb and to divide! And alas! its progress, its actual progress, in this its own profane work! Once there were five broad, beautiful bands of Christianity thrown all around our North and our South: The Presbyterian, Old School and New, Episcopalian, Methodist, and Baptist. Three of these are already ruptured, and how long it shall be ere the very last Christian tie shall be torn asunder who can tell? Once there was a spiritual union in this country as entire as is yet the nominal. But that spirit of union has long been declining. While the shock which the very thought of division never failed to minister to every American heart one generation ago, has almost died away from the masses in our day; on the soil of the North is marshaled one party, on the soil of the South another, whose one only work is to fight for this sad achievement. Do not the calmest men carry about them some sensible testimonies of our decaying union? How it grieves the soul of a patriot to feel his own heart's temptation to withhold the full meed of the nation's glory because, forsooth, the development does not belong to his own section. A few years ago a man of God traversed this country, and many a soul, I doubt not, did delight itself to do honor to the bold, simple, beautiful Christianity which swelled up in his heart as he talked so naturally to large assemblies of the people. He had long been exiled from his father-land, toiling on heathen shores for the kingdom. He had seen splendid palaces, magnificent estates, and many an admirable and beautiful blessing in the hands of men; but he felt no participation in these pleasant elements. They all belonged to the heathen or the heretic. He could claim no estate in them. But now, on his return, after an absence of twenty years, to the land of his birth and of his brethren, why! every thing was *his* because *his brother's*. He felt the tie to his Christian brethren warm, close, and real. He felt all his *brother* had was *his*, his as by an executed deed. Nor did worldly man, in pride of ownership, ever discourse of the magnificent variety and glory of his wealth with a face half so broad and happy, with a heart half so warm and exultant, as did this man of God when he walked the platform and looked out upon a thousand souls and talked of *his* green hills here, *his* beautiful meadows there, *his* splendid mansions, *his* lovely grounds, *his* rich estates, *his* flocks and herds, *his*, HIS, all over the country! Did I say, as though he held them by a legal title! No, no! He felt a far happier, truer property in all the blessings of his Christian brethren than legal deed did ever yet convey to the worldling. Oh! remember! Men can be, and men should be *brothers* by *patriotism* as truly as by Christianity. But ah! that agent, that wicked agent, whatever it be, that shall divide this great and glorious people, this beloved land of promise, this our own native country! What a long black mark shall be drawn against the name of the traitor, for the perpetration of such wrongs, such grievous wrongs against the spirit of patriotism! What a world of property, beauty and glory, shall that culprit destroy! All the North to all the South, and all the South to all the North! I shall not attempt a description of the power for good which shall be laid waste—of the crimes of rapine, blood, and hate which shall be multiplied; nor of the dire curses of heaven which shall be incurred by the fall of this nation. The mischief is certain, dreadful, incalculable! Nor shall I outrage sense and dignity by undertaking a deliberate array of proof, either of the inestimable value of the Union—every heart in the country, and the world, should be a witness of this; nor of the actual decline of the spirit of union in our day—every eye in the land can testify to this; nor that our Modern Reformer promises to be the principal perpetrator of the catastrophe—for all the intelligence of the country well knows this. But I will record this last fact as one grand condemnation of this enterprise. Its fruits proclaim it politically and religiously *divisive*, and therefore every way *hostile to the prosperity of the country.*

II. THE SLAVE.

It is in behalf of the slave that the Reformer takes his stand before the world. If there is a blessing in his work, surely it should reach the slave. Has it served—

1. His *religion?*—The Reformer has never preached the Gospel to the bondman of the South, either in person or through effective public countenance of missionary institutions. He has indirectly cut off the Gospel from the slave by generating (if not always approving) that excess of fanaticism which at one time has broad-cast incendiary publications through the South,* thus provoking home legislation, in designed self-protection, to prohibit literary teaching to slaves, except by masters; which at another, has converted pretended assemblings for divine worship into occasions for the secret dissemination of insurgent doctrines—thus prompting home legislation to attempt self-protection by forbidding assemblies of

* Appendix C.

blacks for any cause without the presence of whites; and which, in its various developments, has generated a common suspicion of all Northern agency in communicating religious instruction to the slave. Again, he cuts off the Gospel from the slave, indirectly, by refusing to encourage Christian organizations at the North and at the South, which commission ministers of all denominations, unexceptionable in character and competency, to labor for the slave in preaching the Gospel, pastoral visitation, catechising the children, visiting the sick, and burying the dead; and directly, by averting from the South those channels of missionary supply which the men of other times and another spirit had opened to bear the Gospel to the destitute within the United States.

Our Reformer sprang into life purely to befriend the slave. From that hour, his almost every breath has been spent in the belligerent advocacy of his cause. His conscious sincerity we would not question; but what a melancholy response comes back upon the soul to such questions as these: What solid acts of service has he performed for his beneficiary? What has he done for his religion? What soul of a slave has he personally converted? What destitute bondman do his principles supply with the means of salvation?

2. His *liberty*. Large sums of money have been expended for the redemption of slaves. It is not pretended that the Reformer has had any very considerable agency in this operation. A home of liberty

has been founded for them across the ocean on their own native shores. To the honor of participation in this movement he makes no pretension. Perpetual contributions of prayer and faith, toil and money, have been necessary in all the progress of this noble enterprise, from its foundation to its present dimensions. The Reformer will acknowledge that he has contributed nothing but opposition to this good cause. What then has he done for that liberty of the bondman which has called him out to take such determined ground in his behalf? It were easier to find an answer to the opposite inquiry. Unintentionally doubtless, but what has he *not* done *against* his liberty? He has frequently defeated broad and grand projects for the liberty of the bondman, started up on the soil where he dwells. Again and again some border State—Virginia, Maryland, Kentucky—by the voice of her population, have come up so near to the passage of gradual emancipation laws, that had there been no such agent in the land as this Reform enterprise, or could its malign influence have but been restrained, freedom to the slaves of a State had been repeatedly proclaimed. He has frequently, though indirectly, inflicted upon the feelings of the slave, the most uncomfortable infringements of his ordinary liberty. Whenever the Reform spirit has swelled up high at the North, and rolled down some great adverse wave upon the South, this very spirit has never failed in its influence to sharpen the tone of authority, tighten the fetters of the subject, curtail his present privileges, and for the time dismiss from the master's heart every incipient thought of future manumission. This Reform spirit has lately struck a blow upon the liberty of the slave, such as no other power on earth could have inflicted. On the day when our Northern brethren landed the first slave on the shores of the South, there simultaneously sprang up in the bosoms of Southern men an embryo reformation principle, if not as deep and strong as it should have been, yet pure and wholesome, whose guardian virtue and power, in spite of all opposition, have been bearing along the religion, the liberty, and the hope of the slave through a slowly, steadily improving process to the present day. Most unhappily, for years past, in Church and State, the Reform temper has never ceased to fling out upon the world the bitterest denunciations against the South, and to repeat its formidable purpose to agitate and agitate until it wakes up a commotion which shall shake off the fetters of the bondman and drive oppression from the world. By an ever ready and powerful law of human nature, this adverse pressure has driven the most violent of the assaulted into an attitude of self-defense, whose defiant spirit now speaks out to the assailant in the bold justification of the institution attacked, as natural and necessary, with nothing to regret and nothing to reform—an institution, therefore, which it shall be their purpose to perpetuate for ever. Now the origination of this new type of Southernism is indeed a mighty blow upon the liberty of the slave, because it falls directly upon his first, best, last hope—even upon that early spirit and principle of self-prompted, slow, steady progress at home, referred to above. Just so far as this new spirit shall embarrass the old, so far it will imperil all that has been won or may be hoped.*

Thus valuable agencies are at work in our day for the liberty of the bondman; but we have seen that our Reformer has no hand in the movement. He furiously debates the cause of the slave before the whole world, we readily admit; but wherever his peculiar spirit and agency reach the slave, we have seen that they never fail to obstruct and imperil. These two facts indicate the probability that in the nature of things as they lie in the constitution of man and the government of God, this Reform agency works damage and not deliverance to the liberty of the slave.

The Christian should look for the sound advance of man's natural liberty, only on God's plan. God requires all his servants to appreciate natural liberty, dear and precious as it is amongst the elements of its

* By birth and sympathy a Southern man, yet I can not forbear to say of this Anti-Union party springing up at the South, that while its organization is perfectly natural, in principle it is as unjustifiable, and in operation will be found as disastrous, as is the fanaticism of the North. For while its principle crosses the plan of Providence, and thereby gives up the only comfortable view which can be taken of the subject of slavery, its action surrenders the Constitution of the Union, the most powerful protection of slavery in this state and age of the world.

own category, as but a *secularity* at last; and therefore as infinitely unimportant when compared with that *spiritual* liberty which God, at so great a cost, employs the Gospel to promote. Now, our Reformer has misled his own mind into such a state that he can not help feeling and acting as if natural liberty were every thing and spiritual liberty nothing. Can it be that God will permit his servants to accomplish any great and good results by reversing the grand order of appreciation and action upon which he himself has laid such stress? While my brethren all around me, talented, noble men, with whom I should delight to fraternize heartily in every legitimate work of our great calling, have been stepping aside to embark upon the mighty political flood which has dashed over this country for years, and while they have been giving their choicest and boldest strength to promote the secular freedom of the bondman—in the calm, unuttered retirement of my own heart, I have enjoyed this conviction: If in sincere obedience to God's order I love and long for the temporal liberty of our African brethren in its proper *secondary* place, and if I give to the immortal emancipation of their souls from the course of sin, its own high, *primary* position—for aught I know, single handed, I shall do more for the social liberty of the slaves of the country than the whole body of my clerical brethen put together, who work for this end by reversing God's order. God says: "Secular liberty *second*." The man of God who practically says, "Secular liberty *first*," may ultimately find himself very, very far second in all the good work achieved in this important field. For surely the men sworn to God—sworn to one thing for God—sworn to seek first the kingdom, as above all secularities—sworn to stand by God's spiritualities before men with all their souls even unto death—if they studiously separate themselves from all the agencies set up by their fellow-servants to send salvation to the perishing bondmen of the country; if they seem to testify no sympathy with God's great work of saving hundreds of thousands of them in our day; if God's mighty movement from generation to generation, of floating this people across the ocean back to their own home, designed peradventure like the exodus of Israel, to spread a great light over that quarter of the globe, (a thought which has sent an augmenting thrill of hope into the hearts of God's people, from the days of George Whitefield to the present hour;) if even this fails to stimulate them to take part with us in working to regenerate these fellow-men under God for their high mission; on the contrary, if, before the whole world, our brethren go forth amongst carnal men, and seem rather to give their whole heart, voice and hand, to drive on the *temporal* emancipation of this people, why, surely God will never permit them, in neglect of their sworn work, to ride over his spiritual establishment, and thus accomplish a secular achievement to which he never called them, and in a way which he had pointedly forbidden. Never! never! I am speaking very boldly; but if our Reform friends will bear with me, I will go yet a little farther, and venture the utterance of a private thought. When the wild political extravagances of our clerical brethren have been echoed back upon us from the hustings of the country, after the first sad impressions had passed away, a gentle smile has sometimes come over my spirit, as some such vision as this sprang up to my fancy: A female falls into the river, and is drowning. A man on the bank flies into a perfect frenzy; he shouts and leaps about and wrings his hands, and scatters the remaining wits of the poor woman, which might perchance have helped her. And why all this ado? Why, forsooth! Because she has soiled her garments, and is likely to lose them. Now, he who springs down the bank and plunges into the stream, saves the *life* of the woman, 'tis true; but I insist upon it this is not *all* he does. He does more for the *garments* than does the poor man upon the bank. Clearly *he* stands upon the wrong platform. He acts upon the wrong principle. He wastes his breath to no good purpose, surely; for he stabs his own propriety, helps not the inferior cause which concerns him, and only damages the more sacred trust he stood pledged to protect.

We have seen that this Reform movement accomplishes nothing for the *religion*, nothing for the *liberty* of the slave; but in its (well-meant) violence throws itself in the way of both. We must therefore record it as an enterprise every way hostile to the welfare of the cause it has undertaken to plead.

III. RELIGION. No man ever perpetrated so great a blunder as to suppose that love, joy, peace, are the fruits of this spirit; nor so violent a disregard of truth as to deny that hostility, confusion, and rupture, are its ordinary products. We have glanced at its mischiefs to the spirit and order of families, churches, and societies; of conventions and parties, literary, political, and religious. Its frequent personal shipwrecks of industry, morality, and faith; and its resurgings in infidelity, atheism, and violence, are equally notorious. These obvious fruits suggest the inquiry whether irreligion is not, in various ways, the natural result of the causes set in operation by this movement. Let us discuss this precise question—How does the Reform enterprise affect the great working power of Christianity?

1. It *tends to overthrow the* BIBLE.

You will not forget that two things define fanaticism. It is unreasonable in its position, and impracticable in the defense of it. The body, soul, and spirit of this Reform lies, first, in ascribing to the instantaneous liberty of the slave a most exaggerated importance; and then in the reckless overthrow of every obstacle to its achievement.

(1.) Let us seek a clear view of the Reformer's unreasonable assumption. We shall facilitate our investigation by renewing our inquiry concerning the relative value of spiritual and natural liberty.

What does God teach us concerning the importance of *spiritual* liberty? To fix man's mind upon spiritual liberty, its every constituent element is distinctly held up to him from the beginning to the end of Scripture. To secure man's just estimate of spiritual liberty, while God affirms the supreme obligation and preëminent preciousness of its every property, he pronounces all else "vanity of vanities." To enforce man's personal appropriation of spiritual liberty, God enlists all the atonement of his Son, all the sanctions of his law, all the counsels of his wisdom, all the encouragements of his grace, and all the energies of his Spirit.

What now does God teach us concerning the value of *natural* liberty? It would seem as if God esteemed it relatively so infinitely unimportant as hardly to be worthy of one distinct notice in the same book; as if God judged that, like the duty of self-defense, it was distinctly recorded in the structure of the soul, and needed no additional demonstration or stimulation from his word. The tyrants and masters of old were daily invading the natural liberties of men before the eyes of Jesus and his Apostles. They did not seem, however, to have entertained the most distant imagination of any wild enterprises to subvert the order of society for its protection, but ever commanded subjects and servants to obey their superiors. Who stands before Peter? (2 Pet. 2 : 18.) A slave! What is his character? He "does well!" Who is his master! A "froward man." What is his conduct! He "buffets" his slave until he causes him "to endure grief, and suffer wrongfully!" Shall not such a causeless abuse of natural liberty warrant some setting aside of this relation; at least some momentary interference with the order and peace of society, to punish such cruelty and deliver the oppressed? No! Peter and the Gospel command that the injured man "take it patiently," and be "subject to his master" still.

Now I hold all this the most natural and powerful indorsement of that most simple and explicit teaching of Holy Writ heretofore referred to, wherein God once for all contrasts earthly and heavenly liberty. "Art thou called, being a slave?" (*Doulos*, 1 Cor. 7: 21.) This man, you perceive, has lost his natural liberty. How shall he graduate this calamity? What shall he do? Shall he lay it to heart as though he had lost his all? Shall he up-turn the whole framework of society in order to regain it? No, indeed! It is God who says: "CARE NOT FOR IT." (1 Cor. 7: 21.) Naturally enough, just at this point is one of nature's most reckless and hopeless rebellions against God. It is in vain that God, in the spirit of Scripture teaching, thus reasons with man. "Feel not for an instant as though all good were gone. They deceive you who tell you so. Slave though you be, every supreme good is left you. You can be like me. You can love me. You can serve me. You can enjoy me. You can have a record in heaven, and heaven's God in your heart.

You can show men true religion, and help me to save men. All this just as well where you are, as anywhere." But is not personal liberty a most precious right, and in itself vastly preferable to a state of slavery? Yes! most assuredly! And should it come in your way consistently with the rules of the Gospel and the order of society—"*if thou mayst be free, use it rather.*" But so sweet is liberty to fallen nature, that these divine conditions are an insufferable bondage, and man exclaims: "Why may I not get into an agony, and break my way out of this horrid oppression?" Because you thereby perpetrate the monstrous madness of our Reformer! You thereby perpetrate an act of injustice as far surpassing that of the slave-maker, as in dignity the mind surpasses the body! Pause and reflect! If you are only converted, though a slave to man, you are "the Lord's freeman!!" THE "FREEMAN" OF THE LORD. (1 Cor. 7 : 22.) This is the boon! This is the great thing! This YOUR ALL IN ALL! Observe now! If you will not realize this divine teaching; if in judgment, feeling, and practice, you will not give to *spiritual* liberty that supreme importance which belongs to an infinite and eternal good; on the contrary, if you will practically, rebelliously insist upon according to *natural* liberty the supreme concern of your soul, though it is but a transient, secular blessing, then mark these three results. You irreparably destroy the *order of your mind.* The working of any rational nature with such a prodigious dislocation, must up-turn it from its foundation. What grand truths must be thrown down! What stupendous errors set up! What mighty interests trodden under foot! What sacred obligations cast aside! You irreparably destroy the *life of your soul.* To the mind that works with this dislocation, religion is a precise impossibility. Your supreme affection, bestowed upon the infinitely inferior carnal object, can not at the same time rest upon the infinitely superior spiritual object; and were there no natural impossibility in the way, would the God of heaven give his salvation and himself to a rational creature deliberately, inflexibly bent upon practically pouring such awful contempt upon both? You irreparably overthrow the *grand platform of the world's redemption.* The principle of this dislocation carried out, necessarily overthrows the order of society. In the nature of things, the peace and order of society is indispensable to the progress of the plan of salvation. To reach and enjoy spiritual liberty, we know that by a mighty change, as from death to life, the heart must give to religion its supreme affections first, and services next. Clearly, therefore, the soul must enjoy *facilities* for so doing. Facilities for reflection, reading, hearing; for the calm carrying out of conviction in faith, repentance, and obedience; facilities for all the undisturbed mental processes, and all the consistent practical exhibitions incident to the acquisition and exercise of true religion; in a word, facilities which demand a settled, orderly, social state.

He therefore wrongs heaven and earth who makes all things tributary to the building up in his soul of this predominant sentiment, namely—*escape from slavery is the one thing needful; therefore the pillars of society, and all else in the way, may be up-turned to reach it.* Study acutely the condition of this mind. The man is fearfully blind. He does not see the relations of God and man; the great end of all things on earth; why time was placed before eternity; why Jesus Christ came into the world. He does not see that earth, air, light; food, raiment, shelter; ranks, trades, professions; blessings, curses, changes; liberty, slavery, law; yea! all things and states on earth, are but a *staging*, a *great platform*, built up at infinite cost, simply that in the calm, undisturbed use of the Word, Son, and Spirit of God, man, before he is to-morrow destroyed for eternity—accountable, immortal, blood-bought man—though he lose all else, may come to acquire *spiritual* liberty! No, he does not see that for the work of the Gospel, for the progress of God's great plan of mercy, society must be kept quiet, and its order undisturbed, even though many inferior matters be left in disorder for the present. In fine, it comes to this—this man does not see that the religion of Jesus Christ is the supreme good of man, but in his blind outrage of all justice and reason, he casts down all the great things of God and his kingdom, to lift up in their stead an overrated, transient, earthly good.

Thank Heaven! whatever be the blindness of

man, there is no darkness in the Scriptures. They teach explicitly this doctrine. On the one hand, slavery, independent of circumstances—slavery in the abstract—is both a clear wrong and a great mischief; and consequently, as a natural right and a most valuable earthly good, we are bound to secure to every child of Adam his natural liberty, so far as this end can be effected wisely, quietly, legally. On the other, to be a *freeman of the Lord*, is, beyond all comparison, man's first great duty and blessing; and lest we depreciate and every way damage the infinitely more important right and good of spiritual liberty, in ourselves and others, we are not to unsettle established order; we are not to disturb the peace of society; we are not to risk the foundations of the cause of Christ, in order to free the slave. Rather, for the furtherance of the paramount interests of the race, and the glory of God, for the present "*Let every man abide in the same calling wherein he is called.*" (1 Cor. 7 : 20.)

I need hardly say that the truths advanced have reference to all ordinary states of society. Whenever there arises such an extraordinary state of things, that universal advantage would be the clear result of a general change, that moment "the powers that be" have no legitimate authority, and the right of revolution vests. Of this, the word of God says nothing, probably for two reasons—such a state of society rarely occurs; and when it does, man will be prompt enough both to see and to improve it.

(2.) Let us now seek a clear view of the Reformer's impracticable maintenance of his unreasonable assumption.

Observe his dilemma. In his fanaticism, he has taken wrong ground. He practically places man's social liberty high above his soul's salvation and all the immortal interests of Christ's kingdom. This is his first grand mistake. The Bible, you perceive, lies directly across his path. He can not get by, to reach his end. What will he do? Will he bow to God's word, and give way? Never! if his fanaticism is mature. Fanaticism is impracticable. *The Bible must give way.* This is his second grand error, and completes his mental disorder. To a sane mind, he can never justify his course. To sustain his own, he flies to a two-fold philosophy. He affirms first: He who gave man his nature, gave him for his government, great "*natural feelings*," *mighty*, *invincible* "*instincts*." By these, as a last resort, he must judge all things. Therefore, if the Bible crosses his instincts, the Bible must be set aside. This ground our bold Reformers assumed early in the controversy; to this ground men in better standing, and even ministers of the Gospel, under the influence of a growing Anti-Slavery feeling, have been ever since insensibly tending; and this ground some of our best men, yet more deeply impregnated with the virus of this epidemic, have recently avowed.

In matters of life and death eternal, man, then, is to find a guide in *his instincts*, is he? Wretched delusion! Preposterous argument! I defy any mind on earth to trace out the gulfs which separate the *greater* violence of man's instincts against *God's* invasion of his liberty, from the *lesser* violence of his instincts against *man's* invasion of his liberty! God made man holy, and gave him a perfect law. This was justice. God brings me into the world without a solitary remnant of original holiness, and full of all sin, and *yet holds me to the same law!* Where is justice now? He first destroys all my power, and then commands me, under peril of hell, to do as if I had all power! Oh! the instincts! the *strength* of those apostate instincts which *fly in the face of God* at the very thought of the stern, unreduced demands of his law!! If, now, man is to go by his *instincts*, away! away! for ever, with the rectitude of God! Is this, my friend, your *progress?* To get off from the *terra firma* of God's omniscience in the Bible, to the crazy instincts of a fallen nature! Yes! It is the progress of the ship which has parted her last cable and like lightning is driven by the gale directly upon the *breakers!* God save his Church in our day, from the *progress* of this Reform! But you see how it is. The man who will advance this Reform, must leave the Bible behind.

To support his reckless assumption, the Reformer flies to his second defense. *The developments of providence! the light of the age!* demand that we place this high estimate upon the value of natural liberty. The Scriptures were given to man in a dark

period of human history. God gave light to men as they were able to bear it. Little was said of liberty then, because little could be appreciated. But—we of this nineteenth century! We—of this age of progress! We—especially, of this only free country under heaven! By the discussions which have been evolved, the principles which have been reached, and the instincts which have been awakened, we do certainly feel and know more of the natural equality of all men, of the inalienable right of every child of Adam to a personal liberty instantaneous, unabridged, and perfect; far, far more than any prior generation. So clearly do we see and feel the broad, deep, impregnable foundations of truth, of heaven's truth upon this subject of liberty, that nothing could increase our conviction that the Apostles and the Saviour himself, were they present, would take ground instantly and indignantly with us.

But say, friend! does not the light of revelation exactly extinguish your light of providence? Does not the Bible bring up this whole subject, in all its governing relations? Does it not treat of natural liberty—of natural liberty as affected by slavery—of natural liberty in its relation to spiritual liberty? Does it not decide clearly their relative importance? Does it not teach us undeniably that the one is of small value, that the importance of the other is incomprehensible? Does it not teach that the one is therefore to give way to the other in all things? Does it not require the slave to be content with his

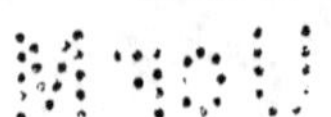

condition, and neither take nor be allowed to take any such steps as would endanger that peace and order of society so necessary to the progress of the paramount cause of man's spiritual liberty? To secure this end, does not the Bible enact a class of rules for the conduct of the slave, and therefore for his continuance *as a slave?* for the conduct of the master, and therefore for his continuance as a master? While these rules faithfully carried out will assuredly work off the worst evils of the relation now, and ultimately the relation itself, and all in the happiest possible manner, does not the Bible at the same time condemn and forbid all agency upon your doctrine, since the first attempt to enforce it disorganizes society? We affirm now, that these teachings of the word of God do take up and settle these questions for ever. Do you deny it? Say, friend! Was not natural liberty then—what natural liberty is now? Is not spiritual liberty now—what spiritual liberty was then? Are the natures and relations of these two elements one whit changed by the flow of time? If Divinity itself were now to speak out, would it inform us that providential developments had so lifted up natural liberty essentially toward the essence of spiritual liberty, and so degraded spiritual liberty essentially toward the essence of natural liberty, that old laws must be abrogated, and a new code introduced to meet the necessities of the case? Preposterous conception!

Besides, if such a doctrine is to be endured for an

instant, where is my Bible? What solitary inch of sure footing have I in all the word of God? If a matter so clearly, so finally settled by the old light, is at the mercy of any new light which may be started up in the successions of time by a fallen heart ever leaping into false discoveries all around me to relieve the embarrassments of its depravity, what one truth have I that may not in like manner be taken from me? Yes! and what do you bring me in the place of my Bible? The light of providence! But how do you reach it? Does *God* tell you that *such* is the light of his providence? Come, my friend; march frankly up to this question and tell me. What evidence have you that such is the teaching of God's providence in this day? There are the providential developments, you say! Grant it! But what do they declare? What voice do they utter? What lesson do they teach? You say: "They teach my doctrine." How do you know that? Advance directly to the point, and tell me! How, how do you know it? Why, your *fallible* intelligence *thinks* so. Yes! and this *is all! this is all!* Ah! what have you done? You have taken away my Bible from me! You have taken away from me the *only sure light!* the light of God's *infallible truth!* My fellow-man, did you but know what God knows, you would feel that I have a solemn right to exclaim, "What a *robber* you are!" Nor is even this the limit of your malice! Behold! You have embarked me again on that broad and shoreless ocean of doubt and dark-

ness which overwhelmed my race at the fall, with no *better bottom* under me than your own wretched, *wretched inferences!* My fellow-man! My heart feels no unkindness to you. But I will tell you what I do deeply think and feel. If you but saw what I judge God sees, the conviction would flash upon you, that no fiend of the pit could pronounce a more fearful curse upon our whole race than you have inflicted. This is my judgment. Alas! what a difference between us! You have *given up divine revelation*, and gone back into the *blackness of the apostasy:* And with you, this is coming out into the light, is it? Ah! were your new light doctrine only true, well might we exclaim: "If the foundations be destroyed, what can the righteous do?" Thank God! the foundations are not gone yet. The Bible is the word of God! The word of God, not to a dark generation, but to *man!* to *universal* man! to men of all climes and *ages!* Yes! and this testimony of God is *sure!* "The Scripture *can not be broken!*" "The counsel of the Lord standeth for ever! The thoughts of his heart to all generations." This infallible, immutable record has settled every grand question touching this relation of master and servant—and settled it for ever—and no new lights struck up by man, shall ever, ever unsettle them.

But if the Bible is sure to faith, you see how it is with the friend who would advance this Reform. He must consent to part with the Bible, this one only sheet-anchor for apostate humanity.

2. This Reform tends to the overthrow of *the pulpit.* How deep the need that man should hear the voice of God! Salvation from hell is in it! How deaf the ear of fallen nature to this voice of God! The natural man receiveth not the things of the Spirit. God built the pulpit to meet this case. And what a solemn work God did when he reared that *most holy place!*

God built the pulpit on the *blood of his Son*, that *he* might be allowed to speak; on the *trampled majesty* of his *throne*, that *man* might be spared to hear. What a foundation! What an affluent, awful foundation! That man's ear might not be diverted from the voice of the pulpit, God stills all the noises of earth for four and twenty hours; that man's whole soul might be awed to imbibe its utterance, God built that pulpit in the *heart* of the Holy of Holies, and gave command that every child of Adam, when he touched its sacred threshold, should revere as did the high-priest, on the tenth of Abib, when in his linen garments, with uncovered head and feet, he entered God's awful presence for a moment, with the blood of atonement, to confess his sins, and the sins of the people. What provision this, for audience! What a loud cry from heaven: "Attention, man!" To give sealing power to the pulpit, in the midst of the temple God lifts up his own voice, and proclaims to his *embassador*, "He that heareth you, heareth me; he that despiseth you, despiseth me:" to the *people:* "He that believeth, shall be saved; he that believeth not, shall be damned."

Thus, at an immense expenditure of authority, self-denial, and blood, did God build the sacred pulpit. Why! Why! At the foundation of all this, there must lie a stupendous truth. Man must, must hear it. What is that truth? You find God's thought in man's state. There is one voice to which the earth can not afford to be deaf. What voice is this? It is the voice of *salvation!* Let the world hear it; let the ministry never forget it; God built the pulpit at enormous cost, exclusively, emphatically to utter the *voice of salvation!* Lest all this costly outlay be wasted upon matters inconceivably unimportant in the comparison, lest this august sacredness be destroyed, and the perishing earth fail of the saving blessing that is in it, never, never let the pulpit utter one solitary note but the note of salvation. Preach the word! Preach the Gospel! This, this is the law of the pulpit! Oh! yes, yes! if at such amazing expense God has built up one place on earth where one man may stand and speak for the life of a dead world, never, never let the messenger of God profane that sacred place, and damage the life of the race.

How shall we preserve the costly, invaluable power of the pulpit? The power of the pulpit is largely committed to the keeping of the preacher. Its consecration or its desecration depends simply upon its use. Utter in the pulpit nothing but salvation, and always in the spirit that becomes the manner of its erection, and the magnitude of its end, and you uphold the power of the pulpit. But utter one word else than salvation, or salvation's word without its spirit, and remember this, the constitution of things must be crushed, or you *must* crush the power of the pulpit. The key which unlocks this subject, is this: Man feels the awful authority of God's pulpit, but, a sinner, he agonizes to get away from it. If, therefore, man on earth ever takes an ell, where only an inch was given, it is precisely here. By the introduction of another topic, or spirit, let the pulpit, the awful pulpit itself, but once authorize the hearer to turn aside from the message of God, and for aught I know, that pulpit may thereby have lost its power over that sinner while he breathes on earth. Judge, then, the responsibilities of the ministry, in view of the following facts. It is the hardest task in the world for the minister to enter the pulpit with a heart fired with salvation, and the easiest to enter that desk without a heart on fire, or with the fire of an unholy heart. It is the hardest exploit in the world to lift up the attention of the people to the voice of the pulpit, and the easiest to let down that attention to any other topic. It is the hardest achievement in the world to regain the lost conscience of the people, but nothing is so easy as to drive the hearer farther and farther from the holy power of truth. Experiment upon this subject. Let the man of God profane the pulpit, and display his learning, or try the charms of style, or give himself to speculation, or do aught else than preach the Gospel. It is a grand relief; for man loves sin, and agonizing truth is not now bearing down upon the sinner's conscience: nor is this all; for the sinner is authorized, and authorized by God's awful pulpit, to turn away from salvation and think of something else in the house of God. Yes! only let the hearer feel that what you say is not Gospel truth, or if it is, that your deepest soul refuses to indorse it because you do not press the message for his conviction, and what is the issue? *You* have lost the power to reach his conscience, and *he* the power to feel the claims of the pulpit. Ah! if these things be so, what havoc! what profane and fearful havoc, is wrought upon the sacredness and the power of the pulpit, when by a secular topic the minister takes direct hold upon the secular heart and fires it up with the strong and bitter feelings that are blazing all over the land! Behold that congregation! It is divided into two hostile parties. During the political discourse, while nature in one rises up against the utterances of the desk, and chafes under the consciousness that he is doomed to sit still and hear an adverse, one-sided political harangue, and that from the pulpit; nature in the other triumphs in the hard blows inflicted not by a street politician, but by all the sacred authority of the pulpit. Most clearly, by all the thoughts and feelings aroused in that whole audience, the pulpit, the sacred pulpit, has turned out the soul of salvation, and brought another world on fire bodily into the house of God! God only knows whether there is one man among us holy and wise enough, at such a time, to be intrusted with the delivery of a single sermon on such a subject. I say not that a minister is never, on any occasion, to refer to the acts of the government in his pulpit. But I do say, that in my judgment, such references are far too common and careless in my day. I do say that the sacredness of the pulpit, its power to command the holy attention of the people to Gospel truth—that very power for which God laid out so immense an expenditure—that very power the preservation of which is of such unspeakable import to the earth, is placed in imminent peril by every such discourse. That sacred pulpit must suffer, if the minister is not a man of eminent *personal holiness.* Common political excitement is daily prompting a nation of men to vehement political utterances in every circle and station of life. That God's sworn servant may not seem to profane the pulpit by the introduction of a common worldly spirit, the exemplary holiness of his every day life should protect him from such an imputation, even by the most violent political advocates of the government. That sacred pulpit must suffer, if the *party spirit* of the day has not been most religiously *avoided* by this good man. Since no minister of Jesus Christ may bring into his pulpit one solitary thought which has not been called up by a heart heaving with the love of God, and swelling with the salvation of men, and since every human heart is so deceitful, no servant of Jesus Christ should dare to bring such a topic into the desk, who has not anxiously besought the heart-searchings of his Master, that he might not be left with sacrilegious hand to mar earth's most sacred, mighty, and delicate engine of salvation, by mistaking the spirit of politics for the spirit of piety. That sacred pulpit must suffer, if this good man has not only carefully avoided an evil spirit, but if his soul is not *filled with the Holy Ghost* at the time. At a moment when the hearts of all the people are blazing with the carnalities of the very subject he handles, nothing short of a divine inspiration, nothing short of the very workings of the Holy Ghost in the soul of the preacher, could command the hearer to forget the partyism of the day, and feel himself in the very presence of God. Yes! nothing but the spirit of God himself, could make that tempted mortal so self-governed and solemn, so gentle and charitable, so spiritual and wise, as he must be to save his pulpit from desecration and his people from sin. Finally: that sacred pulpit must suffer, in which political discussions, in party times, are as *common* as are the alleged outrages of the government.

To the frequency of political discussions in the pulpit, it is an objection that the topic is *too secular* in its elements, too far from that Gospel which alone we are commanded to proclaim. God's embassadors are not commissioned to lecture States, but preach to men; an operation, by the way, which the genius of his calling, and the nature of his power pronounce by far his best method of reforming the state. It is too *profanely exciting* in its bearings. Reverence for the pulpit in its nature is a gentle spirit; in fallen man, a feeble one. In the very house of God, where it finds its highest protection, to throw this tender, sacred, precious thing into the jaws of the most violent workings of carnal nature, is the perfection of indiscretion. It tends, too, quite as frequently to *mislead* and to *aggravate*, as to instruct and assuage; especially since the accurate comprehension of the foreign topic often requires a wider, keener, closer investigation, than a minister can ordinarily afford to prosecute. Above all, as an official procedure, it finds but *little countenance*, either in the example or the teachings of Jesus Christ and his Apostles. While they command us to honor our rulers, and forbid us to speak evil of dignities, we search in vain for any clear authority which subjects the alleged misdeeds of government to the arbitrary discipline of the pulpit. Woe to that people, pulpit, and priest, where politics is brought into the desk in an incautious, unanxious, or hard and bitter spirit; where the character and habits of the minister leave a holy man in some doubt whether his pastor watches for souls as earnestly as for the political crimes of adverse rulers; where they awaken a prevailing conviction in a political opponent that his pulpit would not so certainly speak out against the governmental violence if it had been perpetrated by his own party; and where they accustom every member of his congregation to predict that just as certainly as there occurs in the administration of the government, any such movement as arouses the feelings of his party, so surely this man of God shall embark the strongest energies of his soul in fulminating a fiery pulpit assault upon the powers that be.

Happy shall it be for the Church of God if the next generation does not feel the strength of that adverse blow which has been struck directly upon the sacred power of God's pulpit by the frequent and violent Anti-Slavery and political discussions which our Reform enterprise has introduced into the American pulpit in our day. Nor is the *collateral* mischief of this agent less deplorable than the direct. If a minister of Jesus Christ goes so far from straight-forward obedience to God's command—"*Preach to men what I preach to you*"—as to convince his people that political Anti-Slavery-ism is a legitimate element of his message of salvation, he can not limit pulpit discussion to this one point of aberration. In all its nature and bearings this subject stands intimately, inseparably connected with a large class of associated topics not one whit further from the spirit and terms of the Gospel. Foreign immigration flooding the country with Catholics, legislation the only bulwark of the cause of temperance, indicate an endless catalogue of topics belonging to the same category. These will naturally, necessarily be brought along into the holy place, and incorporated as several parts of God's message of salvation to the world. Mark now if you please. By every successive step of this process,you are schooling men to "*itching ears.*" You, the minister, sworn to preach the word, are disciplining your people to feel restive under the old, stale, condemnatory doctrines of the pure Gospel. You have taught them that they may have other supplies from the pulpit, and you will find them growingly displeased with all else save these undisturbing, refreshing novelties. Thus you yourself are driving a wedge which will and must force off the spirit and body of your preaching farther and farther from the spirit and body of the great central, converting facts of the Bible toward the outskirts of revelation. And even this middle-ground preaching between the saving doctrines of the cross and the destructive morality of the world, you compel yourself to adulterate with a nameless host of secularities and abstractions. Are we not approaching some such state of things at this time, especially in those sections of the country where Anti-Slavery excitement and political preaching have been most abundant? Permit a bold imagining. God creates an angel, places the Bible in his hand, and directs him to the page which records the commission of his embassador. Were that spirit now to hear a sermon from every pulpit in the country, I fear he would frequently take up some such impression as this: "These officers suppose that the perpetual reïteration of the awful message of heaven has become irksome to men; that to sustain the interest of the hearer, they must go off to the outskirts of revelation and keep there; must address mankind through some kind of indirect and abstract discourse; must interlard their official communication with all such admissible varieties as promise relief to the tedium of perpetual repetition; must labor to charm men by the accuracies and beauties of style and taste; in a word, they must toil to preach the Gospel so as to avoid the too plain and pungent out-speaking of its commanding topics." God grant I may be mistaken; but I have conjectured that fallen nature's unwillingness to place and keep itself under the full power of God's holy word, powerfully abetted by the authorized introduction into the sermon of the most absorbing and controlling of all secular subjects, is insensibly working to impair the fidelity of the pulpit. It must allow, nay, compel it to employ its high cultivation in such dilutions and digressions as escape the searching, scorching, saving force of Heaven's high message to man, and open the way for the inlet of all manner of organized heresies. May we of the ministry remember that we are embassadors, charged with the delivery of a written message; that the law of the pulpit requires us preëminently to press out upon men the great doctrines of the Gospel; that we may never leave them except when a heart-burning to save souls forces us to some subordinate or collateral matter necessary to the more perfect or pungent expression of its capital points. I know that a wise discretion must govern us in the practical application of this statement. But I will say, that a preaching of the Gospel, which in a far greater degree shall avoid secularities and abstractions, and employ those mighty central truths which better express the great spirit of the Gospel, and gratify the heart that heaves to sanctify the Church and save the perishing, will not only do more to glorify God and save men, but far more to hold the conscience of the community to the supreme authority of the word of God, and leave secularism, new lights, and heresies no footing in the Christian Church. It is a shallow objection that the views expressed imply such a limitation of the pulpit to the two topics of faith and repentance as must disgust the inquiring mind of the congregation by the sameness of the preaching. The fact is, there is no limit to the multitude or diversity of strictly Gospel topics. That man lives who has preached for the half of a century, who never preached aught but the Gospel of Jesus Christ, and who will tell you that it is no uncommon thing in his experience at this day to bring into his pulpit extended and strictly Gospel views never discussed before.

Whatever differences may exist as to the exact line of true scriptural preaching, or the exact degree in which Anti-Slavery discussions have secularized the desk, one fact, we think, can not be questioned: this Modern Reform, by its direct and consequential bearing, has greatly degraded the dignity and damaged the power of the American pulpit.

(3.) The Reform movement tends to *convulse the Church.* If it is no friend of the Bible, and no friend of the pulpit, it can not fail to damage the cause of Christ.

The fact is, it has never ceased to trouble the Church of God since it sprang into life. How sadly church organizations have fared at its hands. It has ruptured the Presbyterian Church, and the Methodist Church, and the Baptist Church; and not content with all this, it has just now ruptured the Presbyterian Church the second time. How sadly our great religious Societies have suffered from its power. It organized a Missionary Society in opposition to the American Board of Commissioners for Foreign Missions. It set up a Home Missionary operation antagonistic to the American Home Missionary Society. Not long since it commenced to disturb the American Tract Society, and is just now carrying out a second convulsive movement in the American Home Missionary Society, by disposing that body to withdraw its missionaries from the Southern States.

This work of abandoning the South was commenced fifteen years ago, when extreme Anti-Slavery men confined the Home Missionary operations of their newly-organized Society exclusively to Northern States. From this period, the same Reform leaven has exhibited itself more decidedly in the language and action of the American Home Missionary Society. About two years subsequently to this division, its records affirm of Southern slavery, that it "enthrals more than two millions and a half of souls in a bondage worse than Egyptian, that perverts the most direct and effectual efforts for their salvation." (18th An. Rep.) After the lapse of a brief period, the slaveholding States are given to understand that the missionaries of the Society were expected "not to close their mouths on the subject of slavery more than other sins," but "to make their ministry effective in enlightening the moral sense in regard to this evil." About this time the Society adopted the rule which refused "to commission slaveholders as ministers," and "dropped from the list of its agents any missionary in its employ who voluntarily or involuntarily became the owner of a slave."

All this did not satisfy extreme Anti-Slavery men. They began to demand stronger measures against the institution of slavery. They charged the Society with "*countenancing*" this wickedness by the manner in which it dispensed its missionary patronage; "with giving aid and comfort to slavery by supplying slaveholders with the sanctions of the Gospel." And they sternly and publicly required the Society to withdraw wholly from the slaveholding States. In its 27th Report, (p. 120–4,) the Society publishes a long and labored defense.

It denies the charge that it countenances the institution of slavery in any form or shape. On the contrary, it affirms that "the number of the Society's missionaries in slaveholding communities is comparatively small;" that these missionaries are stationed, for the most part, in those portions of the slave States "where the system has the slightest hold, and where it must be expected soonest to yield;" that the Society binds its missionaries to "make their ministry tend in the most effectual manner to the removal of this great evil;" that when the missionary "encounters obloquy and opposition in so doing, he is sustained by the sympathies and the pecuniary aid of the Society as long as there is hope of usefulness," and when this fails, "is assisted to enter other fields;" that "many of the churches to which these Southern missionaries preach," are "known to contain no slaveholders;" "some were formed upon the principle of admitting no such members," "others have freed themselves from this embarrassment," while others still are in "various stages of progress toward a similar separation from slavery." "In the progress of this work, the Society has sustained some of its missionaries in the face of strong remonstrances to the contrary." It is "not true," therefore, that the Society "is fleeing from slavery;" nor that it "suffers the subject to sleep." The fact is, "no practicable measure within its legitimate sphere is overlooked." If the Society "has not accomplished all," it is "doing much." "It has made progress," "real and substantial progress," in this cause. "It records grateful advances by individuals, churches, and communities." Indeed, "it is our firm conviction that no other equal number of minds, in or out of the slave States, exert so great an influence as do these same missionaries to bring the institution to be rightly regarded by those involved in it, and to induce churches to free themselves from its taint." We are purposed too "to persevere in thus preaching the Gospel, and to make still more perfect proof of this efficacy." The Society ventures to hope, therefore, that it may "count upon the confidence and coöperation of every true friend of freedom," etc.

But no! Nothing in the way of self-defense ever satisfies the extreme Anti-Slavery man. You must come square up to his mark or take the blow. The Society had ventured on two points to stand out against the protestants. They required that the Society should "make the exclusion of slaveholders from communion a condition of missionary aid." This the Society declined to do, on the ground of its "interference with the rights of churches to define their own terms of membership." It "did not lie within their province." The second demand called upon the Society to withdraw all her missionaries from the South. To this also the Society declined to accede, on the ground that "it did not seem right and proper."

There has existed for years a sharp controversy on these points between the conservative and the radical elements of the American Home Missionary Society. That the strong Anti-Slavery spirit is practically gaining the ascendency, the New Rule of the Executive Committee bears ample testimony. Its language is this:

"*Resolved*, That in the disbursement of the funds committed to their trust, the Committee will not grant aid to churches containing slaveholding members, unless evidence be furnished that the relation is such as, in the judgment of the Committee, is justifiable for the time being, in the peculiar circumstances in which it exists."

I delight to know that those Christian men who take the lead in the affairs of the American Home Missionary Society, indeed in all our great religious institutions, are men who always do what they believe to be right. They are incapable of any thing else. Like other men, they sometimes lack intelligence and firmness, but never lack integrity. They may be unduly influenced, but that which they do, they ultimately deem to be duty.

All this I cheerfully accord to my brethren. They will permit me now to say, in my judgment, they have committed a great mistake; a very natural one, I acknowledge, but a very serious one. I hold them to have been *betrayed* into error *by the spirit of the day.* Invariably this is a strong spirit. It begins strong; it ever works, and works strong. It is always a little fierce, for it gives no quarter; and more than a little determined, for while life lasts, it never gives up its point. It generates a momentum in the masses it controls, all-competent often to overwhelm an opponent instantly under the fierce pressure. Toward the grand enemy, *slavery,* its manner of operation is perfectly natural. Seize it by the throat, and frown upon it, and shake it, and curse it, and press it back, and choke it with a tighter and yet a tighter grip, until you throw it to the ground and crush it to death. Such is the energy of the Ultra-Abolition spirit of our day; and when we look to Boston, New-York, and here and there all over the North, and see this fierce movement headed and urged on by men and women of captivating talents, high position, daring spirit, and triumphant efforts; and when we consider that these agents do consecrate to this cause more than their ordinary ability, since they must imbibe a formidable inspiration both from the genius of fanaticism and the fire of this peculiar theme, it should not surprise us that multitudes are inevitably borne along by the mighty torrent.

A spirit so violent can never do much good in the kingdom of Christ: when God arises to bless this country, he will assuredly set it aside. It is marked by three capital defects. Palpably it lacks *kindness.* This is not the way Jesus Christ and his Gospel handle sin. *Philosophy.* You may crush by this process, you can not convert. And *justice.* There are good men at the South, and they have done commendable things in behalf of the slave. But all that is worthy in their character and works, the spirit of the day sternly ignores.

The New Rule of the Committee is a legitimate offspring of the Abolition spirit of the day. There is no mistaking it. It does certainly wear the hard, condemnatory, violent face of its parent. The history of its production establishes its descent. The strongest Anti-Slavery spirit of the country lives in the bosom of the Society, but never sleeps there. It works, and would cease to be if it did not ever work upon the whole body to bring it to its own spirit and principle. We have seen that this stern and arbitrary discipline has pressed the conservative element of the Society sorely, and forced it, in self-defense, to apologize to the dominant spirit, by recounting all its past oppositions to the institution of slavery, and its purpose of future loyalty. That the unyielding mettle and restless vigor of the master principle should ultimately and insensibly overpress good men, ever anxious to avoid a rupture, into sympathy with its own views and ways, is just as natural as the law of cause and effect. If my good brethren of the American Home Missionary Society seriously question, whether in the New Rule they have thus been betrayed into an unhappy conformity to the violent Anti-Slavery spirit of the day, they may find some pertinent suggestions in the many little wrongs into which they seem to have been unconsciously driven on their way to their present position. God helping, I will speak nothing in malice, and nothing which our common cause does not seem to demand; and my brethren, I know, will do me the justice to believe this. If on an important point, a party right has gone over to a party wrong, we should expect, in the nature of the case, some such exhibitions as these—an eating of its own words, a crossing of its own spirit, a violation of pledges, an affront of dignities, a breach of justice, a forgetfulness of propriety. Such things my brethren of the Committee could not voluntarily do. That they have been betrayed into some such things is, I fear, established by our own history of the case.

1. In view of the Anti-Slavery charge, that the American Home Missionary Society *countenanced slavery*—compare the former position of the Society with the same *position renounced* in the New Rule.

The charge of the objector was, that the Society countenanced slavery by its act of supplying slaveholders with the sanctions of the Gospel. This the Society stoutly denied. What says the New Rule? Is it not built exactly upon the principle that the Society's former method of dispensing the Gospel to slaveholders was—"giving aid and comfort to slavery"? Why change the terms of the dispensation, and require clearer sympathy with Anti-Slavery views, if they do not feel the force of the objection? On this point, manifestly, the Society abandons its defense, and adopts the principle of the objector.

2. In view of the Anti-Slavery demand that the Society *withdraw all its missionaries* from the slave States, compare the former position of the Society with the same *position renounced* by the working of the New Rule.

When this demand was first urged, the Society responded, that such a withdrawment of the Gospel from the South "does not seem to the Society, nor to the great mass of judicious persons, to be right and proper." Yet is it not a fact, that from the date of the New Rule, to all intents and purposes, the Society's missionaries were withdrawn from the South? A few of them in peculiar circumstances, or in locations very near the Free-line, may yet preach to Southern congregations, but who does not know that not a solitary slaveholding church—a fair representative of the great body of Southern Christians, will ever stoop to ask or accept aid under a requisition so humiliating and arbitrary to Southern men, however conscientious and intrepid may have been the intent of its authors! Clearly the Society's New Rule, by its natural, its necessary operation, works out the demand of the Anti-Slavery objector utterly, and abandons the defence of the Society utterly, by accomplishing precisely that which the Society had said "did not seem right and proper."

3. Compare the Society's *spirit of disclaimer*, expressed in its own language, with *the same spirit renounced* by its own act.

In 1828, the Presbyterian Church, through its leading members, was understood to object to the proposed union of its "Board of Missions" with the American Home Missionary Society, on this ground, namely, that the latter was subject to no *ecclesiastical* supervision. Whereupon the friends of the American Home Missionary Society, to meet this objection, employed in response, these very words: "The American Home Missionary Society has *no power*, and can have *no wish* to interfere with the discipline or doctrine of the churches it proposes to serve." Nay! To still the expressed apprehension of the Presbyterian Church, and persuade that body to confide in its honest purpose never to permit the management of the Society to interfere with the established discipline and policy of the Church, the American Home Missionary proceeded to say: "*It has therefore cautiously avoided even the appearance of power, by choosing to exist without a charter and without permanent funds, and having no existence except in the affections and confidence of the Christian public.*" (A. H. M. S., Vol. I., p. 208.)

O my brethren of the Home Missionary Society! Compare all this with the demand of your New Rule, and the spirit of your published defense. Does not the heart and soul of the whole proceeding speak thus: "This is an age of progress! We have seen new light. We must take higher ground. We must fall in with the advancing age. We must bring you up to better principles." Where is the modest, deferential spirit of the Society now? Its repeatedly avowed temper of non-interference? Where is that asserted emasculation of itself, purposely to put away even the semblance of power to disturb the churches it proposed to serve? Permit me to say, brethren, in my judgment, the Society's New Rule, pressing as it does upon the Presbyterian Church—the Society's advanced sentiments upon the subject of slavery, is *in spirit*, a *direct contradiction* of the "*no wish*" and "*no power*" testimony, whereby it sought to persuade the Presbyterian Church to place itself in its hands in the beginning.

4. Compare the Society's *principle* expressed in its

own language, with *the same principle renounced* in its own act.

When Abolitionism began to press the Society to adopt arbitrary measures with slaveholders, and called upon it to give no patronage to churches that would admit slaveholders to their communion, the American Home Missionary Society avowed its doctrine on this point and responded decidedly, It "did not lie within its province" to do so. It would infringe a most important prerogative of church discipline, if it did; for "it would interfere with the right of churches to define their own terms of membership." Remember this explicit acknowledgment of the Society when first tempted to exert this act of authority, namely, *It is a right of every church to define the terms of its own membership.* Where is this principle of the American Home Missionary Society now? Beyond dispute this doctrine acknowledges in every Presbyterian church the right to determine how far slaveholding shall affect the standing of its church-members. Does the American Home Missionary Society practically acknowledge this doctrine to-day? By its New Rule does the Society dispense its patronage to Southern churches according to those views of the church-standing of its members which these Southern churches entertain? Does the Society consider those slaveholding members in good standing, which the Southern Church adjudges to be in good standing? On the contrary, does not the New Rule most perspicuously announce to the Southern applicant this fact: "What the Presbyterian

Church is willing to consider Christian morality on the subject of slaveholding, we are not willing to consider Christian morality on this subject. We demand something more. We require you to leave at home all ecclesiastical indorsement of your good standing, and appear before us, that we may catechise you and see whether you come up to our own scruples as to sound Christianity."

Permit me to say, brethren, in my judgment, this is a direct interference with the acknowledged inherent prerogative of every church to define the terms of its own membership. Let me explain. Clearly, a general discretionary power rests in the Society to determine the disposition which shall be made of the funds intrusted to their hands. Clearly, too, the personal merit or demerit of every applicant is not to be considered as finally decided by his ecclesiastical standing. Should an application be made for missionary aid by a minister or a church known by the Society to be destitute of that orthodox and upright character possessed by associated ministers and churches, and required of all, it would be the duty of the Society to decline assistance. In every such case in Christian charity the Society should presume that the controlling tribunal is ignorant of facts, which have providentially come to their knowledge. This, I take it, is a right always exercised and never disputed, namely, the right to act upon the defective Christian character of an applicant, especially when the Society has reason to believe that the evidence of this delinquency is not as fully before the supervisory body, or even where that evidence, for some special or some unaccountable reason, has been obviously misjudged by it. But if I understand this New Rule, it is an entire advance upon the old *regime*, and defended as such. It is not confined to special cases of known or suspected delinquency. On the contrary, the Committee's action presupposes, that the whole Presbyterian denomination South has failed to present to the Christian judgment of the Home Missionary Society any satisfactory evidence of the sound Christian character and aim of any one of the slave holding members of all its churches. The entire Slaveholding Church is pronounced destitute of good Christian standing, and therefore not entitled to those missionary privileges, confessedly due to Christ ians, until they bring to the Committee additional testimony of their honest Christian principles.

Observe, if you please, what a slaughter of Christian confidence and church-rights this New Rule executes. Every Presbyterian church carries in its bosom a Church Session—a tribunal constituted expressly to pass upon the Christian character of its members and to pronounce their church-standing. Annually every Presbyterian church must appear before its Presbytery, and make such a report respecting the admission and conduct of its members, and of its proceedings in the premises, as involves a distinct statement of their good or bad church-standing. By the act of approving its records, after due examination, the Presbytery indorses the good standing of all the members of the churches under its care. Annually every Presbytery reports to its Synod, and every Synod to the General Assembly, the condition of its churches, and the general character and standing of its members. Annually, by the deliberate examination and approval of the records of the Presbyteries by their respective Synods, and of the records of the Synods by the General Assembly, the sound Christian membership of every individual connected with the Presbyterian Church is measurably indorsed by the highest tribunals of the denomination. When a Southern Presbyterian church, therefore, makes application to the American Home Missionary Society for assistance, it lays before that body a four-fold testimony to the good standing of its members. The constitutionally authorized testimony of its Church Session, of its Presbytery, of its Synod, and of its General Assembly. What then is the virtual language of this New Rule? Is it not practically this: The witness of your Session, and of your Presbytery, and of your Synod, and of your General Assembly, is nothing to me. I am not satisfied. I have no confidence in their judgment. You hold slaves. You must clear yourselves of this *prima facie* indication of immorality. I must examine you and every one of you myself, before I can reach the conclusion that you are worthy to receive the Gospel at our hands.

My dear brethren of the American Home Missionary Society! To induce the Presbyterian Church to give up her "Missionary Board," and commit her missionary matters to your management, remember you avowed that you had "no power," "no wish," "no right," to interfere with the prerogative of every church to settle the terms of its own membership. Permit me to ask, who can interfere with this acknowledged right of every church, if, by your New Rule, you have not interfered with this right of the Presbyterian Church? You expressed the same principle with equal clearness, when you disavowed your authority and your inclination to intermeddle with "the *discipline* or the *doctrine* of the churches" you proposed to serve. My dear brethren! What is discipline or doctrine as applied to the Church of Christ? Is not their end the promotion of the Christian character, conduct, and influence of the members of the Church? Are not their means those Christian truths and laws which decide church-membership and duty, and which govern the Church by the due enforcement of the same? Why, my brethren! who can interfere with the discipline or the doctrine of a church, if you have not disturbed the discipline and the doctrine of the whole Presbyterian Church? I know you did not maliciously intend any such dishonor. But have you not measurably abolished her constitutional standard of church-rectitude? Have you not required that every church-member holding slaves, in all the Synods, Presbyteries, and churches of the South, shall dishonor the highest judicatory of his own Church, and come before you, that he may there find the only tribunal which you deem competent to decide whether he is worthy to receive the Gospel at your hands? My brethren! Bear with me. Does not the American Home Missionary Society, regarded in the light of the principle avowed thirty years ago, when conferring with the Presbyterian Church concerning missionary union, face to the right about in assuming the ground on which she stands in her New Rule? It is a good thing, brethren, to be valiant for truth and righteousness, but we must not permit our ideas of intrepid defense of high principle to mislead us into a forgetfulness of the principles we ourselves have avowed! We must not allow our notions of valiant assault upon a corrupt institution to betray us into the dishonor of our own assurances to Christian brethren, deliberately advanced with a view to secure their confidence.

5. Compare the *contracting mind* of the Society when proposing missionary connection with the Presbyterian Church, with *that mind renounced* in the New Rule.

Let it be premised that missionary union was sought by the Home Missionary Society, and not by the Presbyterian Church. In 1828, the General Assembly arranged to enlarge the operations of its "Board of Missions." The Home Missionary Society anticipated "interference" and "embarrassment." The Executive Committee accordingly conferred with several members of the Board of Missions, who so far encouraged the proposed idea of united operation that the Committee first passed a favorable resolution in its own Body, and then addressed a circular to all the Directors of the Society, and obtained the approval of the majority. They thereupon published what they termed "*a plan and stipulations*," on which they invited the coöperation of several Churches. They discussed in their cotemporaneous publications "the *evils of the present* system of missionary operation," "the advantages of the proposed union," and "the alleged objections" to the same. Having published such an alteration of the Constitution of the American Home Missionary Society as was necessary to meet the case, they proceed to say that the Society hereby places itself "*in an attitude to invite the coöperation of the General Assembly* in effecting the proposed union, and the *way will be opened for that Body to determine on the subject.*" (Vol. I., p. 208.)

The contracting mind of the Society may be simplified to two points:

The American Home Missionary Society covenants that—

1. *No disturbance shall or can arise to the Presbyterian Church, because all authority belongs to the Church, and there exists no disposition to interfere with it in the Society.* In addition to pertinent passages quoted above, many such declarations as the following are found in the publications of the day: "The plan assumes to the Society no ecclesiastical authority." (p. 208.) "The plan and stipulations on which the Executive Committee invite the coöperation of aux-

iliary Societies yield to such Societies, the control within their bounds even of the missionary appointments of the Parent Society." (208.) "If Presbyteries and Synods become auxiliaries to the National Society on this plan, they have all the security for the orthodoxy and correct ecclesiastical standing of the missionaries within their bounds which the Constitution of the Presbyterian Church furnishes, and no power of the Parent Society can impair that security." (208.) In fine, it is argued that the Presbyterian Church should yield to the plan of coöperation, "especially" since that plan "is rendered so unexceptionable and safe to the separate interests of the several denominations embraced in it."

2. That the *Home Missionary Society agrees to assume a relation entirely subservient to the churches whose coöperation it seeks.*

The proposal of the American Home Missionary Society, in its own language is a proposal "to *serve*" the churches. It does not hesitate to call itself their "*servant.*" "Thus the National Society becomes the *servant* of each ecclesiastical body which chooses to avail itself" of its services. When the Presbyterian Church objected to the surrender of the management of its own Domestic Missions, the Home Missionary Society responded that the objection was based upon a misapprehension of the design and effect of the proposed union—"which contemplates not the relinquishment of Domestic Missions by the General Assembly, but *simply the change of its organ.*" "If it makes the change," it "assumes, *as its organ*, the Home Missionary Society." The agents of the Society will then be cordially admitted to all the congregations of auxiliary bodies, "because they will be in fact, *the agents of the ecclesiastical bodies* within whose bounds, with whose approbation, and for whose benefit they will be *appointed to act.*" Thus, by its own explicit statements, the American Home Missionary Society, by this contract, connects itself with the Presbyterian Church in the relation of an *assumed organ*, an *appointed agent*, an *employed servant.* It is true that the General Assembly declined to give up its "Board of Missions;" but the Presbyterian Church extensively accepted the overtures of the Home Missionary Society, and became auxiliary to that body, in view of the published plan and stipulations, through her Synods, Presbyteries, and missionary organizations. This, the publications of the Home Missionary Society abundantly establish. They say: "Large sections of the Presbyterian Church have already become auxiliary to the Society." "*A majority of the Presbyterian Church*, a considerable portion of the Reformed Dutch, and the Congregational churches generally, have declared in favor of a union and concentration of efforts." (P. 210.) Indeed, the refusal to abandon its Board of Missions is represented somewhat in the aspect of encouraging schism, since so large a portion of the Presbyterian Church had already given its adherence to the plan of union. The American Home Missionary Society therefore bound itself to carry out this contract faithfully with that great mass of the Presbyterian Church which accepted its overtures.

Now, my brethren, fix your eyes, I entreat you, upon two points in this history. First. When the American Home Missionary Society approached the Presbyterian Church and proposed union, remember, in all the churches of the South, Presbyterian church-members held slaves just as they do now. Remember, by the discipline of the Presbyterian Church, all these slaveholding church-members were deemed to possess a perfectly unexceptionable Christian standing. And remember, all this the American Home Missionary Society knew perfectly well at the time she proposed the connection. Again, bear in mind that the Presbyterian Church met your proposal with an honest disclosure of her apprehension of you.—There is no bit in your mouth; we have no rein to hold you in; we fear you will disturb the discipline of our churches.—Call to mind, now, your response to the Presbyterian Church: "Brethren! you should indulge no fear of us. We assure you we have 'no wish,' 'no power,' to interfere with the discipline of your Church. It is not our 'province;' we have 'no right' to decide the church standing of your members. To assure you, and all men, of our unobtrusive temper, we have actually renounced the shadow of all power, 'by choosing to exist without a charter, and without permanent funds.' Indeed you should not entertain the very slightest apprehension of trouble from us; for 'we have no existence except in the affections and confidence of the Christian public.' Why should you fear us? We have no '*authority*.' We are simply an 'organ'—your 'agent'—your 'servant.'" Well, brethren! the Presbyterian churches trusted you; they committed their Home Missionary matters largely into your hands. What have you done, brethren? Without one syllable of premonition, at a distance from the point where we should have expected to hear from the Society, there is published upon us a rule of the Committee, (however sincere your purpose to advance the cause of Christ,) yet a rule violently assailing the discipline of the Presbyterian Church, throwing the Body into great confusion, and doubtless contributing its part to the late North and South disruption of our Denomination. Brethren, most clearly the Society had left itself one only just and honorable method in which she could have acted upon her new scruples on the subject of slavery. She should have addressed the coöperating portion of the Presbyterian Church a second time. She should have rehearsed the fact of her early disavowal of any inclination or authority to interfere with the discipline or the doctrine of the Presbyterian Church. She should have announced her supposed advance in Christian knowledge and conscience, and her consequent inability to serve Presbyterian churches as their almoner any longer, since she would be compelled to dispense Gospel supplies to men professing Christianity, and yet holding slaves upon principles which do not accord with her new scruples. Nothing short of this could have reached the morality of the case. Nothing short of this could protect the Society for a moment against the charge of continuing to receive the funds of the Presbyterian Church as an appointed almoner, and yet of assuming such authority over the Presbyterian Church in the disbursement of the same, as amounted to a renunciation of that contracting mind, which, to the Presbyterian Church, was the condition precedent to her employment of the offered services of the Society.

6. Compare the one grand *object* in the formation of the Society, with the *renunciation of that object* in the Society's recent act. The object of the Society was catholic, and covered the whole country. The act of the Society is sectional, and will abandon half of the Union.

There never was a broader Christian banner hoisted in this land than was that of the American Home Missionary Society. If I mistake not, the very first sentence published under countenance of the Society, (certainly in the Society's organ,) is expressed in these words: "The design of the American Home Missionary Society is to promote not the interests of any one section or denomination of the Church, but the religious benefit of a great and growing nation." How much of this wide range will the Society cover now? The very first sentence published concerning the organ of the Society tells us: "It will have none of the local characteristics of many journals;

but like the Society in whose name it is issued, is intended to be truly national." What one mark is left that will save the publication from the characteristics of a local journal now? The very first sentence of its Constitution speaks thus: "This Society shall be called 'The *American* Home Missionary Society.'" Where is its nationality now? The very first constitutional sentence concerning the end of the Institution informs us that: "The object of the Society shall be to assist congregations that are unable to support the Gospel ministry, and send the Gospel to the destitute within the *United States.*" Will the larger portion of the territory of these United States receive its assistance now? One sentence of its own selected preacher which the Society printed and reprinted a few years since, and commended to its patrons as a portion of an able and eloquent exposition of its own principles, may thus be read on the page of its own organ: "Its missionary is to be sent where slavery is not, *but more urgently where slavery is.*" How many of its missionaries from this day shall be sent to those regions where the slave *so urgently needs their* services? Clearly the New Rule has violated a fundamental aim of the enterprise, and transformed a national into a sectional Society.

7. Compare *public positions* of the Society assumed against extreme Anti-Slavery views, with *those positions dishonored* in the defense of the New Rule.

To establish the charge that the Society had changed ground in their New Rule, from Conservatism toward

Abolitionism, reference was had to certain principles and acts of the Society, embodied in an article appended to its Twenty-Seventh Report. I deeply regret that my brethren should have felt it necessary to object to the responsibility of the Society for this publication. That this paper, induced by the arbitrary, unyielding assaults of the Abolitionists, was drawn up by the accredited organs of the Society, in official vindication of the Society, and published by the officers of the Society, with the Report of the Society, is not denied. That by common law, from the foundation of the Society, with the perfect approval of the Society, its officers have been accustomed to append to their Annual Reports such brief publications as they deemed serviceable to the interests of the Society, will not be denied. That all such statements by the Secretaries concerning the regular business of the Society, in the proper publications of the Society, have always been received, not as the private opinions of an indifferent person, but as communications made by men commissioned and accredited to speak and act for the Society, will never be denied. In the publication described, that every principle affirmed was then a principle of the Society; that every act stated is still verified by the history of the Society, so far as my knowledge extends, has never been disputed. Surely it must tend to destroy confidence in Christian men and all Christian agency, if the American Home Missionary Society does not promptly assume all the responsibilities of that publication.

When our brethren, the Secretaries, and the Committee, put forth that paper, they felt for the Society, they stood for the Society, they spoke for the Society; they meant in their souls that those whom they addressed should give to the Society the full credit of all the principles and facts they therein advanced in its defense. When the members of the Society perused these avowed doctrinés and acts of the Society, advanced in its defense by those whom they had appointed to transact all such business in their behalf, doubtless every one of them, the assailants excepted, did not only inwardly acknowledge and approve every asserted principle, agency, and aim of the Society, but thanked their officers for their firm and skillful defense of the Society against these violent opposers. "Qui facit per alium facit per se." Awkward indeed must the position of the Society be felt to be, if it is so important to absolve her from all responsibility for a publication by her own officers, in their ordinary method of acting for her, to which she had never objected, and no one word of which to this day is understood to be disputed. What speaking evidence does this fact furnish that the Society has reached a new position, not by the light of her own arguments, *but against that light*, and through a force which has pressed her on to the new ground by its own irresistible will.

Finally. Compare the face of the *New Rule* with the face of *Southern Christianity*.

Many men of our day, I am aware, entertain the

deepest conviction that the holding of slaves in this age of the world is an insufferable immorality, and many more think very little better of it. They can not stretch their charity so far as to believe that there does or can exist in a slaveholding community any considerable degree of pure, solid, consistent religion. The black portrait of Southern slavery which has been made so unceasingly to horrify the imaginations of the North for the last twenty years, and the consequent diminution of kindness, and increase of prejudice between the parties, must account, in part, for the strength of this sentiment. Be human opinion what it may, one thing is certain: prejudice can not expunge history, nor imagination destroy facts. I do not affirm that the South is superior to the North in Christianity; but I do question any great superiority of the North over the South on this subject. Select an honest, intelligent delegation of Northern men. Command them to devote one year to a thorough examination of Christian society at the South, and an equal period to a similar examination of Christian character at the North. In reaching their conclusion, I am a deceived man if they do not pass through some such mental process as this:

The difference between the religion of the North and of the South is precisely such as we should have anticipated from the respective history of these opposite sections. The population of the North brought with them in their emigration to this country more education and religion, and a higher appreciation of literary and religious institutions. They occupied the healthier portion of the territory, and pursued avocations which threw society together. Consequently, two superiorities have always distinguished the North. They far surpass the South in educational and Christian institutions, and exhibit a religion marked by an equal superiority in three respects—knowledge, organization, and training. There is, however, a defect in the religion of the North. If Northern mind is more inquiring, it is also more inquisitive. Consequently, you will find at the North more speculation and abstraction in the pulpit; and more new lights, heresies, and infidelity among the people. Southern population, on the contrary, brought less intelligence and religion with them, and, very naturally, an inferior appreciation of literary and religious institutions. They settled, too, in a portion of the country where neither the climate nor the soil admitted of an uniformly dense population, and adopted a method of life which threw society apart. Consequently, the Southern Church is decidedly inferior to the Northern, not only in religious and auxiliary institutions, but also in general Christian knowledge and in efficient Christian training. Yet the South possesses one superiority over the North. If they have less investigation, they have more faith. If the Southern pulpit, therefore, is inferior in learning and style, it is less liable to digression from scriptural matter and spirit. And whatever may be said of the lack of the same look of religion on the face of Southern society, of the imperfect knowledge of its professors, and the great prevalence of self-deception, thorough ignorance and enthusiasm, there is yet a confiding simplicity, an unreasoning reverence in the structure and habit of Southern mind; a willingness to hear any thing from God, but nothing from man, which will probably be found to embody quite as much veneration for the Scriptures, the ministry, and universal religion, and certainly a greater freedom from vagaries, heresies, and infidelity. While some such general view distinguishes the religion of the North from that of the South, the great Head of the Church in late years has been pleased to bestow a greater degree of spiritual blessing upon Christian means at the South than at the North. In the following years, 1850, 1851, 1852, 1853, and 1854, the amount of preaching in the Episcopalian, Baptist, Old and New School Presbyterian churches, has been computed to be, at the North, 33,436 years; at the South, 24,918 years—about one fourth less at the South than at the North. Reported additions to the churches during the same period at the North, 164,553 souls; at the South, 214,918 souls—or about one fourth more at the South than at the North. During these five years, in these four denominations, a Christian force at the South one fourth less, works a Christian result one fourth greater. A reliable report of the Baptist Church informs us that three fifths of its members are found at the South, and two fifths at the North; that the net increase of its members in the whole country during the year 1855, was 26,802. In the Southern States that increase was 22,000; in all other States and Territories, 4802. On the last day of public prayer for the colleges of the country, the thirty-one Northern institutions represented—report but 181 conversions, while the sixteen colleges heard from at the South—record 249.

I am aware that depreciating remarks respecting the statistics of the Southern Church are very common in this latitude. You frequently hear it said: "Half of these recorded conversions are spurious." The initiated "are ignorant persons who mistake dreams for experience"—"are received in times of excitement without intelligent and thorough examination," etc. Such observations betray as great a lack of intelligence as of candor. The fact that practical religion at the South compares so well with practical religion at the North, is a triumphant refutation of this uncharitableness. Upon an impartial survey of this ground, therefore, we may very well imagine that the report of the Committee would be something like this: "In comparing the religion of the North with the religion of the South, whether we employ the Saviour's test, 'By their fruits ye shall know them,' or whether we bring the law of cause and effect to bear upon the much larger dispensation of sanctifying power in late years to the Southern Church than to the Northern, we feel ourselves compelled to express this opinion: that there does exist a sincere, a sound Christianity at the South, is indisputable. If in some respects Southern Christianity is not equal to Northern Christianity, it is our confident conviction that thorough examination will never pronounce the religion of the North very far superior to the religion of the South. Let this, then, stand for the true face of Southern society.

What now is the face of the Society's New Rule? It inflicts a broad brand upon the religion of the whole South. It pronounces Southern Christianity so unsound, so suspicious, that even in the matter of dispensing Gospel supplies among the churches of one of the denominations whose almoner the Society is, the Society feels that it can not admit these Southern churches to the common level of the people of God. On the contrary, if Southern churches seek missionary aid of the Society, this is the published decree of its conscience:—Every slaveholding member of the applicant Church, must appear before the bar of the Committee in person, or by testimony, and submit to examination, that the Committee may exercise their conscientious judgment whether in fact the parties do sincerely desire the Gospel at their hands, or whether in truth they do not apply to the Committee for power to *hide the Gospel* from themselves, and from those to whom they profess to preach it. The Executive Committee of the American Home Missionary Society! Let no man suppose from this *exposé* of the voice and bearing of their unhappy

Rule that I dishonor them as men and brethren. I hasten to say, I would not know where to look for excellent men and faithful servants of God, if these men were not enrolled on the catalogue. My good brethren will now permit a fellow-servant, in advocating the cause of our common Master, to speak out his sentiments concerning their recent action in reference to Southern churches. I use the mildest language when I say, that from its earliest publication, their New Rule has never ceased to appear before my mind as a positive indecency!

I know well that the entire difference between us hinges upon one point. This is the very question we have touched—the soundness of the Southern Church. If it is, indeed, a fact, as our brethren doubtless suppose, that the Southern Church is profoundly beguiled and polluted by slavery; that churches and ministers together, by this cause, are so utterly dishonest or deluded, that the Gospel of Jesus Christ is actually suppressed at the South, and can not be honestly preached to the people; if this is so far true, that to send them the Gospel, or, as they would prefer to express the transaction, to assist such ministers to preach to such churches, would involve the Committee in as grand an abandonment of principle as would be perpetrated by employing the funds of Orthodox denominations in sustaining heretical preachers in heretical churches; I heartily accord it to my brethren, if such is the rottenness of the Southern Church, then the Committee have actually done what they intended to do. They have done a deed of sound Christian wisdom, and of noble Christian daring, and no men on earth deserve higher admiration. But, on the contrary, if the Southern Church, of all denominations, is not so rotten as all this; if there is some true religion at the South as well as at the North; if God converts souls there, as well as here; if God's spirit makes men intelligent and honest there, as well as here; if God sprinkles the consciences, sanctifies the souls, hears the prayers, directs the agency, and accepts the persons and labors of men there, as well as here; if in support of the integrity of their effort to serve God and save men, by what they deem an honest proclamation of the Gospel of Jesus Christ, they present to the eye of heaven and earth *an every day religion* which gives but little countenance to the proud phariseeism so prompt to exclaim, "Stand by! I am holier than thou!"—in a word, if there is reason to believe that your power to *judge* right has been more damaged by *your* circumstances, than their power *to do* right, by *theirs,* what, then, shall we say of this *New Rule?* Faithfulness would seem to demand three painful inferences:

1. The Committee and the Society are, measurably, a *subdued people.*

History confounds the man who denies that they have been subjected to the strong and steady adverse pressure of extreme Anti-Slavery men for fifteen years. Candor forsakes the man who contends that they have yielded no ground to their obstinate opponents. The Society protested that their former ordinary dispensation of the Gospel to the South did *not countenance slavery;* but we have seen, that the Society now gives ground in its New Rule, and takes position very much with extreme Anti-Slavery men. The Society protested, that to *withdraw* her missionaries from the South would "*not be right or proper;*" but we have seen, that by the necessary working of her New Rule, the Society now gives ground, and takes position very much with extreme Anti-Slavery men. The Society distinctly disclaimed *every inclination*, and even possibility, of interference with the discipline or doctrine of the churches she proposed to serve; but we have seen that, under pressure, the Society has given ground, and in their New Rule exhibits very much of the opposite temper of extreme Anti-Slavery men. The Society avowed its *principle*, that it did not lie in its province to intermeddle with the right of every church to *define the terms of its own membership;* but we have seen, that under pressure, the Society has given ground, and is now acting very much upon the opposite assumption of extreme Anti-Slavery men. The Society gave to the Presbyterian Church a semi-pledge that they never would exert any such authority as would *disturb its peace and order;* but we have seen that, under pressure, the Society has given ground, and thrown an Abolition brand into the heart of the Presbyterian Church. The Society committed itself to the Church and to the world, that it would preserve inviolate the *catholic, the national character* of the noble American institution; but we have seen that the Society has given ground, and virtually accomplished that limitation of the Society's operations to the North, so long the vehement object of extreme Anti-Slavery men. Finally, the Society is made to *shrink from the responsibility of a recorded defense of her early principles* against the Abolitionist, although that defense was drawn up by her own officers, bound up with her own Report, distributed to her own members, in accordance with her accustomed method of communicating with the public, and while, to the best of our knowledge, not one of the Society's principles or actions recorded in that publication has been or can be denied.

2. The Society has been measurably subdued by the *very power* which she should have most *steadfastly resisted.*

The American Home Missionary Society stood between two antagonistic elements—the slaveholding churches of the South, and the extreme Abolitionism of the North. A crisis arose, which summoned the Society to decide a point respecting her duty as the appointed almoner of missionary funds contributed by the Congregational and Presbyterian denominations. The precise question was this—in sympathy with the conservative Christianity of the country, should the American Home Missionary Society send Gospel supplies to Presbyterian churches at the South, in good standing with their own denomination and all others; or, in sympathy with the extreme Anti-Slavery views of the North, was the Society bound to consider all the churches of the South containing slaveholding members as unworthy to receive the Gospel at her hands, until the applicant church produced satisfactory evidence to the Committee that its members held slaves upon principles which accorded with her own scruples of sound Christianity on this subject? The Saviour pronounced a woe upon the Scribes and Pharisees! But without one whit of religion, they were arrant hypocrites, covetous oppressors of widows and orphans, profane destroyers of the Word, Church, and Son of God. The New Rule of the Society inflicts a public stigma upon a great body of professors of religion, of all denominations; just as clear and consistent Christians, just as good men and women, as are to be found on the face of the earth. What a body of sound Northern testimony has long been entered up, in support of the truth of this declaration! But Northern mind, under strong Anti-Slavery bias, is exceedingly reluctant to credit the clearest evidence on this subject. That persecuted man of God in Boston was never discredited until he visited the South and bore testimony to the pleasant religious developments he there saw, both in the master and in the slave. And yet there stands not a man on American soil more worthy of Christian credence than he. Nay! I exult in the opportunity to record this tribute of fraternal respect: When I consider his

Christian candor—reading Southern society so fairly, through all the prejudices he carried with him from the North; his Christian principle—bearing witness to the truth, in full view of that cross which must be the reward of such fidelity; and that Christian patience—with which he ever bears his most unmerciful martyrdom: My inmost soul exclaims: "The very brightest Christian crown man wears within the reach of my eye!!" The men who bitterly revile Nehemiah Adams! A mania is upon them! They know not what they do! Permit me to advance and say that the strongest Northern testimony to the solid piety of the South is often most unwittingly rendered. By far the sternest Abolitionist who lifted up his voice in the General Assembly of 1850, at Detroit, was earnestly invited by Southern men on the floor to visit them at the South, and go around and survey the relation of master and servant with his own eyes, under assurances of the heartiest welcome and the most perfect protection. The good man, with perfect simplicity, arose in his place, and thus responded: "No! I shall never go to the South! I have known too many men who lost their principles by going to the South." Yes, my brethren, there are sincere, solid Christian elements amongst Southern men and women, which have destroyed the fiercest prejudices, and changed the most bigoted impressions of multitudes of misled men. Very pleasant and perfectly natural was the exclamation of the delegate to the last Assembly from the city of New-

York, a man as distinguished for his extreme hostility to Slavery, as for his devotion to the cause of Christ. "My feelings toward my Southern brethren," said he, "have undergone an entire change: their bearing in the Assembly has been such as to command my confidence and respect. If any one had told me before I came here, that I could have been brought into contact with slaveholders, and those who justify slavery as right, and that notwithstanding all, I could hold fellowship with them, not in form merely, but sincere, heartfelt friendship, I would have said, it could not be; but I am free to confess that such is the case, and that my Southern brethren take back with them not only my confidence and regard, but they take my heart with them also. I feel that I do now love them as brethren."

Such are the people marked before the world by the New Rule as professors whose Christianity should be suspected, whose Christian operations should not be countenanced, even by the missionary supplies of their own denomination, without personal examination. Bear in mind two things. It does not approach to a justification of the act of the Home Missionary Society, that there are some wrong things in the Southern Church. There are not a few wrong things in the Northern Church. But it does clearly establish the unjustifiableness of their act, that Southern Presbyterian churches are composed of men and women of ordinary personal piety. For surely it is an outrage, that an appointed distributing agent should look a Christian denomination in the face, and say: "Your churches are composed of ordinary Christians, but they are not worthy to receive a dollar of your missionary funds, and shall never do so through our hands, until they come up to a standard of Christianity which we shall dictate." The Society, therefore, would seem to have but little ground for opposition to the South.

What, now, are the claims of this Modern Reform enterprise upon the respect and coöperation of Christian men? Have we not seen that its elements are largely, phariseeism, malevolence, tyranny, and prejudice? Have we not seen that its work is damage to the master and the slave, the pulpit and the Bible, the country and the Church—God and man? Yet this is the spirit, this the influence of that formidable agent which, after a long and desperate struggle, has overborne the American Home Missionary Society to stand by its side before the world, and defame the Christianity of their Southern brethren. When we reflect, therefore, that it is the great mass of the best Christianity at the South against which the New Rule discriminates, and the most violent Anti-Slavery men of the North with whom the New Rule takes sides, we are compelled to believe that, in an evil hour, the Society has given way to the very power which they should have breasted with the most unyielding firmness.

3. Under pressure has not the Society measurably

abandoned her old principles, and yet *failed to reach the new ground she* purports to occupy?

The old principles of the Society are mainly defined by its *office* and its *character*. In office, the American Home Missionary Society, in its own language, is a "servant," an "organ," an "agent," which early proposed "*to serve*" the Presbyterian Church. Direction belongs to the employer—duty to the employee. Clearly that *agent abandons his place* who, instead of following long-established directions, assumes the directorship in the business of his employer. In character the American Home Missionary Society is a *Christian* agent. Clearly that *Christian* agent *abandons his principle* who, instead of laboring for the peace and welfare of mankind, gives such strong countenance to the great disorganizing spirit of the day as must feed and fire the most formidable element of strife and mischief in Church and State.

The new ground sought by the Society's New Rule is mainly determined by the *nature* and the *manner* of the movement. In its *nature* the New Rule is an attempt at moral reform. But this effort is an utter failure. In the absence of all evidence of fraternal solicitude, it displays before the mind of the accused such an appearance of arrogant phariseeism as must prompt it to fling back all its reform power in the indignant reply: "Physician, heal thyself." In its *manner* the Reform effort assumes the attitude of *intrepid heroism*. In this aspect, also, is not the movement a melancholy failure? The American Home Missionary

Society, looking the whole South in the face, and practically carrying out a charge of sin, never practically attempted before, has a very gallant appearance. But the claim of moral heroism so distinctly set up in the spirit and language of the defense of the Society's New Rule, is as indiscreet as it is indelicate. In consideration of this high claim, it is neither unkind nor unnecessary to remind brethren of the lights of *history;* to call to mind that *dicsipline* of a dominant power whereby the Society has been brought to this new stand. One extravagance breeds another. To claim intrepid courage for the Society, is to throw into the mind of an objector the story of captives disarmed upon the battle-field, but rearmed by the captors, and stationed in the front rank and commanded to fire into their own army or be shot down from behind for disobedience. No entire conduct of the men of the Home Missionary Society could be fairly represented by such a picture. But a *thought* is often *a world*, such is the infinite mixture of its elements. And most assuredly, our brethren of the Society have come up to this bold stand against the South so slowly, after such remonstrances against its principle, under such applications of hostile fierceness, as exceedingly complicates the question of gallantry, and should have suggested the idea to a discreet advocate that if he could save the Society's independence, he might well afford to withhold its claims to chivalry.

While it is impossible to avoid the feeling of deep regret that the Society should have given way under adverse pressure, yet in its behalf we should remember the importunity to which brethren have long been subjected. Nor have they been called to bear up against the simple dint of importunity, but against an importunity of power—conscientious, violent, determined power. The principal responsibilities of the New Rule, therefore, we need not say, belong to the Reform spirit, the extreme Anti-Slavery temper of the day. The disturbing capacities of this agent are exemplified on every hand. But in all the events which have transpired in the history of the Anti-Slavery movement, there is probably no solitary fact so well calculated to startle the mind in view of its formidable power to *convulse* the Church of God, as is this recent action of the Home Missionary Society in respect to Southern churches.

As for me, when I look at the agents and the action, they seem so widely sundered I can scarcely account for their connection. One thought, a very uncharitable one peradventure, flits across my mind at times. We are instructed, "By their fruits ye shall know them." O the fruits! in Church and State, the unhallowed fruits of extreme Anti-Slavery principles which God has laid before the eyes of this nation! We are commanded: "Have no fellowship with the unfruitful works of darkness, but rather reprove them." Now my thought is this: God may purpose to be heard and felt upon this subject. After all the developments he has caused to be made of an evil spirit; after all his injunctions to avoid such agencies in the earth—if good men will hold close fellowship with this wrong element; if they will bow down to its power, and suffer themselves to be crowded up to do what they themselves had so frequently declared they ought *not* to do, God will leave these men to show to the world that this *wild power* of our day can even make sensible Christian men perpetrate a palpably irrational and unchristian deed.

Now if this Reform movement strikes such a blow upon the authority of the Bible, and such a blow upon the sacredness of the pulpit, and such a blow upon the peace of the Church, are we not bound to regard it as deeply hostile to the best interests of the Christian religion?

IV. Reformation—you will remember, is the end sought, the work undertaken. The last inquiry of importance respects the influence of this effort upon the cause of reformation; in other words, upon all power to effect desirable improvement in Southern society.

Reformation is a delicate and difficult work. It presupposes the existence of a moral standard and the fact of departure from it, and consists in a threefold mental process. It commences by bringing the mind acquainted with the law and its breach; is advanced when conscience is made to feel conviction of sin; and completed when the heart returns to duty. The whole process is unwelcome to the pride of man's fallen nature, and ordinarily requires a variety of favorable influences to secure either its commencement or its consummation. The most common forces which impel the mind to self-inspection and improvement, are suasion, conscience, benevolence, and interest. The kind appeal of a good man has these three advantages—it brings the mind directly to the subject, places convicting truth before it more clearly and amply than the unassisted faculties of the party would be apt to do, and exerts a gentle and genial power to set truth to work. It is perfectly natural, too, when truth shines first upon the standard and then upon the soul's departure from it, that conscience should start the process of conviction and recovery. Nor is it surprising that the disadvantages of departure from duty, contrasted with the blessings of returning to it, should sometimes, in like manner, initiate the process of reformation. So, also, when parties providentially dependent upon us are subjected to privations and hardships through our neglect, calm contemplative benevolence will often suggest a course of reflection well adapted to lead to our improved fidelity. God's truth on the one hand, and the state of society on the other, are constantly before the people of the South. That these moral stimulants should start many a thought of amelioration is perfectly natural. But reformation works up the hill—against the stream. It requires strong facilities, and will bear but few obstructions. One thing is clear, there must be quiet without, to induce the mind to enter upon self-inspection, and that quiet must be preserved or the thoughts will be sure to be withdrawn.

As to amelioration at the South, our Modern Reform produces a paralysis of all reform power at home and abroad.

1. Glance at its bearing upon *Home* reformation. That very moment which records contact between the charge of the Reformer and the mind of the slaveholder, dates the arrest of the process of reformation. The quiet of the soul is broken up. The thoughts are summoned without, and the mind turns instantly from self-inspection to self-defense. What now becomes of our all-important auxiliaries to reformation? Where is truth? Cast out of the mind at once with the outward direction of its thoughts! Conscience? Wounded pride sets it to work at once, not to convince of sin—but of rectitude! Self-interest? Instead of attempting any longer to effect a small improvement of his property and comfort in his slaves by improving their condition, he is called at once to the more important necessity of defending his assaulted title to all he owns! Benevolence? Weaker friendship for his slave must give way now to stronger love for himself. Thus all favorable influences are reversed, and the mind naturally thrown into an attitude diametrically opposed to reformation. Nor does the malign influence of this Reform stop here. Self-righteousness is stirred up and brought on the field to maintain this attitude, for any attempt at reformation now is a plea of guilty to the charge of the Reformer. *Fear of dishonor*, too, is sommoned to take ground by the side of self-righteousness, and cut off all return

to reformation; for he who engages in any decided reform upon the subject of slavery now, must make up his mind to bear the charge of sympathy with the Abolitionist. To put an end to all hope of improvement, *reäction* against the rude interference of the North arrays a new party, strong because by pre-eminence the *home* party, whose motto is: "Reformation is impossible, because all things are best as they are."

Thus in all its tendencies our Reform enterprise exerts a prostrating energy upon all the stimulants, facilities, and powers of *Home* reformation.

2. Nor does *foreign* reformation fare any better at his hand. A stranger to the body to be reformed always labors under two great disadvantages. He lacks *knowledge*. The eye of the man at a distance does not rest upon the immorality to be reformed; upon the circumstances of the case; upon the discouragements to be surmounted, or the allowances to be made. He does not intimately understand the peculiarities of the character he has to deal with; what methods of approach and appeal would be wise, and what indiscreet. On the contrary, he who is a member of the community, and has grown up in daily intercourse with the party to be reclaimed, and in vision of all the circumstances of the case, is much better prepared to work to advantage in such an enterprise. The stranger lacks *influence* also. He has no influence of authority; none of power; none of friendship; none of confidence; none from any

special claim or connection. On the contrary, he who is identified with the party by every tie which binds man to man, is much more likely to secure his confidence and to exert an influence upon him. It is self-evident that a stranger does not know you—that a stranger has no right to interfere with you. With the velocity and power of lightning these thoughts fly into the mind when a stranger, in a bad spirit, undertakes to set you right. If my neighbor across the street disapproves of my method of governing my children, and is daily heard in a loud, censorious, and imperious tone lecturing me upon the proper method of training a family, nature in my heart would fly up in an instant and I should respond: "Sir, you are impertinent! Mind your own affairs." When we reflect that a stranger is so far from the party to be reformed, has so few connections with him or claims upon him, may so very readily offend him, and can hope to accomplish nothing if he fails to secure his affectionate confidence, the first great rule, the all-necessary prerequisite in every such case, is this: the reformer should always be animated by the most respectful kindness, and approach his work and prosecute its every successive step with the most delicate and considerate regard for the feelings, views, and circumstances of the party he would serve. Indeed it may be set down as an axiom, that reformation by a foreign power can never hope for success, except in the exercise of the truest and the wisest kindness.

Who needs evidence that our Reform friends have as thoroughly destroyed reformation power at the North as at the South? As to themselves, none can question their unsympathizing, unsparing, denunciatory spirit. They have thus surrendered all the power to serve their Southern neighbors, which they themselves might have once exerted. By the same spirit, they have destroyed the power of the more calm, conservative person by their side. This man feels all just and proper sympathies with his Southern brethren; and this very kindness assures him that since Northern violence has inflamed Southern mind against all Northern interference with their domestic concerns, and roused the profoundest suspicion of all Northern attempts to reform Southern society, it does not become him to make any advance in this direction at this time. The fact is, the South deserve credit for the attention they still bestow upon their dependent population notwithstanding the discouraging, provoking operation of our Reform movements. For it must be obvious to every impartial mind that all opportunity and power, North and South, to prosecute, or even suggest remedial ideas touching Southern institutions, have been wantonly squandered by this wild, inconsiderate crusade of the North.

The last demand you can make upon a reformer, is, that he should reclaim the wanderer, or work reasonably toward that end.

The last property of our Modern Reformer we are called to record, we repeat, is this: it is *destructive.*

An ordinary benevolent enterprise involves four things: *theatre*, *beneficiary*, *agency*, and *instrumentality*. The theatre of this reform, is our *country*. The Reform has agitated the *country* to its very foundations, periling the Union. Its *beneficiary* is the slave. The Reform has done nothing for the liberty, nothing for the religion of the slave, but deeply damaged both. Its *means* are God's truth. The Reform has struck a blow upon the Bible, upon the pulpit, upon the Church, and thus deeply damaged Christianity throughout the land. Finally, its *agency* is reformation. In the field in which it has wrought, the Reform has laid waste all power of reformation, both at the North and at the South.

CHAPTER VII.

MORAL ESTIMATE.

In the eyes of the world, the *enterprise* we have discussed, sets out to accomplish a *grand reformation.* In truth and justice, what verdict upon its claims shall history record? What are its properties, its impressions, its results?

Were I summoned to bear witness of its *elements*, I should respond: He who would reform another should possess rectitude to command his conscience, and benevolence to reach his heart; should employ suasion to teach his mind, and display candor to win his confidence; that thus he might enlist all reclaiming power and avert all tendencies to mischief. But we have seen that the attributes of this Reform are the precise antagonism of all this. It averts the conscience by an *arrogance*, which does not possess the rectitude it assumes. It shuts up the heart by a *malignity*, which proves that it comes for no good ends. It employs *force*, a witness that it works to execute some will of its own. It exhibits an *im-*

practicability which will hear no truth from him whom it expects to submit to all assumption from itself. Thus, in view of its constituent elements, blessing this Reform can not convey; mischief this Reform can not avoid.

Were I summoned to speak of the *impressions* which this movement makes upon the mind of the candid spectator, I would say: There would seem to be too much *nature* about it. It finds its principle in nature, derives its inspiration from nature, and subjects all questions to the umpirage of nature. And too little *grace*. It does not go to the word of God for its position, nor to the Spirit of God for its strength, nor to the throne of God for its arbiter. There would seem to be too much *glitter* about it. It is ever throwing itself upon you in heroic attitudes, brilliant declamations, sparkling novels, and blazing resolutions. And too little *gold*. Where are its holy promptings, its wise plannings, its solid fruits; what has it done for Church or State, North or South, master or servant? There would seem to be too much *fury* about it. The master is a monster; destroy him it will, if it must outrage all proprieties, perpetrate all profanities, shake its fist in the face of all perils, plant its foot upon the neck of all dignities, and tumble Church and State, heaven and earth, into irrecoverable chaos. And too little efficiency. It is a teacher, but it instructs nobody; a friend, but it blesses nobody; a reformer, but it reclaims nobody; a restorer, but it up-turns every thing; a good-doer, but it does nought but evil, and cripples all that would do good.

Were I called upon more particularly to graduate the *morality* or *philosophy* of this enterprise of my fellow-men, I would say that it is marked by *two* capital *defects*. It lacks the two vital properties of virtue.

1. *Benevolence.*—One simple thought ever thrills the soul of the Reformer—Liberty! liberty! instant liberty! This is the sum of all good to man. Until man feels liberty, light itself is darkness to him. By pure mania this fancy reigns triumphant over head and heart. His love, of course, is first *narrow*. All its scope and range is limited to this one thought and never goes beyond it. Therefore, he never discusses such questions as these: In view of that entire dependence upon another for all the prompting, planning, and energy of life, in which the slave has been educated and ever lived, without some special training for the great change, what will he get when he gets this liberty? As he is, what of liberty is he qualified to enjoy? In what way will he go about to use a liberty which he never knew? A liberty which his powers are in no way fitted to handle! How long will he hold the shadow of that liberty if you give it to him? Who will provide for him now? Who will advise him? Who will teach him now? Who will stand by to pity and to help in the adversities which are sure to overtake and overwhelm him? Assailed by hosts of temptations, no one of which he ever felt before, bereft of every safeguard

ever thrown around him hitherto, what will become of his morality, his industry, his religion? And his posterity, what must be their fate, when the parents feel their utter incapacity either of self-support or self-direction? These are questions, you perceive, our Reformer can not ask. They are all answered in his all-embracing motto: "Instant liberty is all good." By the necessity of his philosophy, therefore, the benevolence of our friend must be wretchedly *narrow.* It has no call, no basis, for the studiousness of love, nor for the comprehensiveness of love, nor for the services, the beneficence of love. The same philosophy, you perceive, must make this man's love as *nervous* as it is narrow. With a glance it covers all its ground. It has nothing to examine, nothing to weigh, nothing to do; no food to take in, no two points to look at. What can it do but yearn, and swell, and fret itself? Pressed by its own morbid heavings for relief, what can it do but break out into all such declamations, denunciations, and strugglings as promise to work toward its end?

2. *Intelligence.*—You perceive from the views presented, that our Reformer does not take up the case of the slave and calmly study it through and through. He does not consider how all good is to come to this uneducated, disqualified fellow-man through his own idolized liberty: How all the bright blessings of this liberty will be made to reach his physical necessities, his social relations, his moral constitution, his personal habits: By what mysterious power of this

liberty he is to avoid all the perilous conflicts of his new position, and sustain his equal elevation among superior men: Provide a wise judgment for every new juncture and meet all his responsibilities to God and man: With such a work to do for himself, and so little capacity to perform it, how he is to transmit all good to his posterity through coming generations?

Doubtless amongst our Reform friends are found men of as broad intelligence as the land can boast; and here we say, for its every exhibition we should cheerfully accord the very sincerest admiration. But whatever be their intellect, the moment these men bring their intelligence to this subject, a strange power begins to work upon it. Forthwith it is placed between the jaws of the popular mania and screwed up within its narrow limits, and,strive as it may, it can not, it can not break out of the iron bondage. Doubtless there are amongst our Reformers men of as enlarged philanthropy as the world can produce, and for every exercise of this benevolence most heartily should we love to honor and admire these fellow-men. But the moment that benevolence is brought to this subject, a malign power hurries it between the jaws of the vice, and this, too, to be screwed·up within the narrow limits of the prevalent fanaticism, and for its life it can never break out. There is a disease in the mind, and to expect its healthy exercise is to deny the fact. But stay! let me pause and remember. All men are fallible! and God may see more of this fallibility in our own mental action on this subject than we are aware of, and less in our neighbors than we have supposed. Giving this peradventure a considerate and honest record, in discharge of duty I must now proceed to say, whenever we calmly inspect the Reformer's mind and heart on this subject, we do believe that the high intelligence which he boasts—is not there; that the enlarged philanthropy of which he seems so conscious—is not there; that the heroic intrepidity in which he so deeply exults—is not there. We would not despise, we would not scorn our fellow-man for this palpable deficiency; for if there is delusion, there is sincerity. But this we must say: to *approve*, to *respect* the actings of his rational nature on this subject, is precisely to part with a sound mind. There is nothing in the view of his intellect to justify the feeling of his heart. The plan of his mind embraces no boon; the exultation of his heart interprets it all blessing. With no wiser, no broader view of the case than his fanaticism permits, that the Reformer should make his accustomed ado about the recreant conduct of other men, his own high-souled sympathy, and the glorious good he proposes for the slave, is simply *puerile.* It should startle our friend to know, what is assuredly the truth, his intellect, heart, and hand are emphatically *behind the times.* They are left far, far in the distance by the delicate and complicated interests of this momentous, this peculiar case. His intellect does not begin to do its work, and come up and grapple with its great facts and truths. His philanthropy does not begin to do its work, and come up and compass all its great and delicate interests! His courage has not started to come up, and dare its high responsibilities. Yes! it is solid truth! The fanaticism of the Reformer has so pent up the workings of his heart, and crippled the traveling of his faculties, that this grave theme has entirely outstripped him; nor do even its great outlines lie to-day within the reach of his severest vision. A just estimate of this Reform movement, I apprehend, is expressed in the following language: In undertaking to rectify Southern society, a diseased mind, destitute alike of sound wisdom and a healthy philanthropy, has not only deeply damaged both patriotism and Christianity, but put back hopelessly for the present, the very cause it essayed to advance. For while it has accomplished nothing for the liberty, nothing for the religion of the slave—it has enraged and prejudiced the master, destroyed facilities of improvement, and crippled every agency which could possibly be brought upon the field.

CHAPTER VIII.

REMEDIAL SUGGESTIONS.

We have been conducted to the conclusion that this Reform enterprise, in conception, is a mistake; in spirit, an immorality; in operation, a mischief. But are we to stop here? Shall we dismiss this investigation without reaching one remedial thought? Do no lights spring up before us which promise ultimate good to the country, and the Church, by the inauguration of a wiser mind on this agitating, perilous question? Two practical suggestions would seem to promise healing of the past, and health for the future.

Set back liberty and slavery to their just and proper places respectively; and restore North and South to such a spirit of mutual toleration and patriotic sympathy as is imperatively demanded by their character, history, political and geographical relations, and universal interest and influence.

I. *Let us seek a juster estimate of the true nature and value of social liberty.*

For a course of years, by the organized passion and vigor of the most vehement and powerful men in her bosom, the North has been compelled to study slavery through its excesses and exaggerations; and, therefore, to define liberty—the right of deliverance from infernal oppression. Nay! under sickly excitement, having stretched out the sins and evils of slavery to an enormous extent beyond truth—out of these false elements they compelled themselves to build a *Liberty Idol*—an idol as hollow as fancy, but as exacting as Moloch—whose grand doctrine is this: "Slavery is the concentrated essence of personal cruelty, national dishonor, and human mischief; and wherever found, must be instantly destroyed at all hazards." By this process, unconsciously to both, the active few have been cultivating a diseased mind, while the addressed multitude have been losing a just one. Under this process, the troubles of American society have found a fruitful parent in *false judgments and feelings concerning slavery and liberty.* In view of this process, it is as unphilosophical as it is unjust, to look for an abatement of our North and South controversy, in requiring the South to open the way by desirable improvements at home. Certainly, the South should do all in her power to promote the best good of those fellow-men the God of love has placed in her bosom. But it is altogether more natural and proper that the *North should take the lead*, by an honest effort to come back to *just views on that general sub-*

ject, her departure from which has been the pregnant cause of so much evil to Church and State.

In seeking a more accurate estimate of the relative worth of social liberty, we object not to its elevation above all secularities; but we do object to such an imaginary exaltation of the idea of liberty, as by the very state of the mind, works a necessary invasion of the spiritualities of the kingdom of Christ. Just at this very point lies the disease. As a philosophical result of the process through which his mind has passed, there is a halo—there is a glory about the conception of liberty, in a Reformer's fancy, which outshines the sun; and he will not, can not tolerate the man for a moment, who should speak out or act out the solid truth that, important as it certainly is, there are things far more valuable. The most rabid Reformer, in language, will not admit that spiritual liberty is incomparably more important; but it will be in language only; for the moment you put an influence upon his soul to cool his rapturous admiration of natural liberty, or call upon him to fire up in his heart a higher glow for something else, and this by abstracting a portion of his inspiration from the object of his idolatry, that moment you are insufferable in his presence. He abhors you! He degrades you! To save his soul, he can not respect and love you. What an astonishing power of self-deception dwells in the human mind! Our fellow-man really thinks that none but himself properly appreciates *liberty*. What is the truth? Exactly this: he has in his soul a principle of liberty *depreciated* in proportion as it differs from that of other men. Could we subject liberty, as a Reformer sees and feels it, to a clear analysis, we should find it largely an unnatural and sickly element. His conception is built up on an exaggerated view of slavery, and is consequently graduated by it. His excited imagination, therefore, imputes properties which the object does not possess. Nor can he escape the necessary result of a mind unhealthy in exact proportion to the overrating of its object. The principle of liberty in the soul of many a man whom he is accustomed to abuse, on emergencies which try men's souls, might read him an instructive lesson. In this man, liberty is not a creature of the imagination, and would certainly be found more modest, and very probably more prompt, vigorous, and enduring. I respectfully invite my Reform friend to the examination of a few thoughts, with a view, if possible, to bring down toward the level of truth, any extravagant conceptions upon this subject, which he may have unconsciously imbibed.

1. Liberty in its nature, as a right and a blessing, is not *immutable.*

On the catalogue of secularities, there are no two elements farther apart than *liberty* and *slavery*. In itself, liberty is a right, and a blessing most noble and valuable. He who does not appreciate both its elevation and its importance, is less than a man. He whose soul does not spring within him at the cry of liberty as our fathers fought for it in the Revolution, as it shrieked and died on the day that crushed out the nationality of Poland, as it breathed in the gallant soul of the Irish patriot when summoned to speak out what he had to say why sentence of death should not be pronounced upon him, or as it is often heard in our day, in the public declamation of our violent Reformers—he who does not feel his soul swell within him under such appeals as these, I will not ask who could honor him, but who could endure the fellowship of such a man? Who would not be afraid to trust him? Let me go further, and say that he who can look over the multitude of our fellow-men in bondage at the South, and behold them, by the necessities of their condition, so largely subjected to the uncontrolled will of fellow-men, so largely shut off from the fountains of elevating knowledge, from the opportunities of high human development, from the sources of wealth, power, and glory amongst their fellow-creatures—he who can survey this scene, and feel in his soul that there is nothing pleasant, nothing desirable, nothing obligatory in that process whereby they shall all be kindly and wisely trained along and progressively educated under providence, until they or their posterity shall come up to that summit level of intelligence and freedom whereon they may stand and share equally with ourselves all the good and the great things allotted to the children of men by a common Father's hand—that fellow-man does not do justice to God's capacious structure of man, God's established fraternity between men, and God's undistinguished distribution to men; neither does he do justice to that Christianity which works to restore fallen man to his primeval perfection, and which sets every man to work in this enterprise, by the command, "Thou shalt love thy neighbor as thyself."

In like manner, slavery in itself, is a wrong and a curse, most unrighteous and disastrous. He who understands these terms, but does not admit this statement, is an unprincipled man, from whom nothing kind, nothing just, can be reasonably expected. He who holds that, of two fellow-creatures made by God, with nothing to justify, nothing to explain his conduct, one may lay a violent hand upon the other, and destroy his will, and force him to move by his own, and work for his advantage; in other words, he who contends that slavery in the abstract, slavery independent of circumstances, is neither a wrong nor a mischief, that man is a monster, whom no fellow-man can either respect or trust.

But precious as is this liberty, in itself, both as a right and a blessing, it is not an immutable good. And dark as is this slavery in itself, both as a sin and a curse, it is not an immutable evil. Liberty and slavery come together on one principle: they are both modified by circumstances. Mark the maniac, the minor, the convict, and that poor slave of a kind master, at the South, destitute of the very first qualification to take care of himself; will any man say that involuntary submission here—is an evil? That arbitrary control here—is a sin? The fact is, both the sin and the curse are extinguished by the circumstances, and it is slavery no longer. Has either of these parties a right to demand his liberty? Would it be a blessing to him if bestowed? On the contrary, circumstances have destroyed both the right and the good, and it is liberty no longer.

We hold, therefore, it should affect every sensible man's estimate of liberty—that its very nature, as a right and as a blessing, is not invariable; that on the contrary, the conduct, history, capacity, and prospects of the party, the laws of the land, the demands of society, and various other considerations, do actually modify both the claim and the worth of liberty, and greatly modify both. For, these qualifying causes, in their degrees and proportions, do work a steadily depreciating change in the nature of liberty as a right and as a blessing, from a slight reduction of both, through every successive grade of depression, down to the absolute extinction of its every claim and good.

2. Liberty is *extinguished by comparison.* Give one man all natural liberty and no spiritual liberty. Give another man all spiritual liberty and no natural liberty. Fix your eye now upon the personification of these two elements—*natural* and *spiritual* liberty. Gabriel was never gifted with a genius competent to trace the gulfs which divide them. The *one* is a *time* thing, the *other* a thing *immortal.* The *one* has all its play within the narrow circle of man's social relations, the sweep of the *other* is as broad as God him-

self, and all the spiritualities of his boundless dominions. The one implies no action of benign power upon man's fallen nature, no change of man's unhappy relations, no improvement of man's eternal prospects. The other brings divinity itself to heave out all destroying corruptions from man's immortal spirit and implant therein the purities of heaven, to set up man's soul in a justified state before that throne of God it had outraged, and to spread out before man's hope the blood-purchased heritage of immortality. The one finds all its good in the unceasing toil of fallen faculties to extract substance from a world accursed by God into vanity of vanities. The other, oh the other! it is heaven's created, heaven's constitutional title to all the good of God and all he owns. The other! Yes! It is a freedom which goes over Creator and creation with the visits of its intelligence, and while it cheerfully accords an appropriate sentiment to every living thing, to every occurring event, it brings back an instructing, developing, delighting, exalting, and impowering good from all that exists and all that transpires. The *one* is the liberty—rather the jail-bounds of a convict who shall be deluded in the chase of shadowy hopes for a day, and then be consigned to a slavery so deep, a bankruptcy so dire, that the very bitterest prayer of his imprisoned spirit shall never procure one drop of water to cool a parched tongue. The *other*, oh! the other! It is the liberty of a son of God, the liberty of a freeman of the Lord! who shall cheerfully serve

God and man through life, and then go to a heritage whose grand, comprehensive scope is written out in four short words: "*All things are yours!*"

Come up, my Reform brother! Come up and place your boasted *liberty of earth*, side by side with this *God-given liberty of heaven.* Compare them keenly in *nature, relations, possessions, prospects;* and what an absolute trifle of trifles is your idol! Oh tell me! Fellow-man, I challenge you, tell me! As is the star lost in the blaze of the rising sun, is not all your earthly liberty utterly extinguished by the transcendent glory of the liberty of the Gospel?

I have another solemn interrogatory to address to you just here. Yes! Hold your gaze upon your short-lived, shadowy, treacherous, yet captivating liberty of earth, and equally upon our immortal, substantial, divine liberty from heaven, and say: How do you feel, my brother, in view of your own conduct in times just gone by? Did you not *sully your sacred pulpit?* Under the unhallowed inspiration of the day, by the frequent introduction and fervid enforcement of your secular liberty, did you not soil that holy of holies where God commanded you to speak out to a perishing world as man's first, last, and best good, His liberty from heaven? Did you not go further, and *sully your sacred calling?* You left that sacred pulpit, erected upon the blood of Jesus, where God stationed you as a Levite, and you went out into town-meetings, into political assemblies, yea, upon the broadest public hustings of the country, and there amid all the levities, profanities, and violence of the secular tumult, you took your equal part with carnal men, and threw out your very loudest tones and richest thoughts to extol and to magnify this liberty of earth! Having gone so far from your consecrated ground, encountered so many shocks and perils to your holy vocation, and uttered so rapturously the supreme glory of this earthly thing, how is it possible for you to return to your pulpit and after all this find an emphasis *exalted* enough to mark before your people the transcendent superiority of the glory of the liberty of the Gospel? Did you not go further still and *wound that sacred heart* which the Holy Ghost gave you to preach this heavenly liberty? Had you found that emphasis, where could you have found a soul to pronounce it? Why, my brother, had you on the ensuing Sabbath, as a minister of Jesus Christ, attempted in spirit, sentiment, language, and manner, to describe the *just superiority* of the Gospel, one thought had instantly sprung into the mind of half of your congregation: "The man's a hypocrite or a madman." Without argument, instantaneously, all nature feels these things are contrary the one to the other. The human mind absorbed and carried away to the loftiest heights, mind you, in *carnal* admiration, can not in the same breath mount up to the infinitely more exalted and perfectly opposite elevation of *spiritual* rapture. It does not lie in the nature of things.

Bear with me, my brother, and I will address yet

another solemn interrogatory to your heart and conscience before our common Master. At that moment of unholy inspiration, in the midst of all the rapturous excitements of public speech to an admiring multitude, just then there came over your spirit a subtle, flattering phariseeism as you caught a glimpse of your own conspicuous, generous daring for liberty, and then it was, in that evil hour, that you turned to your brethren who were too wise and faithful to follow you in your more than doubtful course. And ah! with what a proud and scornful air did you *stigmatise them.* Yes, *stigmatise* them before *strangers!* Pronounce them Pro-Slavery! Dumb Dogs! Recreant to every high and noble impulse! *Traitors* to *liberty* and to *patriotism!* Deserting both through fearfulness, and that in the hour of the nation's extremity! My brother! did you then and there stand to your post as the sentinel of a kingdom not of this world? Did you then and there conduct yourself as one of a band of fellow-soldiers stationed upon the wall to watch and to fight for a liberty not of the flesh, but for that celestial liberty wherewith Jesus Christ makes free? In all this, did you, say! *did you quit yourself like a* MAN *of God!* My brother, be not angry, though I deal plainly with you. Rest assured of this: at that very moment when you were enacting this luckless episode in your ministry, many a faithful man, your fellow-servant, looked upon you with profoundest sorrow, sometimes swelling into indignation. And he spake out—not one word in the ear of man—but in the clearness and depth of his own outraged sense of all propriety, that man exclaimed: "My brother, had you scandalized your ministerial brethren and done no more, your crime had been nothing. But ah! you have wounded, cruelly wounded the sacred cause of heaven and earth. You have sullied, deeply sullied, that high commission placed in your hand by Jesus Christ to save the world. Whether controlled by the dark impulse of a maddened fanaticism or the shallow vanity of a misled boy, nothing short of an honest humiliation can restore you to the dignity of a man of God or the confidence of your Christian brethren."

3. *Liberty is perfectly invisible* by that eye which takes the grandest and the justest view of the world. Every pulsation of fallen nature, from the first to the last, beats after *natural enjoyment* in this life. Nature's universal cry is: "Who will show me any good? Give me wealth? Give me glory? Give me joy? Give me liberty?" Unhappy man! With what a sad sound does this deepest cry of your nature fall upon the pitying ear of Heaven! What can *wealth* do for man? It has never bought him the very first *right exercise* of the powers that once held the likeness of God. What can *glory* do for man? It has never lifted from his soul the very *first look* of his earned everlasting contempt. What can joy do for man? It has never cheered his spirit with the very first *throb* of that *peace* for which God made it. What can *liberty* do for man? It has never produced

for him the very first *free movement* of a redeemed nature. And yet how often does the very Church of God seem to forget her high work and go out of her place to speak her pantings that all men might enjoy this liberty of earth! And what a liberty! Chained by laws of nature on every hand; fettered by laws of providence at every step; crippled by laws of nations, cities, companies in every place; controlled by customs, sentiments, tastes, under all cir cumstances. It is hard indeed for man to learn that earthly good inordinately sought, indicates a fatal misconception of the end of time, of the work of this life. It is hard indeed for man to practise the lesson that no fallen mind ever sees the world aright until it looks upon it not as a field of natural enjoyment, but as *a theatre of spiritual achievement.* This is the great idea. This should regulate the worth and dignity of all terrestrial things. Here the Son of God shed his blood in atonement for sin: What an achievement! Here the Holy Ghost retraces God's likeness upon the apostasy; What an achievement! Here the word of God is all abroad to light up the darkness of the fall: What an achievement! Here the Church of God, with all her ordinances, and every man of God, with all his influence, work together with the Trinity, to save a lost world: What an achievement! The great primary fact in our history tells that the world has been *up-turned*, and we are all in confusion and peril. And sorrows and wrongs abound everywhere at the North and at the

South. But the great work in this life—surely it is not to get back our little rights! not to exult for a moment in nature's joys! No, no! The world is a spiritual wreck. And *spiritual achievement! Deliverance from sin!! Salvation!! Salvation!!! This, this,* is the *great order of the day* here! And all else, valuable as it may be in its place, is a perfect nullity when compared with the overthrow of sin and the salvation of the soul. Now, my brother, by all your thoughts, your feelings, your words, your tones, your looks, your acts, and your aims, you can not help it, you will assure all men of your conviction that the securement of the liberty of the bondman, this is the great work of the world. Or at least you do come fearfully too near to this monstrous, monstrous extravagance. Nor is this all. You *will* push your measures for the practical accomplishment of his rescue, although you unsettle the very order of society, although you break down the platform, the necessary platform, on which holy agency must stand and work to achieve the redemption of the world.

My fellow-man! can it be that there exist no reasons why a class of men around us should take down their exorbitant views of the comparative value of human liberty? Why, surely, *if* it is a liberty that is *extinguished by circumstances! If* it is a liberty that is utterly *extinguished by comparison! If* it is a liberty so small and out of the way, that it *can not be embraced in a right look at the world,* surely rectitude, benevolence, and wisdom, surely patriotism, fellowship, and peace, should constrain us to lay this whole matter to heart; and since God has promised to direct the steps of those who commit their way unto him, should we not, every soul of us, profoundly commend our personal case to God, and try again to listen humbly for that voice of heavenly guidance: "This is the way: walk ye therein."

II. Let us *seek a kinder heart toward the South!*

Were my Maker to call me out before heaven and earth, and say: "My creature! thou shalt not ask a blessing which directly involves heaven's saving agency. What else thou wilt, ask, and it shall be done." As at present advised, I should not hesitate to respond: "O my Maker! for the temporal and eternal good of the slave, for the unity and prosperity of my country, for the best good of the whole world, and all its coming generations, and for thy glory in all, in mercy—*give to the North a kind heart to the South.*"

What a momentous and singular fact! Here we are, a nation holding in our bosom three millions of our fellow-men. Not of our continent; not of our color; at the farthest possible remove from our grade of culture. How comes this? None but God hath planned this movement. And for what end? I believe that great and good man, *George Whitefield*, responded to this inquiry as early and as clearly as has any uninspired man. Slavery was arrested at the line which divided South-Carolina from Georgia. *General Oglethorpe* was the stoutest sort of an Abolitionist. But cunning and time were too much for him. The Carolinians hired their slaves to Georgians; first for *one* year, then for *two*, *ten*, *twenty*, *one hundred*. Still the faithful veteran was fighting off the enemy as best he could, when *Whitefield* appeared before him, and thus gave counsel: "General, give up your opposition to the introduction of slavery into the colony of Georgia. If the slave gets a good master, he will be better off than he would be were he in his own country, or free in this. Besides, I believe that He who commanded, 'Go ye into all the world, and preach the Gospel to every creature,' sees that there is no missionary spirit in the Church, and in compassion to the heathen, He it is who has brought them here, that here they may be Christianized, and then return with the lamp of life, to light up their own benighted native continent." It must be so. Make the most natural record of this transaction from the beginning, and the simple history is neither more nor less than a lucid plan, a statement of the successive steps, peradventure, of the most philosophical and sublime missionary movement under heaven.

The *first* historical fact directs us to the *people*. Who are they? Of all men the very people for the enterprise. Just the darkest and most degraded heathen upon the face of the earth; sitting in the region and shadow of death, without the slightest prospect of a visit from the heralds of salvation. The *second* historical fact records their *transportation* from Africa.

What does this accomplish? A most important and primary part of the work of their evangelization. It rolls an ocean between them and every fountain and even form of their native superstition. Oh! if our brethren on heathen shores could only take the heathen from the heathen, more than half their missionary work would be instantly accomplished. To cut this people off at once and for ever from all support for their heathenism, to cast all the power of its resuscitation to the ends of the earth, and force them to go elsewhere for thoughts of God, what a precise philosophical prescription to open the way for their salvation, by breaking the reigning power of paganism in their souls. But where did Providence land them? The *third* historical fact replies: "Here! here, where the light of *Christianity* shines in all they see, and the voice of Christianity sounds in all they hear. Where their heathenism must get a blow, and their dark souls receive a truth, with almost every successive motion of their faculties and occurrence of providence. What plan to bring men to Christianity from heathenism could possibly embrace a more direct and suitable provision? The *fourth* historical fact incorporates them into our population in the relation of *slaves* to masters. And what a speaking movement is this? Men rise up against this relation most violently on every hand. Against its original institution this violence could not be too decided. In many of its present aspects the hostility is still justifiable. In one point of view it is deeply censurable. It leaves out wholly the comforting, the Christian side of the case. Yes! the great descriptive truth in this whole history men greatly overlook. To this degraded, pershing people, the alternative was this—Slavery, or no Christianity. Savage slavery at home, without the religion of Jesus, or American slavery, with it. *This* was the issue which wicked men called upon God to decide. Who doubts this fact? What if Abolition intelligence had been called to the helm at this time? Why! think, my fellow-men. If the population brought to our shores had been placed in any other—yes, in any other possible position than this very relation of *master and slave*, they would have perished from the earth in the first generation, and the multitudes of them who have gone to heaven had never sung its songs, and God's great missionary enterprise have long since been recorded a failure. I boldly affirm, that in any other possible relation than the relation of master and slave, the imported population could no more have clothed and fed and housed and stimulated and restrained and guided and taught and improved and preserved and multiplied themselves from the date of their introduction into the country, than they could have bailed out the ocean and gone back to Africa. Yes! my friends, this very relation of master and slave has built the only platform, the only platform, on which our imported heathen could have been held up from generation to generation, to be acted on by the saving agencies of the Gospel;

and though we may not form the relation to found the platform, yet, when man engenders a child of the pit, we should shout hearty thanks to God, that he transforms him into an angel of mercy. Nor is this all. The *fifth* historical fact in the case calls to mind another most important end accomplished by this very relation. It secures the favorable influence of *truth*. A master is the strongest earthly power known to the slave. Government by the one describes the life of the other. In general, a master's power aids Christianity. You can find instances enough at the South, I readily grant, where injustice and unkindness on the part of the master obstruct the influence of truth. But the preponderance, thank God! is vastly in the scale of the master's interest in his slaves and kindness to them; and when the master himself is not kind, others are. The slightest investigation will assure us that God has employed the governing relation of the master to lend the mightiest earthly contribution to that glorious work of Christianity most certainly wrought for the man of color at the South. The master's *authority* will generally command the attention of the slave to that which the master or the white man addresses to him. Had all been free, omniscience alone can tell what myriads of Christian appeals, which arrested the attention and saved the soul of the slave, would never have secured the very first thought of the freeman. Apart from his obedience, the slave cherishes a feeling of *honor* for his master. He considers him a superior person, and feels a deference for him. This feeling insures a respectful attention. What multitudes of imported Africans, free, had never had their hearts thus opened to receive the sincere milk of the word? I need not say that there abides a perfect conviction in the mind of the slave of the master's *capacity to teach*, of his superior knowledge. This, too, exercises a most salutary influence. It tends to produce a *teachable* attention, by breaking the power of the love of darkness in the natural heart, and all those counter suggestions so certain to arise, so hard to subdue; and by enlightening his judgment and disposing his heart to receive instruction, since he knows it proceeds from one who has much more light than himself, and would not misdirect him. What masses of good influence thus exerted upon the mind of the slave had been discarded by the pride of freedom. The *gratitude* of the slave, his appreciation of the condescension of the white man, a feeling which had been a stranger to his bosom if free, but now almost universal in the heart of the man of color, can not fail to incline him to *give heed* to the kind counsels of his superior. In a word, the general force of this relation, first to give a directing, governing influence to the master, and thereby to accustom the slave to be controlled and influenced by the master, must exercise an invisible but mighty agency in bringing the slave under the power of the Gospel.

I must step aside, and give my Reform brother a

moment's attention. I know he does not like to hear these things, and will certainly pervert the teaching, if I do not help him. Now, all this is no vindication of slavery in the abstract; neither is it a proclamation that if a child of Adam would be saved, he must go to the South and become a slave. But it is truth, and truth pertinent to the case, and truth that he is sure to overlook, for it is truth that brings up both sides, and shows us that this relation of master and servant, which *man meant for evil, God meant for good.* The wrath was all man's, the praise is all God's.

The *sixth* historical fact summons us to record the providential fulfillment of the prediction of the great patriarch of colonization. A *free* nation! out of these slaves of the South, the very posterity of the African importation. A Free Nation! Christian philanthropy has founded for the man of color on his own native shores. Though not urged with the vigor which its generous, glorious nature demands, this enterprise has been gradually developing in those elements which promise ultimate and thorough success. The *last* fact in this history would seem to call for the *results* of this mighty experiment of importing population from the darkest quarter of the globe. And here we delight to say, they have, in general, been just what we should have anticipated from a divine missionary plan. The operation of each successive step has produced precisely such effects as the plan itself seemed to design. Separation from Africa has worked out of the minds of this people all their inherited idolatries. What a grand beginning! Importation into America has thrown the light of Christianity abundantly into their minds. What a natural advance! The relation of master and slave, on the one hand, has sustained, multiplied, and improved them socially, and on the other, has educated in them an attentive, respectful, teachable, grateful, and abundant reception of the great tidings of salvation; so that, whatever special deductions are to be entered up against the inhuman conduct of some of those intrusted with their management, on the whole, from their earliest landing on our shores, they have certainly been, intellectually, socially, and religiously, an improving people. Oh! what a comforting fact this, on this dark subject! What valuable advancement toward the grand end of God's plan! And, finally, the Liberian enterprise has started in the American heart a pretty strong hope of the ultimate happy social as well as spiritual destination of the colored man; and though a violently divided mind in the country has hitherto greatly chilled and checked this whole movement, yet, even under this heavy disadvantage, the South has been freeing her slaves about as rapidly as the friends of the colored man, North and South, have been ready to meet the expenses of transportation and outfit.

I call now upon all my Reform brethren to ponder this stupendous scheme of Providence! To study out this bold missionary movement of heaven upon earth! To look on and see that spiritual achievement, the religious good of the heathen! This, this is palpably, preëminently the one great object. How all things have been sacrificed to this; all things been made tributary to this! For the salvation of men how willing God was to employ the cruel wrath of human covetousness to inaugurate the great movement. As of old he made Joseph a slave in Egypt, before he made Israel free in Canaan, so now how willing God's providence has been to suffer temporal slavery to be set up on these free shores, that eternal liberty might ultimately reach the native land of the slave. How unwilling, too, God was to shipwreck his great enterprise by adopting our wild, runaway notions of human liberty! How much redemption work has actually been achieved in the past! How much is this day working out in all the South! And above all, what glorious wonderful achievements in the kingdom would assuredly cheer all our future, if this whole nation had but the heart to come up in earnest and work together with the God of providence!

To facilitate this great end, and dispose men to embark in this enterprise, let us seek a more compact view of God's plan, so far as fallible creatures can read its indication in that class of historical facts involved in his wonderful commingling of African and American population. It may be simplified to two points—*ends* and *means*. The chief *end* would seem to be the entire good of the man of color, presently in this country, ultimately in his own. A three-fold good—*Christianity, intelligence*, and *freedom*. Let them all be made Christians, if possible. Let them all be educated to a practical capacity to take care of themselves, if possible. Let them all be ultimately brought to a state of freedom, if possible. And let them all, or at least multitudes of them, be carried back to Africa, that they may officiate in every wise way both to civilize and to christianize their countrymen. The *means*, too, would seem to be three-fold, and largely such as have been hitherto employed. The ordinary operation of Christianity, through the existing relations of society, looking to the continent of Africa as a grand ultimate Christian field. Let Christian example work just as it has done, and be as much improved as may be. Let Christian teaching be prosecuted just as it has been, and be progressively improved and augmented as far as possible. And let a stronger arm be outstretched to build up the Republic on the coast of Africa, and to direct the eyes of the country to the enterprise. Thus, without one solitary belligerent edict of freedom from the North, let all this be done through kind Christian suasion. Let all parties ever cherish fraternal respect and confidence—the North and the South improving opportunities for instruction and general cultivation under the government of that sensible Christianity, which feels that it has no right to interfere with the existing relations of society, which cherishes no disposition to dispute the claims of the master, but which stands ever ready to coöperate with him and all others to do all in its power to advance the great end of African elevation.

In regard to these means, let it be remembered under every disadvantage, they have already accomplished a great work; and with a nation's hearty coöperation these very means will surely, safely, happily, do all that can be well done in this cause.

Who now will not engage with us in this enterprise? Fellow-man! Lift up your eye and look over this lost world! Think—of the myriads of immortalities perishing every hour! Of the multiplied myriads all over the earth who must go down to hell ere, in the ordinary course of providence, the Gospel can reach them, and the dark grasp of the apostasy upon their souls be un-clenched! Think, oh! think, above all good conceivable by man, what unspeakable joy would thrill the whole family of heaven and earth, if our blessed Christianity could only be carried with power to the perishing tribes of our race! Bring now all these Christian reflections to one point. To work in this field and drive on the conversion of the world, tell me where, in all your wide survey, do you behold such a sight as our country presents? "For ask now of the days that are past, which were before thee, since the day that God created man upon the earth; and ask from the one side of heaven unto the other, whether there hath been any such thing as this great thing is, or hath been heard like it? Did ever God essay to go and take him a nation from the midst of another nation, by a mighty hand and a stretched-out arm, according to all that the Lord hath done" for you and for these Africans before your eyes? In view of this most singular fact in the history of God's dealings with this country, what nation on earth has such an opportunity to send the Gospel to heathen men, as we have had to give the Gospel to our embosomed pagans? What nation under heaven has such an opportunity to send the Gospel powerfully to heathen shores as we have, through our Christianized, liberated slaves, to send the Gospel to the dark tribes of Africa? Now, if spiritual achievement, the salvation of man, is the great work of the Church, has not the providence of God opened a field for us—a field so peculiar, so broad, so productive heretofore under all disadvantages, so promising in the future, if faithfully cultivated—that the very thought of it should precipitate us in the dust of his feet, that we have not more heartily appreciated it hitherto; that the very thought of the prolonged opportunity of its cultivation should make us spring to atone for the past, by giving ourselves most earnestly to the work in the future?

Did I say that in the present exasperated condition of American mind, this is not the day for new suggestions upon the subject of slavery? And is it not true that George Whitefield, or George Washington, might be concerned for the issue, if even *they* should attempt to mediate between elements so distantly and decidedly separated as are the North and the South? But, my brethren and countrymen, where are we?

Have we not a *plan* before us? A plan of operation upon the subject of slavery? Has it not all the elements of a plan? Contriver, contrivance, means, and ends? In its scope does it not cover the entire case, the present conversion and elevation of imported men, and the ultimate evangelization of their country? Is it not a plan inaugurated, and therefore free from the objection of novelty; inaugurated by Providence himself, and therefore free from the peril of a proposal by a North man or a South man, or a man at all? Is it not a plan strikingly divine in all its face and agency? God must work up man's wickedness in his plans; no surprise, therefore, that he should employ man's outrageous cruelty in making slaves, to bring the heathen to this country, sustain them in this country, and subject them to the Christian influence of this country. God must work up man's repugnances as well as his benevolence, in his plans. No surprise, therefore, when Christianity shall have qualified them for freedom, that he should employ the one to press the Africans back to their country, since two races so separated never could dwell together on an equality; and the other to co-work to the same end, since their personal happiness and the conversion of their country both call for their return. And is it not a remarkable fact that whatever strife has arisen upon this subject, in our land, that strife has nothing to do with the subject as involved in this plan, *except to establish its efficiency to accomplish its great ends*, since from the beginning, it has achieved so much under so great disadvantage? My countrymen and brethren! If on this perplexing and perilous subject this nation can come together as fellow-citizens, or should work together as fellow-servants of Christ, does it not become us, with an honest heart, to try that plan which God himself has marked out for us so plainly by Christian principle, wonderful providence, natural laws, the remarkable early prediction of an eminently holy and gifted man, and the strong coïncident judgment of so many intelligent and excellent minds in our own day! Yes! that plan which has already received such striking testimony of his favor, notwithstanding all our neglect. I do most earnestly solicit the confirmation of your conviction of the claims of this plan by an examination of two independent and decisive facts.

I. All those classes of American sentiment which have hitherto refused to coöperate with us on this plan, if I mistake not, will be found upon examination not only untenable, but it will be clearly seen that the *very ends* which these objectors seek, can only be obtained by adopting the very system to which they object—can only be reached by hearty *coöperation with us* on the plan of God's wonderful providence.

As we have said before, and must perpetually repeat, the grand truth in a word, is this: All these objections have their *origin* in wrong views upon the subject of slavery, and their *remedy* only in those just views upon the subject which God's plan involves. Specific investigation will indorse this position.

1. The restiveness of my *Reform brother* is ill-content with any scheme which does not *deposit all its blessings upon the slave—instanter.*

One glance should destroy this cherished notion. Outward changes, without inward culture, make no great contributions to human welfare. The good of man lies principally in the position of his intellectual faculties, moral feelings, and practical habits. In each of these respects, the Southern negro needs a great improvement in order to be qualified for a beneficial freedom. To make these attainments, time is indispensable. Disband every University, College, and School, male and female, at the North, and ship all their Presidents, Professors, Tutors, and Teachers to the South, and enlist every additional volunteer or stipendiary you can command. Give them all facilities for their work; and let this be nothing, nothing but the proper education of Southern slaves for their freedom; and long, long years shall pass ere you witness any very sensible progress upon the great mass of the pupils. You can not, in our day, take up the negro and place him in the white family where he shall see all their culture, hear all their words, breathe all their feelings, and have no subsequent connection with persons of his own color. Consequently, every teaching enterprise must encounter this vast hindrance. You put your light into the mind of the negro, he then leaves you and goes down to the people of his own complexion, and they put it out. To lift one, therefore, is measurably to lift all! How clear it is, that preparation for freedom must come to the bondman *by degrees!* He who would indeed befriend our degraded fellow-creatures, must, must come to this palpable, common-sense view of his case. Assuredly, the good the negro lacks, is far, far more a *personal* than a *relative* change. Alter his relations as you may, shower upon him all the franchises of the earth, as you can, if his intellectual and moral cultivation are not brought up to the necessities of his new condition, freedom itself will only curse the beneficiary. He, therefore, who conceives that the needed good of this population—*Christianity, cultivation*, and *freedom*,—can all be well secured in one generation, instead of getting into the privileged period of light and progress, has gone back eighteen hundred years, and resurged in the age which justified faith in miracles. Nor should the tardy action of moderate views tempt you for a moment to abandon them. Why not abandon the whole system of Foreign Missions? How protracted its agency—how contracted its results! Why not give up the Bible? At work ever since the fall, it has not vanquished all sin yet! Connecticut had but three thousand slaves to set free; she has completed her work only within the last ten years. Only exercise your good sense, my friend, and the kindness of your heart, and it will not cast the slightest shade of depression over your spirit that these fellow-men obey God and abide in their calling yet a little longer. You forget where you are! We are not in heaven yet. We are all on this upturned earth! Every thing everywhere is out of order. You can not set all things right in a day. Let us take care of the best things first. Come up, then, like a man, and lay your shoulder to this good work, and with a good heart let us all heave together; and heave not for your fanciful liberty, but for spiritual achievement! for spiritual achievement just there where our great Leader in person stands and heaves! Yes, my brother! if it is indeed the best good of the black man that you seek! just do this, and you shall see that fellow-man rising before you; rising soundly to all the good he needs. Nor is this all the reward. Bear with me; and I will reveal you a secret. This, this only way to help that man, will give your own soul *a freedom* from that fretful bondage to which your fanaticism has consigned it, and put you in possession of a holy, benign satisfaction you never have felt, and never can feel in any other way. Surely, we may *count* upon *you* to go with us in this enterprise.

2. An analogous obstructive sentiment amongst our countrymen, objects to the continuance of slavery—more on the ground of its working *national dishonor*, than violating natural rights. It is the black spot of the nation. It puts us in bad repute with the world. It brings down upon us the reproach of England.

The reproach of England! Let England hold her

peace upon this subject. If she would set her eyes upon disgraceful national injustice to dependent men, let her review her own conduct to India! Her treatment of China! Her botch-work of freedom in the West-Indies, where she never paid that *twenty million* pounds, and never will! and let her remember this, where she never ministered that preparatory Christian labor which alone could have made freedom a blessing! Let her look nearer home, at her *Three Millions of Paupers!* the mass of whom, through her long neglect, will not receive the Gospel from her hand; the mass of whom would leap this day, to change places with the slaves of the South; the mass of whom are supposed to be the regular descendants of her own *Feudal* slaves. If she dishonors us because we have not emancipated our bondmen, we boldly demand why those whom she has liberated, are not to-day as happy as they are (nominally) free? Why are they crushed, from generation to generation, into starvation, and all such miseries and degradations, dark and dreadful, as no children of Adam should ever be suffered to endure? Simply because she liberated her slaves as Abolition (God willing) shall never force us to liberate ours! England liberated them without the necessary preparatory work of Christian philanthropy in the case; without the necessary preparatory work of a sound common-sense judgment in the case; in a word, without the *absolutely necessary preparatory discipline of the subject in every such case.* She liberated them too much from considerations of political convenience, social necessity, and natural promptings. Consequently, a wretched work she did; for she liberated them hastily, and cursed them deeply through following generations. No! let England hold her peace, and no American feel himself unduly dishonored by her taunts on the subject of slavery.

That the continuance of slavery is *necessarily* a national dishonor, is a palpable error. The governing truth is this: Slavery in a nation is honorable or *dis*honorable, according to the nation's conduct in reference to it; according to its benevolent activity, or selfish inaction. National dishonor, on this subject, both real and imaginary, in our day, proceeds quite as largely from misdirection, as from non-action. We can not be too frequently reminded, that our Abolition friends have pressed their inordinate outcry against the outrages of slavery, and shocking outrages that never pertained to it, so fiercely and long that their own minds, and the minds of multitudes, have been unconsciously driven to feel that this, their extravagant picture, *is* slavery, and *all* that slavery is; and no wonder men feel that slavery is a national disgrace. You perceive that in many men, this sentiment is the direct descendant of that fanatical fancy upon this subject which haunts the imagination of a Reformer; in a larger number, it is the unintelligent, timid echo of those fierce outcries, which have been poured into their ears so long that they can not escape a half-way conviction that there must be something awfully wicked in the most justifiable condition of slaveholding. At any rate, it will not do, just now, to think otherwise, and face the storm. Now I submit it to my fellow-men, whether there is not a want of intelligence, and even of virtue, in this morbid impression, and whether it is not much more manly to rise up and fling off the incubus.

Every man knows, had there been one tithe, one solitary tithe of truth in the monstrous picture of slavery which Abolitionism has ground into the imaginations and sympathies of half the North, American Slavery would have disappeared generations ago, and not a solitary sufferer had survived to groan under its diabolical oppression. While the nature of things bears this testimony on the one hand, there is a voice of corroborative history on the other, which no Reformer will have the boldness to dispute. These slaves, in the hands of their masters, have lived along through successive generations, multiplying faster even than their masters; in general intelligence and capacity to take care of themselves slowly improving from the beginning; hundreds of thousands of them liberated; hundreds of thousands of them converted to God; all of them the recipients of an ameliorating discipline from year to year; and the more intelligent, casting their eyes across the waters upon that bright beacon lifted up on their own native shores, to tell of the good things which peradventure a kind Providence has in store for their coming generations. I affirm that all this, as far as it goes, is a solid honor to this country; and if no man has a right to expunge truth, should be felt and acknowledged to be such. Not by any means what should have been done for them; not by any means what would have been done for them, if the South had been less selfish, and the North less hostile; not by any means what I do trust from this day a better spirit North and South will do for them; but still, quite enough to justify a sensible man in relieving himself of some portion of the *national dishonor* of which we hear so much.

If this thought gives you no relief, I am sure you will feel ample deliverance in another. Where are you? In the world, where to get back earthly rights and find nature's blessings is the great end of man? Away with the shallow offspring of a fallen nature! No! Holy accomplishment! Rescue from sin! Return to God! *This* is our work! This is dignity, honor, and glory! Yes! the very substance and brilliancy of it! This it is, therefore, wherewith every sensible and good man graduates the glory of every movement. Oh! now! if our country, our whole country, would but give heed to our earnest exhortation; if North and South, standing together as brethren, would but look to yon dark land where sin unreproved, wreaks its bitterest vengeance, its fiercest cruelties, upon our apostate fellow-creatures from generation to generation; and then look into our own bosom upon the millions of this very people by the marvellous compassion of the Friend of sinners—mark! *under the process of evangelization;* finally, if under this vision they could but feel the heart to reason thus: "By all this, God must be turning our eyes to Africa! By all this, God is surely crying aloud to us: 'See! I have placed in your hand the best instrument, the very brightest lamp on earth to light the darkness of that suffering, perishing people! Awake! Enkindle your lamp! and send it to fling its saving light over that gloomy region and shadow of death, that Ethiopia may be emancipated from her long, dark oppressions, and stretch out her hand unto God!'" Oh! I do say: If the United States of America would only look at her slaves through the light of this vision, and spring to the work with united heart and hand, she would *cover herself with a glory, a substantial, elevated moral glory,* which would not only sweep away the shallow obloquies of inconsiderate men, but secure to herself a standing before heaven and earth which no *nation ever approached!*

Strict history I suppose it to be, that no considerable body of slaves have ever yet been emancipated in this world, to their own advantage. The reason is simply this: *Christianity* did *not* do the work. Indirectly, she may have worked out necessities felt by selfish considerations, by political convenience, morbid imagining, or unreflecting natural sensibility; but Christianity herself did not deliberately take the case in hand, and go to work as we recommend, or rather as God's plan proposes. Oh! the glory!

the national glory of this work! If I have one spark of patriotism in my soul, nothing in all the compass of national doings could *so cheer it* as a *nation's union* to work out conscientiously, kindly, firmly, that great spiritual achievement to which our embosomed nation of foreigners summons us. Our revolutionary struggle was nothing to it. Our victories in Mexico, nothing to it. Our free institutions, broad territory, boundless wealth, bold enterprise—all nothing, nothing to it. The judgment, generosity, fidelity, faith, and felicity of such an accomplishment! Why, it would compose a far brighter diadem of glory than ever adorned earthly sovereignty. I confess, with vehement indignation my soul has often *burned* within me, as I have listened to my countrymen and Christian brethren, who so far from the slightest sympathy with the view presented, have been calling out impatiently for an instantaneous emancipation of all our slaves simply that we might thereby throw off at once the heavy national disgrace of the institution. Do your work! Free all the slaves to-day! Where are the slaves to-morrow? Where are the whites to-morrow? Where is the peace and order of society, to-morrow? Where is the prosperity of the nation, to-morrow? I freely acknowledge it, my mind is the very antipode of this thought. I do hold, in this nineteenth century, in this age of Progress and New light, this nation could never survive the disgrace—I repeat, it could never survive *the disgrace, the sin*, of such an edict! In our *personal con-*

duct, it would be the throwing down of a cross by refusal to enter upon a long line of arduous and self-denying, but most obvious, honorable, and profitable duty; in its *universal bearing*, it would be murder of our slaves, confusion to the master, affliction to the country, desertion of Africa, and condemnation of providence.

This class of our countrymen will certainly go with us. It is the honor of our country which they seek. Not one spark of national honor on this subject is accessible, except through this very plan. No possible escape from national disgrace, if we neglect it any longer. Surely, surely, *you* will go with us!

3. There is another class of public sentiment which declines to come up to our help, for a very different reason. They say: "*The work of removing our colored population to Africa, is too great.*"

They enter into calculations. They compare the magnitude of the operation with the feebleness of the agency. Three millions of slaves—if the cost of transportation and outfit for each is reduced to the sum of fifty dollars, the enterprise will demand one hundred and fifty millions of dollars; and where shall we look for such a mighty mass of means?

This view chills the soul. Its advocates judge our notions a little wild and uncalculating, the creature of enthusiasm, destitute of a sound business view of the case.

Our fellow-men, I think, are mistaken. What has been done in the past, may be done in the future.

During the last thirteen years, we have imported into this country three millions six hundred and thirty-five thousand four hundred and sixty emigrants, and this without effort. Should it please God to open a profitable field of labor in the bosom of Africa, in the course of a very few years, why may we not transport to their native shores the entire colored population of this country, and never feel the withdrawal of a solitary dollar of the nation's wealth?

Does not the whole question turn precisely on this point? Who is the agent? When God commanded Gideon to expel the Midianites, he responded: "But, O my Lord! wherewith shall I save Israel? Behold! my family is poor in Manasseh, and I am the least in all my father's house." But God replies: "Surely, I will be with thee; and thou shalt smite the Midianites as one man."

If Gideon alone is to fight the Midianites—this is one case. If God is to fight with him—this is quite another! What was the issue? God made lamps and pitchers, without a sword or a blow, vanquish the most powerful and victorious army on earth in that day. Inadequate means should never discourage men in any field where God sets them to work. God has made the sound of a ram's horn throw down the wall of a city. Jesus made clay and spittle give vision to the blind. Be it remembered, in the great work of African elevation, *God is with us!* Assuredly he is an agent! It is his work eminently. He planned it! He commenced it! He has prosecuted it. He will never desert it. We may not, we do not see how this work is to be accomplished. Neither did Gideon comprehend the method of victory when he attacked a great army with a few lamps. It was enough that God's command and promise were on his side. The same command, the same promise work with us in our good and noble cause. It may be, that God will send all our slaves back to Africa, or employ a part of them at home or on another field. It may be that he will do this work through the Church mainly, or bring up the strength of the State to the enterprise. But we have nothing to do with these inquiries. "Secret things belong to God; things revealed—to us." "Thou shalt love thy neighbor as thyself," is revealed through every part of our work; and depend upon it, we shall hide this revelation from our consciences, if we allow ourselves to be discouraged by any unbelief on this head. God has good, and great good in view. He can accomplish all his ends, whatever they are. We have nothing to do but to trust God and go forward. If we will only deny ourselves, and take up our cross, and set to work, he will avert all perils, provide all supplies, give wise direction as we need it, and bring out a most glorious issue. Yes! just as certainly as we prove faithful to duty. Surely, then, our fellow-men will not suffer any idea of impracticability to keep them from a prompt and energetic coöperation in this noble cause! Power to do the work is all they ask; and is it not an all-relieving truth, that what we can not do in our way, God can do in his? On this glorious Christian principle of fidelity to duty and faith in God, the principle which has achieved all the work of the kingdom hitherto, the principle all-competent to do all the work of the kingdom yet to be accomplished, certainly, certainly, *this* class of our fellow-men will take courage, and instantly join our ranks.

4. The last adverse sentiment which occurs to me, would express itself in this language: "You will effect nothing. The South has too little sympathy with any such movement. In general, they hold their slaves for gain, and the mass of the population are bitterly opposed to any enterprise that looks to liberation, however remotely.".

If the South refuses to come up to an enlightened view of the law of love to our neighbor, will you condemn them, and yet do the same thing? You have not advanced a thought which does not bind *you* to coöperation. You say that the masses do not act upon Christian principle on this subject; then does not the law of the kingdom command us to use the wisest influence to bring them to duty? Will the work of the kingdom ever be done in this world until by some means they are brought to this light? Do you know one objection to the method of operation we propose? Again: you admit there are those at the South who are ready for this movement. Does not the *law of reformation*, then, command us to proceed? All sound recovery to virtue must be gradual. Nor is there one point of progress, however early, at which you may stand by, and in reason or conscience, fail to exert your influence to advance the work. When Luther, on Pilate's staircase, received that memorable lightning inlet into his mind of the spiritual import of the text, "The just shall live by faith," the great Reformation commenced, so far as he was concerned. Will that good man be justified in the day of judgment, if such a man there was, who declined to encourage Luther and coöperate with him on this ground, namely, that when he looked over the earth, he felt that mankind had no such sympathy with Luther's spirit and principle as promised the slightest prospect of success against the formidable power arrayed in deadly opposition to both! Be the case as it may, your ground must be abandoned. Let it be that not one solitary right thought concerning the claims of the African population in this country, is entertained south of Mason and Dixon's line, obligation to send that thought to the South as early as it can be wisely done, will rest upon us while we live. Let it be that the leaven of truth has commenced to work in the Southern mind,—obligation to give it our countenance and aid, we can never neglect and be innocent.

But we are happy to believe that the elements of Southern character and the condition of Southern society is entirely misapprehended by the objection. Man at the South is like man at the North; he loves the world, and will fight for his worldly interests, and will neither see nor perform the duty which calls for their sacrifice, as early as he will discover and pursue those things which promise their improvement. But the Southern man is neither destitute of sympathy nor conscience; and has exhibited both on this subject to such an extent, and in such a variety of ways, as constitute grand encouragement to lay before him any scheme to promote this enterprise animated by Christian wisdom and benevolence.

Inspect the legal archives of the South!* Examine the constitutions, laws, and judicial decisions of the several States. They certainly constitute a reliable index of the principles and temper of a community. Whatever may be charged against special acts of unkind legislation, Southern law will be found to provide a scrupulous protection for the social welfare of the slave, extending to his body, living, labor, and comfort. This it does, not by commands only, but by severe penalties also. So faithfully have these statutory regulations been carried out, that in some districts the master who does not make suitable provision for the maintenance and comfort of his slave, or otherwise abuses him, will be more certainly presented by the Grand Jury as an offender against law, than the white parent who is guilty of an equal outrage against his children; while in others, he who takes the life of a man of color would find it more difficult to escape condemnation than if he had been charged upon the same evidence with the murder of

* Appendix D.

a white man. It may be said, in general, that in almost every part of the South, public sentiment works so efficiently to protect the slave from violent abuse, that from the earliest days the slaves have constantly multiplied, steadily improved, and are generally pronounced a happy population. May nothing be expected in the way of *humanity to the slave,* from a people who have framed such laws for their dependents and executed them to such a result?

Southern States have been compelled to pass laws forbidding emancipation, in order to discourage that sympathy of the master which would otherwise inordinately augment in the bosom of Southern society a shiftless and wretched population. The border States, Maryland, Virginia, Kentucky, Missouri, have seen the day when the whole population have been brought very near to a proclamation of liberty to all the captives within their bounds. The South are supposed to have freed near *three hundred thousand slaves.* If we value them singly at the sum of five hundred dollars, (and this ratio has been suggested,) we are then authorized to affirm that the South have substantially surrendered the sum of *one hundred and fifty millions of dollars* in testimony of their sympathy with the freedom of the race. This is a practical expression which more than triples the same kind of testimony given by North America for the conversion of the world. Can nothing be expected for the *liberty* of the slave, from a people who have made such demonstrations of their sympathy in its behalf?

I have been refused a contribution to send the Bible to *China* by a Southern gentleman who made no profession of religion, but who forthwith, at his own instance, paid me for five hundred Bibles, and the cost of their transportation from New-York, to distribute amongst his own servants, and those of his neighbors. I have arisen early on a Sabbath morning and gone down to the quarters with a gray-headed planter, and sat by for an hour or two, while he catechised his negro children, sometimes with tears in his eyes as he spoke to them of Jesus; and then accompanied him to the neighborhood colored church, where, preparatory to preaching, I have heard the missionary instructing a large number of colored boys and girls, before a mixed congregation, in Scripture doctrine and history, receiving from them public answers to his interrogatories. I could readily conduct you to large sections of the South, divided into districts, each of which is supplied by such a missionary conveniently stationed and supported by the adjacent planters, the sole business of whose life is to furnish all manner of pastoral service to his colored charge. Put me down in any portion of the South where the negro population abounds, and I venture to imagine that it will not be long before I shall be enabled to point you to twenty churches built by unconverted men for the religious comfort of their slaves, and supplied with preaching; most of them plain, 'tis true, but all of them commodious, and some of them tasteful and even costly. These persons, in general, make this contribution cheerfully to the religion of their people; a few, because they are unwilling to bear that odium which the public sentiment of the neighborhood would assuredly bring down upon their neglect. There are Societies at the South organized to promote the religious culture of the slave, which have published their Thirtieth Annual Report; have never been without the services of a superintendent of high ministerial qualifications; and which have imparted a wholesome impulse to the work of religious colored instruction, by occasionally reading, publishing, and distributing valuable tracts on the degradation of the slave, the obligation of the master, scriptural expositions and catechetical manuals. There are ecclesiastical bodies at the South which require every minister subject to their jurisdiction, to preach the half of every Sabbath to the colored population. There is no religious denomination at the South which does not cheerfully devote a portion of its ministry to exclusive labors for the spiritual welfare of the servants of the land. Not to multiply details on this head, suffice it to say, that there stands on record this day in the Southern churches a slave membership of near Four Hundred Thousand souls—a number which greatly surpasses the heathen church-membership of the world. May nothing be anticipated for the *eternal salvation* of the slave, from a people whose history for long years supplies such facts as these?

But to advance precisely to the point in hand. You speak of a lack of sympathy at the South with enlightened views upon the subject of slavery. I venture to affirm that there is a sentiment upon this subject at the South as enlightened, conscientious, and Christian, as is to be found on the face of the earth. The *end* is always the same, the best good of the slave as a fellow-man—but in this very class of men you will find great diversity of sentiment as to the best *means* of promoting it. If you will pardon my egotism, I will briefly sketch a specimen of various subdivisions of this noble class of men. A wealthy planter who had long been laboring to train his people for a change in their condition, but who made very little progress as he supposed, constructed at length a special system of management consisting of a general code of laws and privileges designed to educate his slaves to self-dependence in the shortest time. He first subjected to the working of this plan, one hundred of his servants best prepared for the discipline of such an experiment; a few years after, one hundred and fifty more. The last tidings from this enterprise indicated that it had not given the satisfaction anticipated. This class of men seem to have done all that could have been done for their slaves. Nay! This gentleman affirmed that he lived for little else. But it might be questioned whether their interest in their welfare does not tempt them to *haste* in pressing their slaves forward toward freedom. "No human being knows it," said a Southern Christian to me, "but my slaves never serve another master. Doing all for them in my power while I live, I know it will be a dangerous experiment to emancipate them at my death. Some of them will not be able to support themselves. But I have concluded, on the whole, I can do nothing better." This man felt that the longer he could keep his slaves under his guidance and government, the better it would be for them; and though he deeply desired to protect them from possible mistreatment, like many others, might fear, after all, to risk his own method when brought to the moment of decision. A larger number may be represented by the mental condition of one of the best men on earth. Said he to me one day: "I am ninety years old. I must soon meet God. I have various anxieties, but one disturbs me more than all others. What shall I do with my servants? You know I love my servants. What shall I do with them? If I free them here, I know that most of them will go to destruction. I can not do this. Mr. Wilson, you know, tells us not to send them to Liberia unless they can take care of themselves and get a living at home. If they can not do this, that they are better off here, temporally and spiritually, than they would be there. What shall I do with my servants? What do you think of Liberia for those who have no better qualification than mine?" This was the precise condition of a strong natural mind apparently freed from all temptation to misjudgment either by *worldly circumstances*—for by a special deed of gift he had already given to each of his children all that he expected to give them—or by *lack* of *reli-*

gious conscience, for he gave every indication of the residence of God's spirit in his heart touching duty to servants. "Next to the salvation of my only unconverted child," said he, "nothing on earth could give me so much pleasure as the conversion of William. He is an excellent servant, but a great sinner. I will send him into your chamber every morning to make a fire. Do talk and pray with him." "How does William feel this morning?" was ordinarily one of his earliest inquiries. He solicited my conversation with a second and a third, and could always tell me their precise states of mind. Did not this good man desire to know all his duty to his slaves? Had he not sought counsel of God as well as of man? And yet in their present condition he feared to free his slaves! He could not do it.

This sketch of the treatment of slaves at the South, and of Southern sentiments upon the subject of slavery, I do not present as a fair picture of all Southern society. But I do suppose that such facts and sentiments as these find a considerable representation in all parts of the Southern country. One thing I apprehend is perfectly clear. These facts do constitute satisfactory evidence of an all-sufficient sympathy in the Southern mind with truth and righteousness in the premises, to warrant the hope of good from kind, judicious, moral appeal. Truth pertains to the mind, and may be legitimately addressed to it, even when there is no truth in it: Indeed, *must* be, for nothing but truth can bring mind to the attitude of virtue. To hold, therefore, that a people who have given such abounding evidence of their interest in the social state, the liberty, the religion, and the universal weal of the slave, have no such state of mind as should encourage a proposal to develop their philanthropy toward the man of color, is preposterous. What! not sympathy enough at the South with the spiritual condition of the slave to justify you in countenancing our effort to work with God and his people, North and South, for African elevation? Not sympathy enough to encourage your Christian prayer, faith, and liberality, in multiplying Christian privileges amongst these perishing bondmen! Why, they themselves originated this very scheme, and have been carrying it on to the present day, through all discouragements. The fact is, we desire nothing more than to enlist the warm, active, fraternal coöperation of the North. True, all human virtue is progressive! There are always some truths to be advanced to a stronger hold upon the mind; some sentiments to be enfeebled in their influence upon the heart; some new principles to be introduced. Doubtless Southern mind has progress to make in this great cause. Unless, however, you insist that the Gospel does not belong to sinners; that man must be sanctified perfectly, and the work of the Gospel completed, before you send the Gospel to them; unless you hold that so long as there remains capacity of moral improvement in the man, there is no encouragement to use reformatory truth, you are bound in principle, my friend, to go with us. All you have a right to ask, is, that there should exist some foundations of knowledge, conscience, and kindness in Southern society, which may be appropriately addressed with a view to benevolent improvement. Here you have ample evidence of its existence to an encouraging degree. From this hour, then, you will cheerfully take your place by our side, and cordially assist us in co-working with our Southern brethren to carry forward God's missionary plan. *You* will not, you can not refuse to do so.

In laying by the first of our two grounds of appeal, we beg leave to repeat, we do hold it a conclusive argument for God's providential plan, that every opposing state of mind, honestly examined, can find the good it seeks in one only way, and that is, by giving in its earnest adhesion to the enterprise. As the colored man's friend against the oppressions of slavery, do you wish to advance his best good? You can truly befriend him on no other plan. As the nation's friend against the dishonor of slavery, do you desire to wipe away all its stain from her escutcheon? You can never promote our national honor in this connection, save by hearty coöperation on this very plan. Do you wish to secure an efficient power to move against this dark, massive mischief? You will never find the coöperation of God except in carrying out his own providential plan. Do you desire to secure the sympathy of the South as necessary to all desirable success? You will find the hearty sympathy of the South with this very plan and with no other.

II. But the crowning argument in behalf of God's plan lies in the *distinguished blessings*, which nothing but this very plan can shower upon the *great interests of the American people*, and which this plan can not fail to dispense *to the world* as well as to the nation.

Were God to dispatch an angel from heaven under a commission to make a thorough survey of this nation in all its capacities, relations, condition, and prospects, with a view to ascertain the changes necessary to its very highest rectitude, happiness, usefulness, and glory, methinks it would not surprise the reflective mind if the celestial delegate should return and hand up this report: "Let that plan of benevolent procedure indicated by God in his early providential introduction into the country of a large African population, be heartily and faithfully *carried out by the whole country*—and the nation's *great evils* are all averted, *great duties* all discharged, and *great blessings* all secured." Call up the intelligence, patriotism, and piety of all sections and parties of the country, and propound this inquiry: "What does this nation need above all things?" Its every day observation and reflection have long since qualified the soul of this country to respond: "Three things; first, *heal the dissensions* of the nation; these seem to imperil its very existence. Second, that we may have no more trouble from the same cause, *discharge duty to the man of color*, and to *God's voice* in his importation.

And third, Oh! let *not* this nation *fail of her high mission* to scatter around the world earth's highest blessing—political liberty, and heaven's far surpassing gift—the freedom of Jesus Christ the Saviour."

1. *National harmony* is the alone *fruit of obedience* to God's great providential plan.

Let our Northern friends remember that their fathers took part in the importation of the slave; that God's voice, summoning this nation to discharge duty to the man of color, in order that his own benign decrees connected with his introduction, may be accomplished, is addressed to *them* equally with their Southern neighbors. In a word, let them feel that they themselves have *their* responsibilities to meet in this case. And now, just let them advance and take their place and work for the accomplishment of the ends of this divine enterprise. Let them encourage those who have to bear most of the heat and burden of the day, and say to them: "Southern brethren, you have long had a heavy responsibility upon your shoulders; nor have you been entirely unfaithful to your trust! By the constitutions, laws, and courts of your several States, you have thrown a strong legal breastwork around the temporal rights of the slave, and largely protected them from the necessarily perilous power of the master. This was well, brethren! You have advanced more than one hundred millions of dollars in securing the freedom of your slaves. This was well, brethren! You have been the favored instruments of converting to Christ hundreds of thousands of the souls of your slaves. This was well, brethren! You have elevated such masses of them to the possession and enjoyment of Christianity, that our own Northern missionary brethren on the shores of Africa, comparing the dark impenetrable mind of the heathen around them with the enlightened and shouting Christianity of *these very heathen under your training*, have been compelled to publish their wish to the world that every black man in Africa were a slave at the South.* This is well, brethren! By your principles, sympathies, and toils, they have been regularly rising from the profound degradations of their first estate toward the rich blessings of a higher condition. This is well, brethren! Most of you are sensible that, like fallen men, you have looked too much to your own worldly interest in your servants, and too little to the infinitely more exalted interests of their immortality; and many of you are deeply inquiring after all the responsibilities to which God holds you in this matter. All this is well, brethren! There are particulars, 'tis true, connected with your views on some branches of this great and intricate subject, and with your conduct in others, concerning which we shall venture to tender to you, anon, our respectful, fraternal suggestions. But go on, dear brethren, and be encouraged. We have a great work to do. Our God, who called us out to this work in so extraordinary a manner, will surely go with us. And we shall enjoy the

* Appendix E.

high satisfaction to feel, when we commit this enterprise to our posterity, that we have been privileged to contribute some degree of self-sacrificing effort and wholesome progress to one of the very largest and brightest Christian movements of our generation. Yes, brethren, you have our hearty approbation, our prayers, our sympathies, and our faith. And you must allow us to send down liberally our material contributions in all the blessed work of applying to the dark minds of our *protégés* the power of that one great and all-perfect elevator of fallen man, the Gosgel of the Lord Jesus Christ. We need not say, from time to time we shall hope to hear from you of the progress of our noble cause, and may God's richest blessings rest upon your labors."

O my dear brethren of the North! come up thus manfully to clear duty by God's plan, and where are the dissensions of this country? Where now are our sectional alienations; our congressional conflicts; our newspaper wranglings; our party malignities? Where now are our mutual depreciations; our personal disputes; our Anti-Slavery mania; our organizations for disunion? In fine, where is all the bad blood of the nation, North and South? This sacred plan of God, honored by the North: What a healer! what a healer of all the strife of the country! And what else, oh! what else, can heal it half so well?

2. *Duty to the man of color; duty to God's providential voice in his introduction!*

How can the nation expect to prosper if unfaithful

here? This thing, remember, was not done in a corner. When God brought Africa across the ocean to America, every eye from one end under heaven unto the other beheld the mighty movement, and sought the object. Surely it was for some great end that God did this great thing. Surely it was for *no trifle* that God permitted all that cruel rending from kindred and country; those dismal, dreadful forebodings, those bitter shrieks and tears, that mournful, awful breaking of hearts which marked the hour of embarkation from their native land. Surely it was for no trifle that God subjected such a multitude of human beings to all the nameless horrors and deaths of that infernal compression and oppression on shipboard, universally adopted to escape the perils and secure the profits of the voyage. Surely it was for no trifle that God has passed this people, from father to son, through successive generations of toil, trial, and degradation, in the bosom of a country where they must be the observed of all observers, because palpably suffering the privations of those natural dignities which we of all men profess to appreciate. God's object! God's object in all this? Assuredly it was well worthy of all the suffering man was called to endure. What was that object? God brought Israel out of Egypt, that by his liberty he might shed a salutary light over the world. God brought Africa into America that, by bondage, her sons and daughters might here catch that light which was sent to lighten the Gentiles, and ultimately, through proper training, reflect it over the land of their fathers.

But, brethren and countrymen, our nation's conduct in the premises! What tidings has this conduct announced to a beholding world respecting our views of God's grand and sacred designs therein? May not the Lord bring up the North to testify against the South, that she has been faithless to God, in that in her *selfishness*, instead of working for God's ends, she has employed this mighty doing of God too much to gratify her own covetous and worldly aims? May not the Lord call up the South to testify against the North that she too has been faithless to God, in that in her selfishness she has withdrawn and otherwise invested her proportion of the capital in trade, and now, forsooth, instead of working for God's ends in the conversion of the people, and the enlightenment of Africa, because the South will not adopt her sentiments and follow her dictation, gratifies her own morbid views of other men's duties by withdrawing herself almost wholly from the work; indeed, is just now cutting off her last channels of missionary appropriation. Most assuredly God must have a controversy with our people on this account! On all sides, there has been a wicked abandonment of his most generous purposes. Nor need we, as a nation, expect any great blessing from his hand, while North and South perpetuate our disgraceful differences, and practically refuse honest coöperation with God to secure those broad and gracious ends which he seeks through Africa in America.

But, O my friends! only let the North and the South come up to a hearty co-working, side by side, in God's providential enterprise, and where is God's controversy with his people? Let both sections study to feel the full power of our fellow-man's claims upon us for himself and for his pagan country. Let both sections study to cherish a due regard to the high claims of God, not only to our notice, approbation, and sympathy touching his great plan for the conversion of the heathen, but largely for the *divine honor*, the *divine honor* put upon us in our being permitted to stand by God's side, and be co-laborers with himself in such an enterprise! Yes, let us but do this, and how it will delight our heavenly Father to cheer us with the refreshing visitations of his grace in all this field! How he will make us to delight ourselves in one another! For now, instead of seeking that which assists to dishonor a brother, each will find heavenly cheering in enriching himself with his brother's excellencies.

3. *But how! how shall this nation do her great work?*

The United States of America is the singular nation of the world! You can find pagan nations enough; and between them and us half-evangelized nations enough. You can find tyrannies enough; and between them and us half-free states enough. But where is there on the face of the earth such another country as ours! Our country, thank God, is singular in her position, and singular in her history; singular in the genius of her people, and singular in the structure of her institutions; singular in her liberty and her religion, and singular in her power and her progress. Surely God has raised her up, and placed her at the head of the nations, to do a singular work on the earth! There is principle, and intelligence, and wealth, and enterprise, and power enough to do a great and a good work for God and man. Yes! and the earth shall suffer, and suffer deeply, both in her politics and in her piety, if she fails of the wholesome power of this people. God forbid that this nation, so largely endowed and so solemnly charged, should prove recreant to her high calling! But there are signs of the times, numerous and ominous, which make us anxious for the issue. The diabolical bent of man's heart in our day to seek gain, as though it were godliness; our base corruption in politics, and dishonesty in trade; the shocking immoralities of our great cities, and our host of organized heresies and new lights throughout the country; our oversight of God's end in slavery, and the consequent abuse of the institution at the South, and our fanaticism on this subject at the North, with its private murder of charity and peace, and its public shocks in Church and State; and by all this and the like, our constant provocation of God, and exposure to his righteous judgments! If these evil elements and tendencies are not corrected; if they are suffered to be progressively developed, woe to all high hopes of good from the peculiar properties and power of this country. Where! where are we to look for protection against all this brewing mischief?

The enlightened, sincere coöperation of the nation in God's providential plan! Will not *this* go far to secure that holy power of our country, that promise of mighty beneficence, so dear to every enlightened patriot, to every sincere Christian! If it heals our dissensions, think, through all the land, what a wicked waste of virtuous principle and power it will arrest! What benign and holy agencies of charity and peace it will renew! If it brings us to a just consideration of God's providence, and conformity to its dictates, think, what an impediment to God's blessing upon the nation's work it will remove! How much nearer it will bring us to God and God to us in all our aims, agencies, and influence! "Behold! a man turned aside and brought a man unto me, and said, Keep this man! If by any means he be missing, then shall thy life be for his life, or else thou shalt pay a talent of silver." Behold how far the Lord turned aside from his ordinary providence when he brought the black man to our shores, and left him in our hands with a solemn injunction of special duty to the captive! If this nation returns to her commanded vigilance and fidelity to this man, think what a qualification will she thereby acquire to feel for all the captives and pagans of the earth! Oh! what a rich missionary spirit will she thereby necessarily imbibe!

Without enlarging the detail of favorable special influences which must follow the nation's return to duty, there is one general view in which national fidelity to God's providence would seem to constitute the precise qualification to resuscitate and perfect our very highest national power for the conversion of the world.

Activity in evil is the necessary result of inaction in the good principle. Activity in good is the direct overthrow of evil agency. Behold that large, wealthy, powerful, but impotent Church! It is orthodox and orderly! and this is all. It has no faith, nor prayer, nor liberality, nor language, nor life. But let that Church colonize! let it set up half-a-dozen mission schools! let it set out to raise funds for a professorship! start it up to do any great thing for the Lord! By all the laws of nature and of Scripture, this very movement shall work a resurrection of that dead body. Formality, pride, coldness, covetousness, unbelief, and every other evil thing, is worked off by the good working of love, faith, zeal, and prayer. Our nation, our beloved nation, after all our pharisaic opinions of its orthodoxy, piety, and usefulness, is not a little like that magnificent, over-grown, half-dead Church. The feeling and the working of this nation in the kingdom, what is it in comparison with what it should be in view of these four things—the light in our minds, the power in our hands, the necessities of the earth, and the claims of our Saviour! As a nation, we have a little interest in Foreign Missions, and a little in Missions at home; a little interest in the cause of the Bible, and a little in the Tract cause. Indeed, we have a little interest in many good things. But a *large heart*, or a *powerful arm* for *any thing*, any thing in the kingdom, we have not. This nation has never yet been stirred up to the foundations, and shaken and started to her lowest roots as she should be by the boasted light of this nineteenth century. This great New light, this light of Progress, makes us Reformers, but does not rectify us; disputants, but not doers. Our religion is shamefully querulous, but feeble; wordy, but empty. Oh! this nation needs to be worked over by God's mighty truth and Spirit, that she may work off her vicious features by working out naturally and powerfully the great elements of love to God and man. Now, what more suitable means to accomplish this can man conceive, than fidelity to God's great Africo-American missionary enterprise! If we can not move in view of such a cause, what can start us? Only let this nation lend her eye, heart, and hand to this noble, neglected work. Let her take in all its great thoughts, high duties, rich promises, bright prospects, and feed upon them. Let her fill her private meditations, the converse of the parlor, the car, and the workshop, the worship of the domestic altar, and the exhortation of the pulpit, with the fire of this great topic. Let her do this, and the result is inevitable—she must stretch herself up toward God, and spread herself out toward the heathen, and work mightily and gloriously for the conversion of the world.

Tell me, my dear brethren, can you believe it but the vision of an earnest fancy, that if this whole nation, honest as in the very sight of God, would throw away her sectional prejudices North and South, cost the sacrifice of pride what it may, confess her guilty deficiencies and sins in the past, be the humiliation what it must, and come up to the help of the Lord; if she would first inquire concerning the sons and daughters of Africa in the midst of us, "Lord, what wilt thou have me to do?" and then set to with all her heart to do the work of the Lord; tell me, I say, under God, would not this, the nation's fidelity to God and his imported man of color, would it not avert her great perils, discharge her great duties, secure her great usefulness, and verify the report of the angel?

Survey, then, God's providential plan connected with the slaves of the South, means and ends, as interpreted above. Brethren and countrymen, distinctly respond to these three inquiries. On the face of this transaction is there not a light which forces every soul of you to say: "This thing proceedeth from the Lord"? Have you not seen, too, that every *objection* to coöperation, examined, proves an *argument?* Have you not seen, again, that national union, in obedience to God's providence, naturally and beautifully works out all the great ends the Church and the nation should desire? Where, then, is that man's refuge from condemnation by conscience and by God, who does not instantly lend a hand to this most noble work? By that help and blessing waiting for us from above, shall not our whole country, from this very day, move up into the light of God's countenance, and side by side, commence to struggle earnestly with heaven for the accomplishment of this divine, this wonderful enterprise?

What a question is thrown upon us at this point!

Where lies the impediment? Eminently just here, in the lack of a *kind heart on the part of the North toward the South.*

But is there no lack in the heart of the South toward the North? Certainly, certainly. Why, then, do you exclude the South from your statement concerning the grand necessity to the nation's welfare? I will tell you, my friend. Bear in mind, I am now particularly addressing the North. It is proper, therefore, that I should give prominence to the deficiencies and duties of the North. Again: Anti-South is rather more chargeable to the North, than is Anti-North to the South. Not hatred of the North, but love of her own institutions, is the distinguishing feature of the Northern charge against the South. This the language of the North admits — "*Pro-Slavery.*" Not retaliation of Southern assault, but opposition to an institution of the South, from the beginning was the distinguishing feature of the Northern spirit; this, too, universal language concedes—"*Anti-Slavery.*" The opposition of the South to the conduct of the North is the *resulting*, not the primary attitude of Southern mind; whereas, opposition to Southern institutions was the *primary*, not the consequential, attitude of Northern mind. In the beginning, the South did not set out to force the North to adopt her principles, but the North to bring the South to hers.

Again. Duty, as indicated by our construction of God's providence, the Christian South has not entirely neglected; but duty, as so indicated, that portion of the Christian North I address, has utterly abandoned; and therefore it peculiarly becomes them to study to cultivate a kinder feeling toward their Southern neighbors.

The all-governing reason, in my view, however, I desire to be understood, is this: the kindness of the South toward the North, though it must do good, never could do for the kingdom in this country and the world, what must instantly follow the kindness of the North to the South. In advancing the proof of this important position, namely, that almost all good in the premises depends upon the *conduct of the North*, permit me to say:

1. That a kind heart cherished by the North toward the South will measurably *secure to America, Africa, and the world, all the glorious blessings* promised to that course of duty which was providentially imposed by the introduction of slaves.

We have seen that the South are doing something to free their slaves, and more to Christianize them.

We have seen too, that the class of men at the North whom I address, have set themselves against every Southern movement on the subject. They seem to say practically, we will even withhold the Gospel from you, if you come not to our views. Thus they throw the nation into conflict on the one hand, and embarrass the Church in her obedience to God on the other. Oh! if all our Northern fellow-men could only be persuaded to exercise a little patience on this subject; could only be induced to bear with the shortcomings of their neighbors as God bears with theirs; could but be influenced to unite heartily with Southern brethren in doing all for the slaves which the present condition of society will allow—what then? Why, then, the whole nation would place itself, measurably at least, in the attitude of obedience to God's great providential mandate. Mark, now, the natural result: all the prominent blessings of God's great missionary movement are earned, the nation's perils averted, the nation's duties met, the necessary influence secured.

Observe, more particularly—

2. That a kind heart cherished by the North toward the South is the only *safeguard against great national peril.*

In marking the course of this North and South controversy, you have not failed to observe, that precisely what the Northern mind wants, dwells only in the Southern mind; and precisely what the Southern mind wants, is to be found only in the Northern mind. Put into the Northern mind two truths which the Southern man does most clearly know from his own observation and experience, namely, the utter impracticability of any such thing (in general) as a judicious dissolution of the relation of master and servant instanter; and again, that degree of benevolence which he himself truly feels and daily tries to exhibit toward his servants—and the Northern mind will be brought instantly to some greater toleration of the Southern man. Put into the Southern mind two facts of which the Northern man is perfectly conscious, namely, that in his (Northern) mind, below his violent denunciation of the master, there are many lines of generous sympathy with the man of color,—and beside that ignorance of the slave's unfitness for a present change of condition, there dwells a clear discovery of many incongruities of slavery with a perfect state of human society, by no means so clearly seen by the Southern man—and the Southern man must feel that more allowance should be made for the vehement oppositions of his Northern neighbor. How singular is the work of providence! Here are two sections of a great nation in a hostile attitude. What shall prevent their shameful, perilous collision? Mark! God has intrusted to the South what should restrain the North, and to the North what should restrain the South: while the elements of self-restraint, evil feelings have largely shut out of the minds of both. What a call to union! Disobey this call: aggravate this controversy: mark the issue! You throw the

South back upon herself, and not only cut her off from all the valuable enlightenment which she might have received from kind association with the North, but you place her in an attitude to misunderstand the North and be provoked by all her conduct. You throw the North back upon herself, and in like manner not only cut her off from benefits which she might have derived from the South, but you expose her to increased dissatisfaction with her neighbor. What is the result? You have pursued precisely the only philosophical process to breed a national rupture. But give a kind heart to the North toward her Southern neighbor, and the parties will commune with each other. They will interchange thoughts and feelings. They will look deeper into each other's minds. They will be drawn toward each other. And if, by the nature of man, any thing can avert the calamity of national disruption, this will. But observe yet more particularly—

3. That a kind heart in the North toward the South is the *one only way in which the North can bring to the South* her great and greatly needed help in that great work with our African population which God has intrusted so largely to the hands of the South.

Permit me to attempt a yet more particular analysis and comparison of Northern and Southern mind upon the subject of slavery. There is, on this subject, a right and a wrong mind at the North, and a right and a wrong mind at the South. These grow naturally out of the relation of the parties to the institution. The Southern man stands in a *two-fold* connection with slavery. The first is that of *practical acquaintance.* He handles slavery every day intimately. While he has, as we have said, a perfect knowledge of the slave's unfitness for present freedom, and best understands how to address him, he handles no other species of labor, and therefore, the moral, economical, and miscellaneous disadvantages of slavery, he does not so perfectly comprehend. The second is a *pecuniary relation* to slavery. The natural tendency of such a connection must be to blind the mind and blunt the conscience, and thus measurably obstruct the clear sight and sense of high Christian duty to a fellow-man. The Northern man sustains also two relations to this institution, and these the precise opposites of those of the Southern man. He is personally disconnected with slavery; consequently he can not know the slave as well as the master does, his capacities, inabilities, and temptations; and may, therefore, very naturally mistake as to the proper course which an enlightened conscience would pursue in the treatment of the slave. On the other hand, the Northern man has no pecuniary interest in the slave, and is, therefore, free from all bias upon his judgment or his conscience as to what a good man should be willing to do for a fellow-man in such a relation. On the whole, while the Southern man, from his intimate connection with his slave, has his great advantages over the Northern man, the Northern man may be supposed in general to possess two advantages over the Southern man. By his personal separation from the institution, a stronger conscience as to a man's duty to his slave; by his perfect acquaintance with *free labor*, a superior knowledge of the comparative economy, morality, comfort, etc., of these opposite methods of accomplishing the manual work of society.

He who examines Southern society closely, I am persuaded, will learn two things—that the mind which comes nearest to Christian perfection on the subject of slavery, in knowledge, sympathy, and agency, is to be found at the South; and that all the properties of sound Christian morality on this subject are scattered through Southern society. Indeed, I see no injustice in the statement that the mind of the South is on the way toward Christian perfection on this subject. It certainly has these two all-embracing elements: partial knowledge of the evils of slavery; incipient conscience of the obligations of the master. It wants two auxiliary applications—the one to increase its knowledge of the evils of the institution, the other to strengthen its conscience to discharge its duties. Now, the *intellect* of the North! It has no material interest to prejudice its action, and abstractly has a clearer view of many of the relations of this subject than the Southern man possesses. The Northern mind, therefore, is exactly fitted to supply one of the elements needed at the South. The *conscience* of the North! This, too, is free from the enfeebling influence of a proprietary interest in slavery, and therefore has less to prevent its prompting rightly and strongly on the subject. The Northern mind, therefore, is exactly fitted to supply the second element needed by his Southern neighbor. The *mistake* of the North, how palpable! how provoking! By its uncharitable violence it destroys all sympathy and intercourse between the opposite sections of the country, and thus excludes from each that needed good which it could only derive from the other. The duty of the North! how obvious! Cherish a *kind side toward the South.* Believe all things, hope all things, endure all things. Feel for the high responsibilities of your Southern neighbor, and place your shoulder under his burden. Envy his exalted opportunity of serving God, man, and himself, by heroic, self-denying virtue under great temptation, and spring to his side that you may share his honors. Bear in mind, whatever be his weaknesses, the Southerner is a frank and warm-hearted man. Nothing is more sure than is kindness, to win his confidence. He will readily open all his soul to you, and take in all yours. See! see what love can do. You will lay all your advanced views directly in his intellect, and help him there; you will place your solemn conscience directly by the side of his, and strengthen him there. Thus you *have* just what that man wants, but will never, never *get*, until you *love* him.

Yes, you must permit me to repeat the affirmation, —I can scarcely conceive of an event within the easy compass of human power, which promises a greater blessing to America, Africa, and the world, than the growth at the North of a fraternal spirit toward the South. I pray God to shed the spirit of love upon my country, both upon the North and upon the South. Surely mutual love will never harm us! Surely it is the very element, and the only one, that can save us. Many a great and good man of this nation has seen this clearly, and left the world longing for it deeply. *Leonard Woods* of Andover ever breathed the spirit of a little child; and yet it was as near to the *spirit of wisdom* and the *spirit of Jesus Christ*, as was that of any fellow-man whom it has been my privilege to know. What a beautiful heart did long beat in the bosom of the good old man, on this very subject! How simple, earnest, opportune, were his thoughts, words, and feelings, just before he left us for heaven. On the 23d of September, 1853, in a letter addressed to myself, he employs this language: "I have long been sick at heart to hear ministers and churches at the South denounced and treated in such a manner, as to injure them and injure their brethren at the North, and offend the God of love. Most heartily shall I rejoice in any measures which may be adopted to promote the spiritual and temporal welfare of the South, which is just as worthy of regard as the welfare of the North. How much do we need to have *our hearts enlarged.* It is impossible to tell how much the North might do to benefit the South, by the *feelings and the language of love*, by cordial sympathy and co-operation! And ministers and Christians at the North would thus benefit themselves as much as others. I wish we could all understand what is the mind of Christ, and just what he would say to us if he should come as in his former visit to this world, and should walk through the North and the South, and tell us what he would have us to do, and what would be his prayer in our behalf. I think we find in his Gospel, and in John 17th, what his instructions would be, and what his prayer. '*Love one another*,' would still be his great and last command. And his prayer would still be, '*That all his disciples may be one*.' But I need not say this to you, or to those who feel with you. It is all in your minds and in your hearts. The Lord be with you and your brethren, and in his own way do more for the cause of truth and love than we can ask or think."

The Lord answer the prayer of the good old man in heaven, for the greater harmony of the North and the South! A man should work for the answer of his prayer. My suggestions, I repeat, are two. The violent men of the North, who have done so much harm by misjudgment! let them labor to form a *more accurate estimate of liberty*, natural and spiritual. These fellow-men who have it in their power to do so much good by benevolence, let them strive to cherish a *more patient and fraternal spirit* toward their *Southern* brethren.

If the wise counsel, the proper temper, upon this

great subject, have not been presented by these pages, the Lord in mercy speedily bury this intruding volume, forgive one who has lived to do very little else but perpetrate blunders and sins, and in his own perfect way, accomplish that great kindness for which the nation and the earth so deeply long.

CHAPTER IX.

FRATERNAL EXHORTATION.

MY heart yearns for a private interview with two of my neighbors.

And first, my Anti-Slavery brother, permit me to have a word with you.

I have dealt very plainly with you, perhaps you think harshly; if so, I am wrong. God judge between us and forgive and reform the sinner. I would come nearer to you. I would tell you, as it were, alone, all I think and feel about you. Permit me, then, to say with perfect familiarity, that in late years I have become more thoroughly dissatisfied, both with your principle and your spirit. I was born at the South, and have spent most of my life there. My judgment may have been too much influenced by my circumstances, to justify so bold an expression of my sentiments in this latitude. It is certainly true that I have had much to do with slaves; nor have I been so fortunate as to escape animadversion upon my treatment of them. I have been more seriously troubled, however, by accusations of sympathy with your views. In those days I was no nearer to conviction of the truth of your grand tenet of immediate emancipation than I am to-day. But this thought separated me from most of my brethren. I could not sympathize with the violence of their denunciation of men of your faith. I felt and said, however indiscreet the measure proposed for the good of the man of color, I could not but appreciate what seemed to me the all-sufficient evidence of a magnanimous sympathy with a fellow-man who needed human kindness. I could see no possible selfish consideration for this interposition, and therefore felt it my duty to give to the Abolitionist the credit of a generous heart and a manly friendship. I have not lost this conviction in regard to very many who hold your views. I now confine it, however, chiefly to those who dwell at a distance from sources of knowledge, but are constantly reached by your party activities. For the last eight or ten years, my position has been changed. Formerly I was not brought into contact with the spirit and movements of the Modern Reform, and knew but little of the character and workings of the system. Of late I have been embosomed in the midst of its operations, and have added a new idea to my former stock. I suppose that you probably commenced your connection with this cause in that spirit of manly benevolence which I have commended. But I imagine what was then amiable in your temper, has since become greatly obscured by the manifold unamiable developments of that epidemic mania which I doubt not works strongly within you. I do verily believe that there is a virus abroad upon the subject of slavery which impregnates the mind and tends directly if unconsciously to corrupt the virtue which comes within its range. My dear brother! Have you never feared this? Have you never had misgivings on this subject? Whether you have or not, will you engage with me in an honest investigation of the precise state of your own mind, so far as it stands affected by the subject of slavery?

That you are a Christian man I have no disposition to question, but I invite your examination of this precise inquiry: Does not all the Christianity of your soul sternly affirm, "I will have nothing to do with your Abolitionism?" Understand me. That you have humility, and charity, and patience, and teachableness, and every Christian grace, I do not doubt; but are these things found in connection with your spirit on the subject of slavery? On the contrary, does not your own Christianity keep clear of your Abolitionism? This is our point. Permit me then to press the following inquiries.

On this subject—the subject of slavery—do you find any *humility* in your spirit? Do you ever doubt yourself in this matter? Do you ever fear that you may be wrong? Do you know such a state of mind as this: "After all, my brother's view may be right! My sentiments may be wrong.

As he says, I may be harming every good thing in connection with this subject. I am certainly a fallible creature, and it behooves me to cherish these thoughts." On the contrary, is not *this* your unvarying temper? "I *know* that I am right. I *know* that every slaveholder is wrong." On this subject, is there any *charity* in your spirit? Can you suffer long and be kind? In sympathy with the slaveholder do you find it easy to believe, hope, endure all things? Have you ever felt any thing like a sweet and cheerful patience toward them that differ with you concerning the qualities and bearings of the institution of slavery? Any thing like that tender respect and deference toward these persons, which you would be sure to feel if your diversity of sentiment respected any other topic? On the contrary, have you not marked in your own spirit such an uniformly hard, censorious, and uncompromising temper as sometimes surprises you into the soliloquy: "Why, on the subject of slavery I scarcely know myself."—On this subject have you any *teachableness* in your spirit? Do you ever yield to opposing argument? Has your tongue ever said, or your heart ever felt: "Truly, my neighbor, that view of yours looks reasonable. Give me a moment to think of it." My Christian brother! Do you know what it is in very truth to struggle with God for light on this subject? Do you ever subject the very sentiments you hold, to his inspection, and feeling that you know nothing, do you anxiously inquire of him whether they are indeed so unquestionably and importantly true, that you may, as it were, sword in hand, cut your way for them through the world? On the contrary, have you not at times been more than a little startled at the impracticable self-reliance, intolerance, and recklessness which always mark the workings of your spirit on this subject? Have you any *reasonableness* in your spirit on the subject of slavery? What say your *judgments?* You hold a sentiment touching the stupendous elevation of natural liberty, which in the practice degrades spiritual liberty in the same proportion. You hold a sentiment concerning the rights of man which in practice works out the precise process to breed an insurrection and shoot down his life. You hold a sentiment concerning national glory which in practice must philosophically rupture the Union and destroy society. You hold a sentiment concerning true religion which in practice profanes the pulpit and abolishes the Bible. You hold a sentiment concerning love to your neighbor which in practice is an exact war of extermination. What say your *feelings?* You are the friend of the slave! But is it not a fact that the morning paragraph concerning the Southern master's cruel blow upon the body of his servant, did more to rouse your indignation against all the South, than did the announcement of the hopeful conversion of 400,000 souls to thrill you with gratitude to God for the salvation of the man of color? What say your *prayers?* Do they not anxiously beseech the slave's deliverance from those troubles about which God tells him not to trouble himself; while your heart—be your language what it may—is scarce ever conscious of a sincere yearning that the slave might come to possess that spiritual freedom which God says is his all in all! What say your *actions?* You well remember the day when you sent a pecuniary contribution, perhaps a rifle, certainly a strong heart, to defend liberty against Ruffianism in Kansas; but is it not a truth that to save the perishing souls of the millions of the slaves of the South, you never yet contributed as many dollars, performed as many acts, or uttered as many words; or at least would you not be ashamed to lay the very little you have felt, said, and done for the eternal salvation of the slave, by the side of all you have felt, said, and done to break the master's transient hold upon his service? How clear it is, my friend, that your mind is out of order on this point! It does not work reasonably. It does not weigh truth duly. It does not appreciate things according to their importance. Permit one more inquiry on this subject. Is there any *self-control* in your spirit? Do you not feel that your passions rise quicker and higher on this topic than on any other? Have you not just on this point less calm self-approbation, less desirable self-control, than you readily command on any other conceivable subject? O my brother! Does not God know that you have had many secret admonitions from heaven on account of the actings of your soul on the subject of slavery? Not that you have been much distressed by these compunctions; certainly not that you ever spake to man of them! But is not this the truth before God, that you have been compelled, all your life long, to make little apologies to conscience for the rude, contradicting, violent, unchristian outbreaks of your temper in conference with your fellow-men on this maddening subject?

What do you learn, my brother, by this self-inspection? Does not a close investigation of the state of your soul assure you that even *your own Christianity* will not keep company with such a mind as you have *on the subject of slavery?* How then can you expect other men to tolerate you? My dear brother! I hold you to the teachings of our investigation. The argument is irresistible. Know this: The Spirit of Holiness and the Spirit of Truth are one and the same Spirit. They always go together. Now if you have found that the humilities, and the charities, and the candor, and the judgment, and the self-possession of Christianity do not dwell *round about this subject* of slavery in your heart, then you have expelled the *Spirit of Holiness* from your heart *just there.* And depend upon it, the Spirit of Truth has not remained behind. Depend upon it, you have driven out the Spirit of Truth too; and you *are in error!* Yes, my friend. Just *on that point,* rest assured of it, you are IN ERROR. *Your doctrine is as untrue as your temper is unholy.*

Come, my friend! For a long time you have been

bearing violent public witness against all the good men who entertain more moderate sentiments than yourself. Place your hand in mine and let us go to God. Here alone, before our common Maker, Saviour, Master, as your fellow-servant in Jesus Christ, I bear solemn testimony to you of my conviction, that you are wrong in spirit and wrong in principle: That you stand in the way of the natural rights and the Christian hopes of the slave: That you stand in the way of the political union and moral power of our country: That you stand in the way of the sacredness of God's pulpit, and the authority of God's word: That you stand in the way of God's great missionary providence, and the conversion of the world.

The heart is deceitful above all things; who can know it? I trust I would not wrong you. Surely I ought to love you, my fellow-man. Will you take a little advice from me? Daily for the space of a month, enter thy closet. Bend thy knee. Utter not a word of prayer. Mean to meet God. Tarry in his presence, seeking, expecting light from him alone. Let whatever thought enter thy mind that will. Only be a little child, and long for truth, the very truth, of God, be it what it may. Peradventure, God will have mercy upon thee—and if we, thy brethren, have indeed received his guidance—lead thee too into our more excellent way.

O my dear brother! how happy should we be to have you by our side in this great field. While we admired the vehemence and vigor of your coöperation, how inexpressibly grateful would be our experience that you could now talk and work with us and our Southern brethren, and exhibit the very same kindness and patience which always adorn your spirit on every other subject. May the Spirit of Truth and Holiness teach and unite us.

My Christian brother! *whose Anti-Slavery sentiment is advancing toward the extreme views we have discussed;* permit me in Christian frankness to tender you three points of fraternal counsel. I entreat you consider:

1. The *peril of your position.* You are pressed by a strong power from the North, and have no adequate brace against the pressure.

Anti-Slavery strength finds its basis in two properties, vehemence of emotion and vigor of action. The strongest impulses of the human soul heave on this enterprise. Indignation in view of what is deemed oppressed humanity, condemnation of what is considered wicked principle, fierce purpose to carry a point, all a little maddened because fed by a vision of greater ills than exist. These energized emotions speak powerfully to conscience, to shame, to fear, to irresolution, and to the love of peace. The stern look, the flashing eye, the condemnatory tone, the dogged intent of a Christian man, all pressing the vindication of crushed liberty, and this, as with a sword drawn under the high banner, "Instant and perfect submission or no quarter," make a tolerably formidable array. Remember, too, that these elements act as constantly as they do vehemently. They never fail to speak or act when speech or action is called for. They never fail to work when the slightest door is opened for their agency. Nay, they often break through proprieties, to wave their banner and press their cause.

What a prodigious energy have we here! The feeblest cause is powerful if perpetual; far more powerful than any single action of the strongest element. The fiercest bolt of lightning that ever fell from heaven scarce ever did more than crush an oak. The little axe in perpetual motion shall cut down the world. Annex the power of perpetuity to the action of a powerful cause, and what a power you secure. Repeat the shock of heaven's bolt as regularly as the blows of the axe that clears the world, and what a crushing work you make. Such is the nature of the power of this Reform enterprise. *It is a strong cause, ever acting strongly.* And such, remember, is the agent that works upon you.

Where now is your protection against this power? In self-defense you work to great disadvantage, both in the nature and in the circumstances of the case. In the twinkling of an eye the entire blow of the Reformer is upon you. Only let him utter his watchword, "Slavery," and the work is done. The great right of liberty, the great wrong of its oppression, and the shriek of the soul for justice, are all instantaneous. Now it is not so with you. You can not avert or beat back this blow with a word.

You can not state your defense in a sentence. You must bear the blow and suffer on, advancing one idea and then another, and then a third, before you reach the thought that rallies your soul against the assailant. The power of the Reformer, you perceive, is vastly more available than yours; and far better adapted to the kind of combat which he naturally gets up. Ordinarily this is not cool investigation in search of truth, but a furious onset to put down a foe. This, you know, nature expects you to repel at once.

Circumstances, too, are equally against you. Survey the relative position of yourself and your antagonist. You are the defendant, he the assailant. Nothing prompts you to wield your weapons upon him, nothing can keep him from employing his sword upon you. Your mind is feeble in this conflict, because indifferent here and occupied with other things; his, always meets you in its strength, because impowered both by decision and emotion. Your mind is not well supplied with truth, and has no established channel of supply; his, has laid out all its strength in acquiring armor for his work, and keeps itself ever active in the acquisition. You begin the conflict under the disadvantage of seeming to contend for the worst of causes; he, on the contrary, for the best. You set out with a long catalogue of admissions–the actual existence of slavery at the South; the natural wrong of slavery; objectionable elements in the system of slavery; cruel acts perpetrated in the practice of slavery; the duty of seeking the removal of slavery. He, on the contrary, strikes his first blow in the consciousness that the battle is half won already; for press him as you may, he falls back at will, and finds ready shelter under any one of your recorded admissions. Controversy on your part is always reluctantly commenced and painfully prosecuted, because you know he will import a spirit as unwelcome to your quiet taste as it is unpromising to your hope of good. But controversy is his very life. He ever feels that he can do God and man no better service than to overthrow all who oppose his glorious cause of "liberty." How feeble is your hold upon your arms! The utter unfitness of the slave for present liberty—of this you have no personal knowledge. The constantly improving condition of the slave—this is not before your eyes. The commendatory deeds of the master—with these you are not familiar. The word of God! You almost fear to touch it, lest he fling the scornful charge into your face: "You prostitute Scripture to uphold slavery." But while you handle your own weapons so feebly, how pungently he makes you feel the force of his! That serious countenance, those stirring tones, that vehement testimony against oppression, those rehearsals of blood-stirring cruelties to the innocent and the helpless! Oh! your disadvantages in the conflict. And what inducements to submission! Throw down your arms to the Anti-Slavery banner, and you escape from the most grievous disgrace upon the face of the earth, "*Pro-Slavery!!*" Ground your arms! and you escape that war to the knife with the Abolitionist, which, otherwise, nothing but death itself can conclude. Think how powerful the pressure on the one hand, how feeble the resistance on the other, and tell me, my brother, are you not in peril of falling under this adverse influence?

Nay! Are you not more than half subdued this very moment? Analyze the exact condition of your mind. Your intellect sees clearly, and can demonstrate perfectly, both from Scripture and reason, that there is no necessary sin in the holding of a slave; but is either your heart, conscience, or agency, under the influence of your judgment? Those most earnest outcries against the *awful sin* of *slavery*—against the *heart-rending cruelties* of *slavery!* You have heard them for so long a time, from such influential sources, and with such a feeble capacity of effective resistance, that they have actually built up in your soul a species of *superstition.* Where your judgment sees with perfect clearness that there is no sin, just there your heart and conscience forebode fearful sin! If this is not superstition, it is worse. The fact is, though you know it not, your strict mental rectitude on this subject is a little disturbed. You often exhibit a singular intellectual phenomenon. Through a steady process your mind slides down into extreme Anti-Slavery views, while, to the amusement of your brethren, you are all the way indignantly repudiating the very slightest sympathy with sentiments so absurd. My brother, the calm spectator sees clearly what you do not realize. He sees the Reform power actually radiating increasing degrees of epidemic influence into your very soul, through your unprotected sympathy with its reïterated, its indignant protests against the crimes and cruelties of slavery. Yes, my brother, study the peril of your position!

2. Consider the *character of your agency.* Is it not unjustifiable and injurious?

It is scarcely possible that such a mind should act right. It does not move by its own light. It does not work by its own reason. It is measurably spell-bound, and must yield unreasonably to the malign influence that acts upon it. My brother! condemn the nature of slavery—slavery in the abstract—and God helping, neither you nor the strongest Reformer on earth shall condemn it more promptly or sincerely than I will. Condemn the cruelties of the master to the slave. You are a bad man and no Christian if you do not. But, my brother, you must not stop there. You must not be *one-sided* in your condemnation. You must act out a fair, a just mind. Therefore, you must *as* decidedly condemn the extravagances of those fellow-men who have gone beyond all Scripture and reason, all the good of the Church and the world, in carrying out their philanthropy. If they have started a Reform movement in the earth, which, examined, must be pronounced arrogant, and malignant, and belligerent, and headstrong, is not this wrong? If in its execution they are hurting the country, and the slave, and the master, and religion, and the power of helping all the great and good interests of the earth, is not this wrong? Do we right, then, if we do not decidedly condemn it? But do we condemn it, as by our judgment we should do? Do any of us testify against their wrong management of slavery as intrepidly as they make us testify against the wrong elements of slavery? It is very natural and very certain that we are a little overawed and unfaithful in the premises. Nay! Instead of bearing a decided and discouraging testimony on all proper occasions,—to a guilty extent, in many ways, by omission and by commission, we fall in with them and decidedly encourage their intrepidity and enforce their mischievous power over men. I speak it cheerfully, no man can be too kind to any Reform brother on earth; but I speak it seriously, in this day when God is laying before us such developments of their spirit and their work, and they are yet exhibiting such marks of power, no man can be too firm in his purpose and effort to make the Reformer feel that, in his furious philanthropy, he is sinning—sinning against God and man. I believe we often offend by failing to speak such words, to take such stands, to do such things, as are directly intended to disapprove, discourage, and defeat. In my opinion, we as often offend by being led to take so abundant a part with them in their published sentiments and practical measures. I have no doubt, that for many years, the conservative element has inordinately encouraged and invigorated this enterprise in the Church and country by coöperation in their agitating system of discussion, resolution, and testimony. Their whole operation, however benevolent its ultimate ends, is too unchristian in spirit, principle, and influence, to justify such a fellowship on our part.

Besides, it has operated to inflict a positive injustice to our Southern brethren. "The welfare of the South," says Dr. Woods, "is just as worthy of regard as the welfare of the North." Our ecclesiastical course has heretofore embarked too little sympathy with the welfare of the South. There is another principle just as clear. The man of the South has his rights, as well as the man of the North. I hold it one right of every man upon earth, North or South, that *he is just as much to be approved for his good acts, as he is to be blamed for his bad ones.* Call up distinctly this self-evident truth, and settle your conviction of it. It will go far to settle our judgment on this whole point. I affirm that by the constitution of man, the good of society, and the word of God, we are precisely under the same obligation to *bear a favorable testimony in view of the good a man does, as we are to bear a condemnatory witness of the evil he perpetrates.* You say that the nature of slavery is wrong! Grant it. That there are wrong things in the system of Southern slavery! Grant it. That many cruelties have been perpetrated by the slaveholder! Grant it. That you have a right to bear testimony against such things! Grant it. Straightforward for thirty years, with little intermission, our Assemblies, Synods, Presbyteries all over the North have been bearing such adverse testimony, solemnly, earnestly, vehemently. I call you now to witness that there are good things at the South as well as bad ones. Southern men have paid down a very great sum of money toward the freeing of their slaves. I say, this is a good thing. Under God, they have converted hundreds of thousands of their souls, and sent them to heaven. I say, this is a good thing. They have been lifting up the great mass steadily toward all temporal and all spiritual good, from the day that your fathers landed them on Southern shores. I say, this is a good thing. They are doing more for them this day than they have ever done before. I say, this is a good thing. Some scanty allusion to all this may, peradventure, be found in the bosom of condemnatory testimony: But say, brethren, has our General Assembly on any one occasion come out before the Church and the world, and borne prominent witness to their high and encouraging approbation of these noble doings of Southern men? Since they felt themselves bound for so many years to condemn so many things in connection with Southern society, have our Northern Synods and Presbyteries been accustomed to delight themselves in holding up before all men the generous, useful, Christian deeds of their Southern brethren? No, my brother, no! From year to year, in spite of all their remonstrances, we have held up all that we could find to blame in their condition and their conduct; to their suffering, shame, ay! and the *deep damage of their Christian influence*, we have held up our condemnatory testimony before the whole world, while their noble self-sacrifices, Christian fidelities, and the blessings of God on their labor for their slaves, we have been quite willing to pass by unnoticed. Undeniably all this is unjust. I say it is unjust. Nor can it fail to be true that this very neglect has done much to harm the Church and the country for the last quarter of a century. I will take it upon me to express the fear that at the bar of God, this very neglect may have something to answer for in the sundering of the Presbyterian Church at our last General Assembly. Just imagine that our dear brethren of the North had pursued a perfectly opposite course. Suppose that they had felt and said: "We have been testifying and testifying against slavery at the South for thirty years. Surely, all the South and all the world have the full benefit of our condemnatory testimony on this subject. No man under heaven can doubt where we stand, how we feel. We have been no Delphic Oracle on the point of our abhorrence of this institution. But the evil of slavery is not all the truth of the world. Nor all the truth of the South. We have brethren there, and good brethren. Neighbors, and good neighbors. And if wrong things have been done at the South, so have right things been done at the South. And since we have long been faithful in condemning the wrong things of our brethren, at last let us be faithful on the other side, and begin to approve their right things. Yes! In even-handed justice, in obedience to self-evident duty, in approving the right as well as condemning the wrong, we will fix our eyes upon another aspect of this mighty subject. We will look our good brethren of the South directly in the face, and love them. We will think of all their responsibilities, and encourage them. We will inquire into all their trials, and sympathize with them. We will study out all their noble Christian deeds, and admire them. We will survey all God's blessings upon their labors, and rejoice in them. And we will summon this General Assembly to the discharge of a long-neglected and a most happy duty. Yes! We will cease our condemnatory testimony for once, and we will stir up our souls to take great delight in bearing most hearty, fraternal witness to all in the character and conduct of our dear brethren, which our Christian discretion commands us to approve." Oh! had our brethren of the North but possessed a heart to do this! How just! How wise! How salutary! It would have saved the Church. It would have staunched long-running wounds. It would have cheered all good hearts and works in Southern lands. It would have locked the arms of the South around the North. Yes! Yes! It would have accomplished the great work and hope of the country. For it would have thrown the kind heart of the North upon the South, and thus brought North and South, side by side, to work with God for the slave, for Africa, for the holy power of our country, and for the conversion of the world.

Our agency! Has it not been wrong? Our influence! Has it not been pernicious? We have suffered the strong spirit of our deluded brethren to bear us away too far from a wise and just Christian course on this subject. We must love them with all our hearts, but from this day we must change our policy. We must take a new stand. We must tell our brethren frankly and firmly, that they are wrong. That they have the wildest men of the nation in their lead, and though they mean it not, the darkest doom of Church and State for their work. We must make them understand that the time past shall abundantly suffice for our countenance, our toleration, of such an enterprise, direct or indirect. And while we will not be what they unrighteously charge, "*Pro-Slavery*," we will yet try to persuade them to part with their wretched extravagances, and come up and join us in working for the slave and for the master, and for the country, and for the Church, and for ourselves, and for them, and for God, and his lost world. We will exhort them to enlist under our banner and join us in carrying out that calmer, kinder, wiser course, which promises to accomplish all God's most humane designs in introducing Africans into America. My brother! has not your agency been wrong and harmful?

Finally. Consider your *solemn future duty.* You have long been standing in unprotected peril. You must seek protection. You have been doing an unjust and injurious work. You must learn to do better.

For your protection see to it that you *rectify your mind.*

You have long felt that there is a mighty power in the Reform cause. Mark! To an enlightened Christian there is no power there. This Anti-Slavery movement is wrong in principle. It sets out to reform God's heritage, but it takes up the very opposite of every radical element of reformation, and goes to work with these carnal weapons. Surely it must do harm. The nature of things makes mischief its necessary result. Now fix the fact for ever in your mind, that this *Anti-Slavery movement is a wrong thing, doing harm.* So root and ground this truth in your mind that your soul shall rally upon it instantly and strongly. Dwell upon its arrogance, its malevolence, its belligerence, its prejudice, and so incorporate its every feature with your mind that you may readily fall back upon each and all at any time, and bring yourself to an intelligent and decided opposition. Carry in your soul, too, the witnesses of its danger to the country, damage to the slave, injustice to the master, disturbance of the Church, desecration of the pulpit, and dishonor of the Bible. Nor forget its overthrow of the liberty of the soul, in its idolatry of the liberty of the body. Only do this:

Only thoroughly instruct your mind concerning the character and influence of this movement, and you have destroyed its power. You have disarmed your adversary. Be not content, however, to stop here. Build well your own foundations. Study the word of God, and fear not to say as did Micaiah: "As the Lord liveth, *what the Lord saith*, that will I do." Follow firmly the plain teachings of Scripture. Instruct your mind too in the fact that of a truth the Anti-Slavery disposition of the bondman would perpetrate the clearest injustice, because it would inflict the direst results upon all society. Acquaint yourself with all of duty which the South has done and is doing, that so far you may approve and find encouragement to work, and pray, and hope. Above all, never forget God's providence in bringing the black man so far from his own home, to the home of the white man. Surely it is, that we might use his bondage as we use the subjection of the child, to teach, to train, and to christianize; and, all this, largely that we might thus impower him to teach, train, and christianize the man of his color in all the world. Ever bear in your mind that, touching duty to the slave, this is the great work, this the great end. And never forget this, that to fail to feel for the slave, work for the slave, send down the Gospel to the slave, stand by and encourage those Southern brethren who are directly and daily toiling for the best good of the slave,—to fail to do this, through any Abolition influence, direct or indirect, is to be shamefully recreant to high duty. This decided repudiation of extreme views, intelligent adoption of just sentiments, and hearty, steady coöperation with the men who are not clamoring but working for the man of color, is the one only position that should never be changed on this subject, the one only position where a man can stand firmly.

Finally. For the good of the kingdom see to it that you *rectify your agency.*

To do this, allow me to repeat, you must kindly and firmly maintain an active disapproval of the Reform movement.

Just as certainly as Christianity prospers and God reigns, just so certainly this violent spirit will be overthrown. The only proper way to accomplish this end, is to treat it as it deserves. All reason and conscience charge us to see to it, that we decidedly discountenance it as a wrong thing.

We owe it to *ourselves* in self-protection. Sin finds a sympathy within us—therefore, if we do not resist sin, we yield to it. Man's nature can not be indifferent to the Anti-Slavery appeal. To seek to be neutral, or to suffer ourselves to be so, is, to give way to its power, and adopt the system. We must destroy its power by disapproval, if we would not be shaped by its influence. We owe it to ourselves in moral principle. We are under law; built to stand by truth and righteousness. This Reform is wrong in spirit and principle, decidedly, mischievously wrong. We are unfaithful to conscience and to

God, if we do not make men know that, in our judgment, every man should do what he can to reform it.

We owe it to *every fellow-man under its influence.* We are our brother's keeper. He is injuring himself and all mankind—deeply injuring all. We owe it to him to seek his deliverance from evil. There is no possible method of effecting this end if we withhold solemn, downright condemnation. Strive to be neutral! You encourage him, for he will be sure to think that your heart fears public opinion, but your conscience is on his side. With prompt and profound seriousness unbosom your conscience to him, and bear testimony against his ways as he does against yours. Nothing short of this will ever bestow upon him that very kindest service it is in our power to render.

We owe it to the *cause of Christ.* We are put into the vineyard, fellow-laborers with our brethren. They are most mischievously mismanaging our Master's interests. Kindly, but firmly, we must object, remonstrate, and withstand. Through our remissness and lack of decision they have deeply damaged the Lord's kingdom. Its only protection lies in our faithful remonstrance.

We owe it to our *country.* What a troubler of Israel this spirit has been in Church and State? It is an instrument which chafes and divides all it touches. It does not simply destroy kindness and respect, it breeds scorn and rage toward all who fail to abet its cause. It has thrown the nation into a state of universal turmoil, nor will it ever come down to the temper of reconciliation, reflection and reformation, until this violent spirit is subdued. For the union, the peace, and the moral progress of the nation, therefore, this element of alienation and strife must be decidedly discountenanced.

We owe it especially to that cause which the Reform has taken in hand—the *cause of the slave—the cause of Providence.* No solid advantage can ever accrue to the slave until he finds a better friend than his Reform patron. Clamor about liberty will never make a slave a freeman or a Christian. The reason is obvious. Clamor can not work. Nothing is done without work—quiet, steady work. The spirit of this enterprise is restless, noisy, quarrelsome. It will never sit down to teach the dull slave from year to year. It will never quietly do its little part of contributing regularly to preach the Gospel to the bondman. It can never compose itself to construct a calm and suitable prayer, and offer it daily and quietly in the closet. In a word, it is utterly destitute of that patient spirit, that self-denying labor, which alone can save the slave. The heart of our neighbor has a good meaning at the foundation, but the good will never reach the slave, because his mind is disordered by the control of a fanatical element. If you doubt it, give yourself the help of observation. Look around you. Exactly in proportion as men are noisy against slavery, they do nothing for the slave.

The fact is, the *principle* of the Reformer as well as his spirit, works out this issue. He holds, that to send the Gospel to the South by men who do *not* entertain his views is—"*Pro-Slavery.*" By a double necessity this doctrine bereaves the slave of every good. The master will surely expel the agent, and the Reformer will as certainly withhold and discourage all kinds of practicable service. Indeed, I doubt not the decided tendency of the Reformer's principle to chill even prayer itself, or convert it into a boisterous outcry against that which he hates. Give way, therefore, to the Reform power of the country, and individual sympathy, liberality, and activity in all the North will never be educated to those wholesome, practical habits which promise to bear substantial blessing to the man of color. Nor is this all! Give way to this extreme Anti-Slavery temper, and what becomes of a kind heart between the North and the South? that indispensable pre-requisite to the prosperous fulfillment of providential designs in behalf of the African. Certainly there is no one cause which works so effectually to embroil the North and the South, and to obstruct national coöperation with God's missionary providence.

By the most solemn obligations, therefore, to God and to man, we are bound to bear kind but faithful testimony to our Reform neighbors, that they are wrong, and doing wrong. We must do this, that we may break that power which they have with the world through our neglect to take decided public ground against them; we must do this, to assist them to see the error of their way and bring them toward the only position which, by any possibility, can accomplish the good they seek.

Oh! that God would shed upon our country a spirit of calm and serious reflection! On every hand glaring are the signs that we have left the old paths: That we have done wrong: That God holds us guilty in his sight. Many nations have been destroyed for sin. Critical indeed, is our condition. But three possible courses lie before us: We must be left of God to go on to destruction. Or we must be sorely chastised by God into reformation. Or if there yet remains a sufficient conservative intelligence and piety in the land,—in the fear of God, in mutual respect and kindness, we must employ it in habits of teachable and prayerful thought. Where shall we begin? Were I summoned to express the promptings of a fallible nature, I would pray that God in mercy to us, to our country, and to the world, would be pleased to imbue all moderate men with that mingled wisdom, kindness, and firmness, which would qualify us to bear truth most effectually to the mind of our Reform neighbors and brethren; that in the greatness of his grace he would kindly teach them that more excellent way wherein they may retain all their principles of justice and philanthropy without defeating their influence; may accomplish all their ends by lending to wiser methods the hearty contribution of their own intrepidity and vigor. We know nothing: but surely it would seem to us—secure but this, and instantly by its most happy bearing in a thousand ways, we should be transformed into the happiest people that ever shouted thanksgivings to the Father of all mercies. The country agitated no more! The Church distracted no longer! The North and the South meeting in kindness, and co-working in cheerful prospect of our permanent national and Christian prosperity! And the slave, the innocent cause of all our troubles, by the happy coöperation of the whole country conducted along wisely through gradations of general improvement, which God shall direct, in God's own best time, shall surely come to take his place among future generations, every way qualified to work with other men for the ultimate fulfillment of God's glory in the happy destiny of the race.

Who am I? A fallen man! Where am I? In a fallen world! Who are these about me? Fallen fellow-men! Oh! then to rise to God, and to raise our fellows, individually and universally, is the great work of man. In *humble* suggestion, because fallible; in *honest* effort, because under duty, I put forth this word. If it is a right word, the Lord in faithfulness impower it. If it is a wrong word, God in mercy bury the work and forgive the workman.

APPENDIX.

A.

At the close of the Revolution, a Convention of Delegates from the thirteen States, sat in Philadelphia, to consult upon the formation of a Constitution for the country. On the 8th of August, 1787, the Committee to whom the subject was referred, reported a draft, of which the 4th section of Art. VIII. ran thus: "No tax or duty shall be laid by the Legislature on articles exported from any States, *nor on the migration or importation of such persons as the several States shall think proper to admit;* NOR SHALL SUCH MIGRATION OR IMPORTATION BE PROHIBITED." The slave-trade by this report is legalized forever. The committee who made this suggestion was composed of five persons, Rutledge, Randolph, Gorham, Ellsworth, and Wilson. The first *two* from the South, the last *three* from the North. The second committee to whom this subject was subsequently intrusted, made the following report: "Strike out so much of the fourth section as was referred to the committee, and insert: 'The migration or importation of such persons as the several States now existing shall think proper to admit, *shall not be prohibited by the Legislature* PRIOR TO THE YEAR 1800.'" The slave-trade is arrested by this report at a time stated. The committee who reported this amendment consisted of eleven persons—Langdon, King, Johnson, Livingston, Clymer, Dickenson, Martin, Williams, Pinkney, Baldwin, Madison. The first *five* represented Northern States; the last *six*, Southern States

B.

An *Anniversary*—a *Convention* of an organized Society—calls out the largest attendance of its leading men. Their addresses and resolutions, their temper, sentiments, and language, on such occasions, constitute a fair type of the spirit and principle of the enterprise.

At a meeting of the Anti-Slavery Convention in Boston, in May, 1856, *Charles L. Remond*, a colored man, said, remembering Washington as a slaveholder, he "could *spit upon Washington.*" [Loud hisses and applause.] "The hissers," he said, "were slaveholders in spirit, and every one of them would enslave him if they had the courage to do it. So near to Faneuil Hall and to Bunker Hill, was he not permitted to say that that SCOUNDREL *Washington* had enslaved his fellow-men." [Hisses and applause.] Wendell Phillips followed Remond, and said: "Washington was a sinner. It became an American to cover his face when he placed his bust among the great men of the world, for it was stained with a great gout of blood; yet he was a great man, had great virtues, and he would not give him the name of scoundrel, because there were too many for whom they should keep that name." On the same occasion, W. L. Garrison attacked Mr. Everett for his lecture on Washington. Report in the *Boston Traveller*, May 29, 1856.

Henry C. Wright said in his speech before the N. E. Anti-Slavery Convention, in Boston, May 28, 1850, in answer to the question, "Who is the God of humanity?"

"He is not the God of Slavery. He is not the God of Daniel Webster. He is not the God of Moses Stuart, or of Leonard Woods, or of Ralph Emerson. I do not mean Ralph Waldo Emerson, but the Rev. Dr. Emerson. He is not the God that is preached in Winter-Street Church, by Rev. William M. Rogers."

* * * * *

"Shame on the nation, and shame on its politics, and shame on its religion, I say, and shame on such a God. I defy him,

I scorn him, he is not my God. I will never bow to his shrine. My head shall go off with my hat, when I take it off to such a God as that;" and much more in the same style.

The speech is published in the *Liberator*, Garrison's, of June 7, 1850, (phonographic report by Dr. Stone.)

In the same paper, same date, Wm. L. Garrison is reported to have offered several resolutions. The 16th was as follows:

"*Resolved*, That if the BIBLE sanctions slavery, and is thus opposed to the self-evident truth that 'all men are created equal, and have an inalienable right to liberty,' *the Bible is a self-evident falsehood*, and ought to be, and will ere long be regarded as the enemy of nature, and nature's God, and of the progress of the human race in liberty, justice, and goodness."

At the same Convention Henry C. Wright said: "If you would see what slavery is, look into your hearts. What use, then, is it to ask, whether the *Bible* sanctions slavery or not? for your heart has decided the question. The book (the Bible) if it sanctions slavery, is a self-evident falsehood, and should be treated as such, so far as slavery is concerned."

* * * * *

"The question is often put to me: 'Would you believe slavery to be right, if *God* should declare it right?' 'No!' 'What would you do?' 'I would fasten the chain upon the heel of such a God, and let the man go free. For such a God is a *phantom*. I would discard the phantom, and liberate the slave.'" [Cheers and hisses.] This Mr. Wright was formerly pastor of the First Congregational (Orthodox) Church in West-Newbury, Mass. He now has no connection with any religious denomination.

In a letter dated May 21, 1851, writteu to Rev. Henry Ward Beecher, and published in the *Liberator*, of June 20, 1851, are the following sentences of Henry C. Wright:

"Anti-Slavery will triumph; but only on the ruins of the American Church. Humanity will surely come off victorious over what this nation *calls God*, and hurl him forever from his throne of blood; simply because that God has staked his claim to our worship on the support of slavery."

The same paper reports Rev. Daniel Foster, of Concord, Mass., in the course of an earnest Anti-Slavery speech, to have said: "He stood on that floor as an Orthodox clergyman, but he did not come to indorse the conduct of his brethren of the denomination. He had often said to his people, and he repeated it here now, that he would as soon exchange with the devil as with one of these hireling priests, these traitors to God and humanity." [Applause.]

He considered the professed Church of Christ false, and its hireling priesthood utterly unworthy of confidence; but, God be thanked, the Anti-Slavery people were in the field! They were the true Church of Christ, and aim to carry out the true design of the Gospel of Christ. [Great applause.] This Mr. Foster was one of the chaplains of the Legislature of Massachusetts, in 1855 6. He is not now connected with the Orthodox Congregationalists.

At the New-England Anti-Slavery Convention, held in Boston, May, 1852, Mr. Garrison offered the following among other resolutions:

"*Resolved*, That it is still sacredly imposed upon us, by a scrupulous regard for the truth, by strict fidelity to the cause of the perishing slave, by all the aspirations and claims of oppressed humanity, universally to declare that the American *Church* is the mighty bulwark of American slavery, the haughty, corrupt, implacable, and impious foe of the Anti-Slavery movement, whether in its mildest or most radical aspect—the defender and sanctifier of colossal wrong and transcendent impiety, and, consequently, that its pretensions to Christianity are the boldest effrontery and the vilest imposture."

In the same Convention, Rev. Mr. Griswold, of Stonington, Conn., is reported in the *Liberator* to have said: "For the *Church* which sustains slavery, wherever it be, I am ready to say with another, I will welcome the bolt, whether it come from heaven or from hell, which shall destroy it."

C.

THESE sheets go to press at a season of the year when society on the Atlantic is in a state of unusual dispersion. I have consequently failed to secure that definiteness of statistical statement anticipated.

SLAVES EMANCIPATED.—In 1840 there were 215,000 free blacks in the South. Add all subsequently freed, and all deaths and emigrations for a hundred years before: affix to each any reasonable appreciation, exclusive of outfit, and you make both the number and the value of slaves liberated largely greater than the statements of the text.

2. COLORED CHURCH-MEMBERSHIP.—In 1855, *Heathen* church-membership is set down at 180,000. The present estimate of colored church-members in the *Methodist* Church, South, is 175,000. Eight or ten years ago the *Baptist* colored membership at the South was recorded as only 4000 less than the Methodist. When to these two numbers, you add all the colored members of other un-included organizations of *Methodists* and *Baptists*, also of *Episcopalians*, *Lutherans*, and *Presbyterians*, *Old-School*, *New-School*, and *Cumberland*, you readily reach an aggregate of colored church-membership near twice as large as the strictly Heathen, Orthodox church-membership of the world.

INCENDIARY PUBLICATIONS—SOUTHERN SPIRIT OF EMANCIPATION.—Occasionally from the commencement of the Abolition excitement in the country—by private hand or channel, and by mail, *disturbing, insurgent, Anti-Slavery documents*, written and printed, have been scattered through larger and smaller portions of the South. One of the most unfortunate attempts of this kind was made in the year 1833 or 1834. The subject of *State Emancipation* had come up in discussion amongst the population of Virginia. The gradual Emancipation Bill was introduced into the Legislature, the whole subject extensively investigated during the session, and postponed for the yet more thorough *examination of the people* during the *interim*, with a view to *final decision*, the next year. *During the interval* the *Anti-Slavery Society*, of the City or State of New-York, (its President then resided in the city,) dispersed over (the whole South, I think, certainly, through) the State of Virginia, incendiary sheets and pamphlets, embellished with pictures of *the slave*, the applied lash, the streaming blood, chains, etc., etc.

These publications were addressed perhaps to all the clergy, certainly to all those who had emigrated from the North, and to a large number of other leading men in community. Mail after mail deposited its insurrectionary sheets and pictures in the hands of the parties. Instantaneously there sprang up a tremendous reäctionary popular excitement. A large portion of the ministry—all the Northern and many of the Southern ministers—left the State, all of them suddenly, some of them clandestinely. Public indignation required those who remained to come out in the papers of the day and denounce this Northern interference. As to incipient emancipation—it perished utterly from the very time of Abolition inter-meddling. Months elapsed before society became composed. The *effects* of this and similar attempts upon the peace of the Southern mind and social state, continue in *the prohibitory statutes* which curtail the *literary* and religious privileges of the blacks.

D.

On the subject of slavery, we do well to bear in mind, that it is the *harsh* side of *Southern* legislation, and the *kind* side of *Northern* legislation, which are constantly before the *Northern* mind. The activity of Anti-Slavery men secures the perpetual circulation of the offensive laws of the South, while the fact that slavery has been abolished by Northern law lies before every man on the face of Northern society.

At a time when the subject of slavery is undergoing such vehement discussion at the *North*, and when the welfare of Church and State are so largely dependent upon the issue, it is important to impartial investigation that the Northern mind —by a glance at least—should *reverse* the position of the subject.

I propose, therefore, to place before the reader a sketch of the *kind* elements of *Southern* legislation upon the subject of slavery, side by side with a glance at those *harsher* statutes which the *North* felt themselves compelled to employ, when called in providence to manage the institution.

Chap. I.—Southern Slave Law.

The *Negro Law* of Virginia, as presented in the following view, was prepared at my request by a distinguished member of the bar, and legal officer of that State.

The laws of Virginia, in respect to slaves, are of two classes: the one recognizing them as *persons*, the other as *property*.

I. As persons, they are recognized as morally responsible beings, as religiously responsible beings; in either case, their rights—secured by law and penal sanctions. They are subjects of legal punishment, and are protected against crimes upon their persons by legal penalty against the offender. Their claim to freedom may be asserted, without cost or charge, and a trial by jury, before a judge, secures their rights to freedom (if any) by a remedy which in practice has been found complete and favorable to their claim.

1. *As moral beings, subject to law.* Of all offenses of which a white man is capable, the slave is. In some cases, with a lighter; in others, with a heavier penalty.

2. *As religious beings.* A master is liable to a fine, if he employ his apprentices, servants, or slaves in labor or other business on Sunday, except in household or other work of necessity or charity. A Jew or other "Seventh-day" believer is not subject to this penalty, provided he does not compel a

slave, apprentice, or servant, *not of his belief*, to do secular work or business on Sunday. Here is a recognition of religious belief in the slave, as well as in the master; the *property* right of the latter is infringed to protect the *personal* belief of the former, and the whole is secured by penal sanction.

While the law forbids *unlawful* assemblies of negroes for religious worship, or for reading or writing, yet there is no inhibition upon the master to teach his slave to read and write, none to teach him religiously, or to permit his attending public worship, where it is conducted by a white person. Indeed, practically, there is no difficulty, where it is conducted by a negro, under circumstances which assure the police it is not perverted to other and illegal purposes.

3. Murder, rape, stabbing, shooting, and even assault, may be criminally committed upon a slave, and the offender is criminally responsible. Subject to the proper and necessary qualifications resulting from the relation of master and slave, the master is criminally responsible for such offenses against his slave, except in the case of assault, where from necessity, correction must be inflicted by the master; and the limitations can not easily be prescribed by the Legislature, but must be left to general principles, as in cases of immoderate correction by a parent or teacher. If the injury done is more than an assault, and becomes mayhem, stabbing, shooting, or homicide, the master is responsible.

4. A claim to freedom may be asserted before our county or circuit court, (our courts of original jurisdiction in all cases.) The claimant has *counsel* assigned to him *without charge*, and has allowed him the service of *every officer of court without cost*. The holder of the claimant is dispossessed, unless he gives bond, that he will have the claimant forthcoming to abide the court's judgment, and to allow him reasonable opportunity to prepare for trial. The case is ordered to be tried as a privileged case, without regard to its place on the docket. If the verdict be for the claimant, the jury is further directed to assess damages for his detention, and he receives by the judg-

ment of the court his freedom, his damages, and his costs. If it be alleged, that the officers of court will be against the claimant, it may be answered, that the only chance for their costs, (usually heavy in such cases,) is the success of the claimant.

5. The mode of their trial for crimes is peculiar, and eminently merciful.

Five justices (such men, any three of whom in our county courts may try any civil cause in the commonwealth, whatever the amount involved) sit upon the trial of a negro slave for felony.

The death penalty can not be inflicted unless the *five justices concur.* In a case where the punishment *must* be *capital*, a *dissenting voice will acquit:* in which the law is more merciful to the slave than to the white man.

In all cases of the death penalty or transportation, the record of evidence on the trial is sent to the Governor. He may commute the former to transportation, or pardon entirely.

The court in all cases assigns counsel, and awards to him a fee which must be paid by the master. Thus the slave is better provided for than the poor white man, or free negro. He has a master, whom the law compels to protect him!

6. The duty of masters to maintain their slaves is fully provided for by our law, in those cases where the interest of the master will not make him do so.

Any person permitting an insane, aged, or infirm slave to go at large without adequate provision for his support shall be fined, and the overseers of the poor shall provide for such slave, and charge the owner for the amount thereof, and recover the same by motion in the court of the county; and to prevent evasion, if such person by gift, sale, or *emancipation*, attempt to avoid this legal duty of support to his slave, the same remedy is provided.

Can as much be said for the hireling of the free States?

7. Our laws do not forbid the negro to be taught to read or write. The restraints upon it were enacted when the Abolition

war began by its incendiary appeals to the slave to rise against his master. If the slave is prevented from reading the Bible, it is because Abolition opposed its peaceful lessons of obedience by incitement to revengeful passions and brutal rebellion.

8. The great defense to the personal rights of the negro slave is in the jurisdiction, under the unwritten common law of our social existence, of the master. Interest, association from childhood to age, the memories in common between the old slaves and the young masters, or the young slaves and old masters, links of sympathy, which none can comprehend but Southern people and those who have lived in the South; these are the defenses of the slave from external wrong and internal oppression. The same motive in kind, the same legal defense from outward wrong, which protects the child and the wife, defends the slave. A trespass to the wife, or child, or slave, must be redressed by a suit by the husband, parent, and master. The master can gain nothing, but loses his money, by the death, discomfort, and inability of his slave. This is the lowest, and is an unworthy aspect, which can only restrain the more brutal of Southern men, and yet it shows what powerful motives of interest guard the slave even against the brutality of such masters.

Among men who have human sympathy, affection, long association, family bonds shield the slave from tyranny. Not one master in one hundred, is a cruel one; not one in fifty a harsh one; more than one half are too lenient for the good of masters or slaves.

II. In the respect in which slaves are regarded as *chattels.*

It is true that slaves are now *personal estate.* At one time they were, in Virginia, *real estate.* Every lawyer knows that these are necessary divisions of all property, to be regarded, in looking to its transmission after death, or its liability for the debts of the owner during life. Slaves are property; now chattels, or personal property.

I have shown that slaves are persons; and *slave persons are property.* They are *persons* and *property;* neither alone.

They are property in the sense that children are the property of the father; the apprentice of the master. The property in each consists in the right of the master or father to the direction and avails of the labor of the slave, child, apprentice. The slave is in *perpetual minority.* His is a permanent subjection; that of the child or apprentice, temporary.

Slaves and apprentices are personal property; that is, they both go to the personal representative at the master's death. In respect to them as property, a few things are to be observed.

1. Slaves shall not be taken under execution, when there are other sufficient goods to satisfy it, without the debtor's consent—a consent which a debtor is loth to give, where he can otherwise save his slave.

2. An administrator or executor is forbidden to sell slaves to pay debts or legacies, until all the other personal property has been sold.

3. Slaves shall be divided as real property is; that is, the widow shall have one third of them for her life, and the others to be distributed among the legal distributees.

In these provisions there is a tender regard to the personal comfort of the slave, even when he is treated merely as property.

Thus when the slave is treated as *property, there is a regard to his interest as a person.* When treated as a person, he has safeguards of law, of family, of courts; for his protection, as a man, morally and religiously responsible; against his own master, for his support; for his defense against criminal prosecutions; and for the prosecution of his own right in law to be free.

The *Negro Law* of KENTUCKY will be found in the language of the State.

Extracts from the Constitution and Laws of Kentucky, in reference to slaves.

I. *Constitution.*

Art. 10, § 1. The General Assembly . . . *shall* pass laws to permit owners of slaves to emancipate them. . . . . They shall have full power to prevent slaves being brought into this State as *merchandise.* They shall have full power to prevent slaves being brought into this State, who have been, since the 1st day of Jan., 1789, or may hereafter be imported into any of the United States, from a foreign country. And they shall have full power to pass such laws as may be necessary to oblige owners of slaves to treat them with humanity, to provide for them necessary clothing and provision, to abstain from from all injuries to them, extending to life and limb, and in case of refusal to comply with the direction of such laws, to have such slave or slaves sold for the benefit of their owner or owners.

§ 3. The Assembly shall have no power (in cases of prosecution for felony) to deprive them (slaves) of the privilege of an impartial trial by a petit jury.

II. *Legislative Enactments.*—(Revised Statutes.)

Chap. 93, Art. 1, § 3. Slaves, after this chapter takes effect, shall be, and held to be, personal estate . . . . to be distributed, *in kind*, WITHOUT SALE, when practicable.

§ 4. Slaves shall not be *sold* by the personal representative, unless, for the want of other assets, it be necessary to pay the debts of the decedent. . . . . Suits may be maintained by the personal representative, for INJURIES to slaves devised.

Art. 2, § 2. No slave shall be imported into this State as *merchandise*, or for the purpose of sale or barter, *in or out of this State*, under the penalty of $600 for each slave so imported.

§ 4. Immigrants bringing with them slaves, ... shall, within sixty days after their arrival, take the following oath:

. . . . "I do swear that my removal to the State of Kentucky was with the intention of becoming a citizen thereof, and that I have brought with me no slave with the intention of *selling* him."

§ 6. Requires the *importer of slaves* to take a similar oath; § 7 imposes a fine of $600 for any effort to *evade* the preceding law; § 8 imposes a fine of $200 on any one buying a slave so imported contrary to law; § 9 provides that slaves, so imported, shall not be subject to sale, or sold under execution or other legal procedure, for the payment of debts, unless "all *other* estate of the debtor, subject to the payment of debts, shall be FIRST *exhausted.*"

Art. 4, § 1. If the owner of an infirm, insane, or aged slave, or any person having such slave under his control, suffers him to go at large, or fails to make adequate provisions for his *support*, he shall be punished by fine, not exceeding fifty dollars; and the county court, or other public authorities, charged with the supervision and care of the poor, or any city, town, or county, in which such slave may be found, shall provide for his maintenance, may charge such person quarterly or annually, with a sum sufficient therefor, and recover it, from time to time, by a motion in the name of the commonwealth, in the county court.

§ 2. If the owner of any slave shall treat him cruelly and inhumanly, so as, in the opinion of a jury, to endanger the life or limb of said slave, or materially to affect his health; or shall not supply his slave with sufficient wholesome food and raiment, such slave shall be taken and sold for the benefit of the owner.

Art. 7, § 20. It shall be the duty of the master or owner, personal representative or guardian of such owner, (in case of charge for felony,) to employ counsel to defend a slave, when tried in circuit court. If no counsel be employed, the court shall assign counsel to defend him. The master, or owner, or his personal representative, or the guardian, shall pay said counsel the sum accorded him by order of the court, for such defense, not exceeding fifty nor less than twenty dollars, and may be attached and compelled to pay the same.

There is no law in Kentucky, and never has been, prohibiting the instruction of slaves in spelling and *reading*.

It is also to be observed that while there is no statute prohibiting the separation of husbands and wives, and especially children and parents, it is within our chancery jurisdiction, and usually acted on by our chancellors, in the sales of slaves made by their decrees, to provide against the separation of these connections, particularly that of mothers from young children.

It may be also observed, as showing the *animus* of our people, that cases of *cruelty* in the treatment of slaves, never fail to carry with them, when once distinctly defined, the *loss of caste*, with respectable society.

The *Negro Law* of Georgia in the language of its legislators and judges.

Extracts from the Constitution and Laws in reference to Slaves.

I. The Constitution protects the life and members of the slave.

Art. 4, § 12. The Constitution declares: "Any person who shall maliciously dismember or deprive a slave of life, shall suffer such punishment as would be inflicted in case the like offense had been committed on a free white person, and on the like proof, except in the case of insurrection by such slave, and unless such death should happen by accident in giving such slave moderate correction." To the same effect is the act of 1799.

II. The Penal Code protects the slave from cruel treatment.

1. By strangers. "Any person, except the owner, overseer, or employer of a slave, who shall beat, whip, or wound such slave; or any person who shall beat, whip, or wound a free person of color, without sufficient cause or provocation being

first given by such slave or free person of color; such person so offending may be indicted for a misdemeanor, and on conviction shall be punished by fine or imprisonment in the common jail of the county, or both, at the discretion of the court; and the owner of such slave, or guardian of such free person of color, may, notwithstanding such conviction, recover, in a civil suit, damages for the injury done to such slave or free person of color."

2. By owners, employers, etc. "Any owner or employer of a slave or slaves, who shall cruelly treat such slave or slaves, by unnecessary and excessive whipping; by withholding proper food and sustenance; by requiring greater labor from such slave or slaves than he, she, or they are able to perform; or by not affording proper clothing, whereby the health of such slave or slaves may be injured and impaired—or cause or permit the same to be done; any such owner or employer shall be guilty of a misdemeanor, and on conviction shall be punished by fine or imprisonment in the common jail of the county, or both, at the discretion of the court."

3. Against Sabbath labor. The Act of 1770 declares: "If any person shall, on the Lord's day, commonly called Sunday, employ any slave in any work or labor, (work of absolute necessity, and the necessary occupations of the family only excepted,) every person so offending shall forfeit and pay the sum of ten shillings for every slave he, she, or they shall so cause to work or labor."

4. Their impartial trial under charge of capital offenses provided for. "Slaves and free persons of color are, in cases of charge for committing capital offenses, to be tried before the superior court *as white persons are*, and the trial shall proceed to rendition of verdict in conformity with the provisions of the Penal Code of the State," etc.

5. Protection against temptations to drunkenness, etc. By the Penal Code of the State it is made an offense, punishable by fine of not less than ten nor more than fifty dollars, (for the

first offense,) and, on a second conviction, by fine and imprisonment in the common jail at the discretion of the court, to furnish a slave or free person of color with intoxicating liquor, except as medicine furnished by the owner, overseer, or employer of a slave, etc. (Cobb's Digest, 827.)

6. Legal sympathy with him *as a man.* "The laws of Georgia at this moment recognize the negro as a man, whilst they hold him as property. They enforce obedience in the slave, but they require justice and moderation in the master. They protect his life from homicide, his limbs from mutilation, and his body from cruel and unnecessary scourging. They yield him the right to food and raiment, to kind attentions when sick, and to maintenance in old age; and public sentiment, in conformity with indispensable legal restraints, extends to the slave the benefits and blessings of religion."

The Chief-Justice of the Court of Errors, whose sentiments are expressed above, seems to entertain the conviction that this benign consideration of the claims of the slave, especially the establishment of the doctrine that *the killing of a slave is murder*, is rather the result of *Southern statute* than of common law. He considers the fact of statutory legislation declaring that such killing shall be murder, in connection with the fact that the judicial history of the State furnishes no evidence of a man's being tried for the murder of a slave prior to the passage of the statute; and especially the tenor of the preamble of the statute, as contributing to furnish conclusive evidence of such an opinion.

"Whereas, from the increasing number of slaves in this province, it is necessary as well to make proper regulations for the future ordering and governing of such slaves, and to ascertain and prescribe the punishment of crimes by them committed, *as to settle and limit by positive laws, the extent of the power of the owners of such slaves over them, so that they may be kept in due subjection and obedience, and owners and persons having the care and management of such slaves, may be re-*

strained from exercising unnecessary rigor or wanton cruelty over them, be it enacted," etc.

The preamble to the section which creates the offense, recites as follows:

"Whereas, cruelty is not only highly unbecoming those who profess themselves Christians, but is odious in the eyes of all men who have any sense of virtue or humanity, therefore to restrain and prevent barbarity being exercised towards slaves, be it enacted, etc.

"Now we say that it is clear from these recitals, that before the act of 1770, cruelties and barbarities were exercised, and that there was no restraint upon the power of the master by law, over his slaves. No other inference is possible." (Georg. Reports, vol. 9, p. 582–4.)

The *Negro Law* of SOUTH-CAROLINA was collected and digested by *John Belton O'Neal*, one of the Judges of the Court of Law and Errors of said State, under a resolution of the State Agricultural Society, read before them at their semi-annual meeting at Spartanburgh, in 1848, and by them directed to be submitted to the Governor, with a request that he would lay it before the Legislature at its next session.

The extracts presented are, of course, in the language of Judge O'Neal, a gentleman well worthy of the high offices which he holds in Church and State.

CHAP. I.—STATUS OF THE NEGRO—*His Rights and Disabilities.*

§§ 1 and 2. Color (black) is *prima facie* evidence that the party is a slave. The offspring to follow the condition of the mother.

§ 6. When the mulatto ceases, and a party bearing some slight taint of African blood ranks as white, is a question for the solution of a jury.

§ 8. No specific rule as to the quantity of negro blood which will compel a jury to find one to be mulatto, has ever been adopted. Between one fourth and one eighth seems fairly to be debatable ground. When the blood is reduced to or below one eighth, the jury ought always to find the party *white.* When the blood is one fourth or more African, the jury must find the party *mulatto.*

§ 22. Under the Act of 1740, 1st section, 1st proviso, and the Act of 1799, it is provided, if any negro, mulatto, or *mestizo* (the offspring of white and Indian parents) shall claim his or her freedom, he may, on application to the clerk of common pleas of the district, have a guardian appointed who is authorized to bring an action of trespass, in the nature of ravishment of ward, against any person, claiming property in the said negro, mulatto, or mestizo, or having possession of the same; in which action the general issue may be pleaded, and the special circumstances given in evidence; and upon a general or special verdict found, judgment shall be given according to the very right of the case without any regard to defects in the proceedings in form or substance. In such case if the verdict be that the ward of the plaintiff is free, a special entry shall be made declaring him to be free, and the jury is authorized to assess damages which the plaintiff's ward may have sustained, and the court is directed to give judgment and award execution for the damages and cost.

§ 26. Proof that a negro has been suffered to live in a community for years as a free man, is *prima facie* proof of freedom.

§ 27. A negro at large without an owner for twenty years —presumed to be free.

§ 29. Any thing which shows that the owner had deliberately parted with his property—enough to establish freedom.

§ 30. The validity of freedom depends upon the law of the place where it begins. Hence when slaves have been manumitted in other States, and are found in this State, their freedom here will depend upon the validity of the manumission at the place whence they came.

§ 35. A slave illegally emancipated was free as against the owner, under the Act of 1800.

§ 45. Free negroes, mulattoes, and mestizos are entitled to all the rights of property, and protection in their persons and property by action or indictment, which the *white* inhabitants of this State are entitled to.

§ 47. They may contract or be contracted with. Their marriages with one another, and even with *white* people, *are legal.* They may purchase, hold, and transmit, by descent, *real* estate.

§ 48. They are entitled to protect their persons by action, indictment, and the writ of habeas corpus.

§ 49. Decided in the court of appeals that insolence, on the part of a free negro, would not excuse an assault and battery.

CHAP. II.—SLAVES.—*Their civil rights, liabilities and disabilities.*

§ 11, Act 1740. Although slaves are declared to be *chattels personal*, yet they are also in our law considered as *persons*, with many rights and liabilities, civil and criminal.

§ 13. The right of protection which would belong to a slave, as a human being, is, by the law of slaves, transferred to the master.

§ 14. A master may protect the person of his slave from injury by repelling force with force, or by action, and in some cases by indictment.

§ 15. By the Act of 1821, the *murder* of a slave is declared to be *a felony without benefit of clergy.*

§ 16. To constitute the murder of a slave no other ingredients are necessary than such as enter into the offense of murder at common law. So the killing on sudden heat and passion is the same as manslaughter, and a finding by the jury on an indictment for the murder of a slave of a killing on sudden heat and passion, is good, and subjects the offender to the punishment of the Act.

§ 17. An attempt to kill and murder a slave—indictable as an assault, with an intent to kill and murder.

§ 18. By the Act of 1841 the unlawful whipping or beating of any slave—subjects the offender to imprisonment, not exceeding six months, and fine not exceeding $500.

§ 19. What is sufficient provocation by word or deed is a question for the jury. The question is, whether, as slave-owners and reasonable men, if they had been in the place of the defendant, they would have inflicted the whipping or beating which the defendant did.

§ 20. The Acts of 1821 and 1841 are eminently wise, just, and humane. They protect slaves who dare not raise their own hands in defense against brutal violence. They teach men who are wholly irresponsible in property to keep their hands off the property of other people. They have wiped away a shameful reproach upon us that we were indifferent to the lives and persons of our slaves. They have had, too, a most happy effect on slaves themselves. They know now that the shield of the law is over them.

§ 23. When a slave has suffered in life or limb, or has been cruelly beaten or abused, when no white person was present, or, being present, shall neglect or refuse to give evidence, *in every such case the owner or person having the care or management of the slaves, and in whose possession or power the slaves* shall be, shall be *adjudged guilty* unless he can make the contrary appear by good and sufficient evidence.

§ 25. Requires the owners of slaves to provide them with sufficient clothing, covering, and food; and if they shall fail to do so, the owners respectively are declared to be liable to be informed against to the next nearest justice of the peace, who is authorized to hear and determine the complaint; and if found to be true, *or in the absence of proof*, if the owner *will not exculpate himself by his own oath*, the magistrate may make such order as will give relief, and may set a fine not exceeding £20 current money on the owner, to be levied by warrant of distress and sale of the offender's goods.

Says the Judge: this provision (leaving out the exculpatory

part) is a very wise and humane one, except that the penalty is evidently too slight.

§ 27. It is the settled law of this State that no owner can abandon a slave needing either medical treatment, care, food, or raiment. If he does, he will be liable to any one who may furnish the same. In the language of *Judge Wilds*, an eminent Christian and patriot: "The law would infer a contract against the evidence of the fact, to compel a cruel and capricious person to discharge that duty which he ought to have performed voluntarily. For as the master is bound by the most solemn obligation to protect his slave from suffering, he is bound by the same obligation to defray the expenses or services of another to preserve the life of his slave, or relieve the slave from harm and danger. The slave lives for his master's service. His time, his labor, his comforts, are all at his master's disposal. The duty of humane treatment and medical assistance ought not to be withholden."

§ 28. Slaves are protected from labor on the Sabbath-day. The violation of the law in this respect subjects the offender to £5 for every slave so worked; and the 29th Section to a fine of £20 for every offense of working them longer on week-days than the law allows.

§ 31. A slave may, by the consent of his master, acquire and hold personal property.

§ 41. By the Act of 1834, slaves are prohibited to be taught to read and write. This act grew out of a feverish state of excitement produced by the impudent intermeddling of persons out of the Slave States, with our peculiar institutions. That has, however, subsided, and I trust we are now prepared to act the part of wise, humane, and fearless masters, and *that this law and all of kindred character will be repealed.* When we reflect as Christians, how can we justify it that a slave is not to be permitted to read the Bible? It is in vain to say there is danger in it. The best slaves in the State are those who can and do read the Scriptures. Again, who is it that teach our slaves to read? It is generally done by the children of the owners.

Who would tolerate an indictment against his son or daughter for teaching a favorite servant to read? Such laws look to me as rather cowardly. It seems as if we were afraid of our slaves. Such a feeling is unworthy of a master.

CHAP. III.—CRIMES.—*Trial and Punishment.*

§ 1. When a slave commits a crime by the command and coërcion of the master, mistress, employer, or overseer, it is regarded as the crime of the master, mistress, employer, or overseer, and the slave is not criminally answerable.

§ 8. The slave may strike in defense of the person or property of his master or employer, and the master in defense of his slave.

§ 23. In all parts of the State, slaves or free persons of color are to be tried for all offenses by *a magistrate and five freeholders. Eight* to be summoned, of whom the slave or his master may select five, and upon good cause shown against any freeholder, another shall be substituted in his place. The jurors to be sworn. The slave must be provided with an advocate by the magistrate, if necessary. Right of new trial, etc. —always time to obtain pardon before the infliction of the sentence.

§ 34. A slave can not be twice tried for the same offense.

§ 39. Duty of the master of the work-house, jailor, or sheriff *to provide sufficient food, drink, clothing, and covering* for all runaways delivered into their custody.

The Judge comments upon many laws upon the statute-book which are no longer enforced, as a dishonor, and should be repealed, and suggests many liberal alterations.

Touching the *constant liability to a change* of owners, he remarks: "This continual change of the relation of master and slave, with the consequent rending of family ties among them, has induced me to think, that if by law they were annexed to the freeholds of the owners, and when sold for partition among distributees, tenants in common, joint tenants, and co-parce-ners, they should be sold with the freehold and not otherwise; it might be a wise and wholesome change of the law. Some provision too might be made which would prevent in a great degree sales for debt. A debtor's lands and slaves instead of being *sold*, might be *sequestered*, until like *vivum vadaum* they would pay all his debts on execution by the accrued profits."

Against the late ANTI-*Emancipation* laws, he says: "My experience as a man and a judge leads me to condemn the laws of 1820 and 1841. They have done more harm than good, and caused evasions without number. They ought to be repealed, and the law of 1800 restored. The State has nothing to fear from emancipation as that law directs. Many a master knows he has a slave or slaves for whom he *feels it to be his duty to provide.* As the law now stands, that can not be done. In a slave country the *good should be especially rewarded.* Who are judges of this but the master? Give him the power of emancipation, under well regulated guards, and he can dispense *the duty which both he and his slave appreciate.* In the present state of the world it is especially our duty and that of slave-owners *to be just and merciful, and in all things* to be *exceptione majori.* With well regulated and mercifully applied slave laws we have nothing to fear for negro slavery. But let me assure my countrymen and fellow-slaveholders, *that unjust laws or unmerciful management of slaves fall upon us and our institutions with more cutting effect than any thing else.* I would see Carolina, *the friend, master, and mistress of all her people, free and slave—to all, extending justice and mercy.* As against our enemies I would say, *be just and fear not.*"

Concerning those State laws which prohibited religious meetings of slaves without the presence of one or more whites, the Judge says: "They are treated now as dead letters, and ought to be repealed. They operate as a reproach upon us, in the mouths of our enemies, in that we do not afford our slaves that free worship of God, which he demands for all his people. This was *never intended.*"

The law which forbade slaves to own "horses, mares, cattle, sheep, boats, canoes, or peryaugers," is obsolete. "Certainly," says the Judge, "no legislator *now* would venture to say to a master, You shall not allow your slave to have a *canoe* to fish with, or to carry vegetables to market, or that he should not be allowed to have a *horse* to attend to his duties as a stock-minder in swamps, or that a family of slaves should not have a *cow* to furnish them milk, or a *hog* to make them meat beyond their usual allowance. Experience and observation fully satisfy me that the *first law of slavery is that of kindness from the master to the slave.* With this properly inculcated, enforced by laws, and judiciously applied, slavery becomes a family relation next in attachment to that of parent and child. It leads to influences of devotion on the part of the slave which would do honor to the heroism of Rome itself."

In February, 1812, Professor Charles Dewar Simmons, on his return from Columbia to Charleston, found the Haughabock swamp entirely overflowing the road. In attempting to cross on horseback he was washed off the road and separated from his horse. He first succeeded in reaching a tree; then constructed a raft of rails tied with his comfort. Three times his slave Marcus swam in to his rescue. His master cried out to him: "You can not help me; save yourself." But Marcus persisted in efforts to save his master until they perished together.

(Traveling a few years since by stage, in Alabama, my attention was directed to a plain looking man conversing by the way-side with a woman of color. Then followed this narration. The white man was the owner of a very excellent and valuable servant, the husband of the woman with whom he was conversing. He was a skillful artist, the builder of all the fine public bridges in that portion of the State. The master commenced to dissipate, and of course to lose his fortune. He loved his slave, and fearing that he might be taken for debt, persuaded the Legislature to bestow upon him the privileges of a freeman. He increased in property as his master declined.

Ere long he testified his attachment to his master by relieving a mortgage upon his estate to the amount of two or three thousand dollars. No very long time elapsed before the freed man advanced and paid down a much larger sum in relief of the master's growing embarrassments. Whereupon a neighbor says to the servant: "Jack, you fool! Why don't you take a mortgage on your master's property yourself?" "Oh!" responds the noble-hearted man: "I *would not like to treat master so.*" Surrender all his fortune rather than subject a kind master to the humiliation of suffering a sense of legal dependence upon one who was once his slave.)

This glance at the slave laws of four States, un-selected—two in the Northern and two in the Southern portion of the territory of the South, will give us a fair view of the fair side of Southern slave legislation.

Chap. II.—Northern Slave Law.

Let us now direct our attention to another aspect of this subject, and observe how naturally our slaveholding fathers of the North fell into the very same class of *apparently cruel legislation*, which *in the South* the Anti-Slavery spirit of this day would fain represent as a series of barbarities unparalleled and insufferable.

What estimate shall we form of the love of freedom, the genuine liberty-spirit of our forefathers? Great efforts are made, very naturally, to exalt the character of our Northern ancestors in this respect. After all, it must be confessed that their spirit of liberty makes a very ambiguous demonstration both in the history and in the enactments of their early days.

I. *History.* In 1641, Massachusetts held the doctrine, distinctly in her statute laws, "that *lawful captives*" "taken in *just wars*," were "*rightfully reduced* to *bond-slavery*." (See Ancient Charters, and Colony and Provincial Laws of Mass., ch. xii.) She practised upon this doctrine and made slaves of the Indians. And so did the other New-England States. At the close of the great Indian war in Connecticut, in 1676, Council met at Hartford to decide what should be done with the many prisoners on hand and with the many others who had surrendered themselves. They sent for *Uncas*, a friendly chief, and said: "The war was the English's, and the benefit should be theirs." To this Uncas cheerfully consented, acknowledging "that all the prisoners and surrenderers were theirs to dispose of at will." The Council ordered "that the right and division of the captives be left to the decision and determination of (three men) who are to dispose of the said captives, whether they be in the hands of the Pequods, Mihoags, or Naragansetts, to such persons to whom they of right do belong, according as the claimers shall make demands." (Trumb. Col. Rec., 473.)

Like Africa, New-England shipped her prisoners to become slaves in foreign lands. At the close of the fight of the Great Swamp, July 13, 1637, between the Pequod Indians and the Connecticut and Massachusetts troops, it is said "that the Pequod women and children, who had been captivated, were divided among the troops. Some were carried to Connecticut; others to Massachusetts. *The people of Massachusetts sent a number of the women and boys to the West-Indies and sold them for slaves.*" (Trumbull's Con., vol. i., 85.)

Where were their sisters, husbands, and fathers? New-England had no great conscience against *dividing families* when she held slaves. No *Southern* master ever separated them so hopelessly. But New-England traveled much farther than this in the violation of the liberty-principle of the present day, and probably farther than any Christian nation ever trespassed. Parties who were not "*lawful captives* in just wars"—and who probably had never been condemned after regular trial by a high court—by statutory regulation, Connecticut allowed to be seized and transported to foreign parts to be disposed of as slaves in exchange for slaves. The Indians, a little restive under the discipline of the justice and freedom which New England slave-laws administered, very naturally became troublesome, and retaliated. Thereupon the Connecticut statute ran thus: "As it will be chargeable to keep Indians in prison, and if they should escape they are likely to bear more malice, it was thought fit that the magistrates of the jurisdiction *deliver up the Indians seized to the party or parties endamaged, either to serve or to be shipped out and exchanged for neagers,* as the case will justly bear." (Trumbull's Col. Rec., 532.)

In one law here is *slave-making*, *slave-exporting*, and *slave-importing*, and hopeless family rupture.

In 1764, certain merchants of Boston addressed to the General Assembly of Connecticut an elaborate document, whose "*sixth*" point the State librarian has been kind enough to put in my possession. It objects to "the *destruction of the fishery*" that it will prejudice the whole trade of the Province. Amongst others, one branch of this trade is represented as of great importance. The Northern colonies supply *Surinam* and the other Dutch settlements almost wholly with all manner of provisions, "for which we receive *molasses* in return; this is distilled into *rum*," and devoted to three uses—"for the fishery—to export to the Southern colonies—*and to Africa, to purchase slaves for our own islands in the West-Indies.*"

Thus New-England not only imported and exported, but *transported* slaves, and this sometimes by distributing an article almost as contraband in our day as slavery itself.

It is true, she made loud protestations of her abhorrence of the crime.

In 1646, the General Court of Massachusetts conceiving themselves bound by the first opportunity to bear witness against the heinous and crying sin of manstealing, etc., "do provide for the release of certain negroes *unlawfully* taken" and for their return "at the charge of the country," to their native region of Guinea, and a letter with them "of the indignation of the court themselves." (Ancient Charters, etc., ch. xii.)

And yet, long after this, in 1708, The same General Court enact that a duty of four pounds per head shall be paid for "every negro or negroes" hereafter imported. But if any negro so imported shall be again exported within twelve months, the whole duty is to be returned. And the like drawback is allowed the purchaser in case any negro sold him die within six months after importation. (Ibid., Appendix, ch. xix.)

These two extremes, *Anti-slavery* and *Pro-slavery*, are brought together, in 1641, by a Massachusetts statute as violently suicidal as was ever recorded by a law-making body. It runs thus: "It is ordered by this court and the authority thereof, that there shall never be any bond-slavery, villanage, or captivity amongst us—(Had the Legislature stopped here, the anti-slavery type of the law would not have been objected to by the extremest abolitionist; and what pro-slavery man at the South is not as well suited by the residue of the very same sentence of the very same law?)—*unless it be lawful captives taken in just wars*, or *such strangers as sell themselves to us*, or *are sold to us: provided, this exempts none from servitude who shall be judged thereto by authority.*" (Ancient Charters, ch. xii.) Surely liberty neither thought nor breathed in Massachusetts on the day when its assembled intelligence and authority commanded that there should be no slavery amongst us, unless it be in one way or in another.

How it must shock the ultra liberty spirit of the day to call to mind a certain officer constituted by ancient society. "Every city, town, or manor may appoint" a Common Whipper; who "shall receive a salary, not to exceed three shillings per head, for each slave whipped." (Laws of New-York, 1691.)

II. The liberty spirit of our Northern ancestors is yet more seriously implicated by all manner of *special enactments.*

What possible aspect of *Liberty* in the eye of the strongest Reformer did not the pro-slavery laws of the North violently impugn?

1. The right of a *free nature.*

The laws of Massachusetts, Connecticut, Rhode Island, New-York, New-Jersey, etc., assume the fact that the complexion of a negro or a mulatto is *prima facie* evidence that the party is a slave.

2. The strongest conviction of man's right to the freedom of his nature, a Reformer would express in this language: No man has a right to make "a *chattel*" of his fellow-man. The strongest right of property in man which I remember to have encountered, was enacted or conceded by the slave legislation of the North. In all free governments, when no offense has been committed, private property can not be taken for public uses without *due compensation.* It is probably quite as universal, that all title to property is destroyed, when that property is demanded by government for violation of law. In the case of *fines* inflicted for offenses committed, of articles forfeited by the violation of revenue or other laws, of estates, in revolutionary times, confiscated for treason, etc., etc., the law destroys all right of property in chattels thus demanded by government. But in early times, when violation of law demanded the life of the slave, the *chattel property* of the master survived, and the law itself acknowledged that it could not destroy it. The Act of the Assembly of New-Jersey passed in 1704, required that "The owner of every man-slave executed should receive £30; and for every woman slave, £20."

3. The right of *free birth.*

By a New-York law passed April, 1691, it was declared that "Every child born of a slave mother shall follow the state and condition of the mother!" Such was the law of Connecticut, Rhode Island, and most if not all the Northern States at one time.

4. The right to *choose one's residence.*

No person, being an African or negro (other than a subject of the Emperor of Morocco, or a citizen of some one of the United States) shall tarry within this Commonwealth for a longer term than two months. "If he do so, he is to be imprisoned in the house of correction, and kept at hard labor till next session of the peace, when, if *convicted of the offense*, he shall be whipped, not exceeding ten stripes, and ordered to depart out of the Commonwealth within ten days; if he does not, the same course to be pursued *toties quoties*." (1788. Laws of Mass., vol. 1.)

Thus, if a human being having any other than a white complexion, should dare to seek a home on the free soil of Massachusetts, he shall be forthwith imprisoned, worked hard, whipped, and ordered off. Should he refuse to go, he is to be imprisoned, worked hard, and whipped until he submits to ignominious banishment.

5. The right of *locomotion*.

"Every slave found out of the town, or place where he resides, shall be deemed a runaway, and any person inhabiting the State is empowered to seize and secure him, carry him before a justice, who shall order him to be whipped." "Any free negro found without a pass, may be taken up by any one, carried before a justice, and compelled to pay all charges." (Laws of Conn., passed during the Confederation.)

"If a slave be found from home after nine o'clock in the evening, any free person may seize him or her, bring them before a justice, and he shall sentence them to be whipped on the naked body." (Ibid.)

Whereas great disorders are oftentimes raised in the night-time by Indians, negroes, and mulattoes, servants, slaves, etc., it is provided that none of these shall be abroad after nine o'clock at night, unless upon some errand for their masters; otherwise they are to be arrested and subjected to the discipline of the house of correction. (Mass. Ancient Charters, App., ch. xvi. 3.)

Any person finding a slave five miles from home without a written passport, is authorized to take up the slave, and whip him or her; or order the whipping on the bare back, not exceeding twenty lashes, and shall have for his reward five shillings for every one taken up as aforesaid, with reasonable charge for carrying them to their homes, to be recovered of the owner as any other debt. (Laws New-Jersey, 1704.)

If a slave belonging to one province goes into another without a passport, any free person is empowered to take him or her up, carry them to the nearest constable, and have him or her whipped on the bare back, not exceeding twenty lashes. The person so taking them up, shall have for reward ten shillings in money for each slave, the constable three shillings for whipping each, to be paid by the owner, the slave retained in prison until all reasonable charges are paid. (Ibid.)

If a ferryman carry a slave who has no passport, he may be fined twenty shillings for the first offense, and forty shillings ever after for each offense. (Conn. Conf.)

6. The right of *personal security.*

Hereafter it shall and may be lawful for any master or mistress, to punish his, her, or their slaves, *at discretion*, for crimes and offenses, not extending to life or limb. (New-York, 1730.)

7. The right of *self-defense.*

Every negro, Indian, or other slave, that shall be found guilty of talking impudently to any Christian, shall suffer so many stripes, at some public place, as the justice of the peace in such place shall think fit, not exceeding forty, every law, custom, or usage, to the contrary notwithstanding. (New-York, 1691.)

Should a slave presume to assault or strike a free man or a woman, professing Christianity, a justice of the peace may direct such corporal punishment as he may think meet or reasonable, not extending to life or limb. (New-York, Ibid.)

If a slave presume to strike a free man or woman, any two justices of the peace may authorize such corporal punishment as they may see meet, not extended to life or limb. (Laws of New-Jersey, 1704.)

If any negro or mulatto shall presume to smite or strike any Christian, he shall be severely whipped. (Mass., 1705.)

If a slave shall *conspire* to kill or murder, he shall suffer the pain of death, in such manner as the aggravation or enormity of the crime, in the judgment of the justice, shall merit or require. (New-Jersey, 1704.)

What a malignant, unguarded law! The slave does not perpetrate murder; he simply conspires against the life of his master. The statute seems to feel that *hanging* is too good for him. What power to oppress is put into the hands of a passionate or cruel justice! The slave must die any horrid death that one man, the very lowest officer of the State, may choose to inflict. (Compare Southern Laws.)

8. The right to *transact business.*

No person shall trade or traffic with a slave without consent of the owner, on pain of forfeiting treble the value of the thing traded for, and the sum of £5 with costs, and the contract shall be utterly void. (New-York, 1691.)

Any free person who shall presume to trade with a slave, shall return whatever he receives, and forfeit and pay double the value over and above; and if the person so offending be unable or shall neglect to make restoration, he shall be publicly whipped as the court may order. (Conn. Confederation.)

9. The right of *equality.*

Northern laws violated this right in every possible form.

Civil equality. They denied to the man of color all the franchises of citizenship. They were neither permitted to vote nor to hold any post of honor, profit, or trust.

Military equality. In 1707, Massachusetts passed an act for the regulation of free negroes, etc., which ran thus: "Whereas, in the several towns, (etc.,) within this province there are several free negroes and mulattoes, able of body and fit to labor, who *are not charged with training*, watching, and other services required by her Majesty's subjects, whereof they have share in the benefits, it is provided that they shall do service equivalent, in *repairing highways*, *cleaning streets*, and the like, and they are to pay five shillings per day for neglect.

In case of alarm, they are to appear at the parade of the military, and do such service as was required by the first commissioned officer, on pain of forfeiting twenty shillings, or doing eight days' work as aforesaid.

If they can not pay fines as aforesaid, or shall not perform labor as aforesaid—shall be sent to the house of correction, receive its discipline, and work double the number of days assigned, or at the rate of one day for every shilling in the fine. (Mass. Charter, ch. xcvi.)

Penal equality. For tumultuous and disorderly conduct when the white man *was fined*—imprisoned, "if the offender shall be a negro servant, in lieu of imprisonment he may be whipped." The same discrimination for similar offenses. (Temporal Acts, Boston, Ed. 1773.)

By the law of New-York, 1788, where the white man was fined £5, the free negro was compelled to pay £10 for the same offense.

By a Massachusetts law, 1698, the Indian, mulatto, or negro, who trafficked in stolen goods, "shall be whipped not exceeding twenty lashes, and also be prosecuted for theft."

This law would seem to reverse the order of justice. First *punish* and then *try*.

Testifying equality. No slave shall be admitted as a witness, except in criminal cases against each other. (New-York, 1788.)

Equality of *indulgence.* No person who is or shall be licensed to be an innholder, shall suffer any apprentice, servant, or negro to sit drinking in his or her house, or to have any manner of drink there without leave of the master. (Laws of Mass. for 1692–1751, p. 94.)

Social equality. No more than *three* slaves shall meet for any purpose except for servile labor, upon the penalty of forty stripes on the naked back. (New-York, 1691.) This statute would seem to interdict amongst blacks social worship and school-teaching.

Christian equality. Massachusetts passed a law in 1705, in which such language as this is found: "If a negro or mulatto commit fornication with a Christian woman," etc. Again: "If a Christian commit fornication with a negro or mulatto woman," etc. Again: "No Christian within this province shall contract marriage with any negro or mulatto." This statute not only assumes that negroes and mulattoes are slaves, but seems to regard them as pagans, especially by alluding to the whites as "*the English or other Christian* nation."

10. The right of *extending sympathy and aid to the oppressed.*

If any person entertain or tolerate any slave in his house after nine o'clock in the evening, he shall pay ten shillings for the first offense; and whatever increase or addition a justice of the peace may think proper ever after. (Conn. Confederation.)

Any person concealing any slave shall forfeit forty shillings for every time so concealed or entertained; and if any person whatsoever shall be found guilty of harboring, entertaining, or concealing any slave, or assisting to convey them away, if such slave shall happen to be lost, dead, or otherwise rendered unserviceable, such person harboring, concealing, or assisting shall be liable to pay the value of such slave to the owner. To be collected by action for debt. (New-Jersey, 1704.)

The New-York law almost verbatim. 1788.

In 1822. For concealing a slave, or assisting in his escape, New-York law inflicted a fine of $300, to be recovered by action of debt.

If any person shall conceal any negro or mulatto slave, or shall in any manner assist such slave in escaping from the lawful authority of his or her master, the person so offending shall forfeit and pay the sum of $300, to be recovered by action of debt. (Laws of Rhode Island, 1822.)

The New-York statute of 1788 went further still, and enacted: Any person knowing that a slave is or has been entertained or secreted by any other person, and does not make it known, shall forfeit two pounds. If he neglect to pay, or is unable to pay, he shall be imprisoned until he pays forty shillings and all costs. Harder legislation this than the Fugitive Slave Law.

11. Right of the master's *emancipation spirit to all legal encouragement.*

"Whereas great charge and inconvenience have arisen to divers towns and places by the releasing and setting at liberty mulatto and negro slaves;" it is provided, that no mulatto or negro slave shall be manumitted until sufficient security be given to the town treasurer that the same shall not become a town charge. And no slave shall be accounted free hereafter for whom such security shall not be given. (Mass. Charter, App., ch. xviii.)

Slaves set free to be maintained by the late owner. If he refuse, to be relieved by selectmen of the town, who shall recover the charge of the owner on execution. (Conn., 1718.)

By the law of New-Jersey, none to be manumitted unless security given for the payment of twenty pounds annually.

And be it further enacted, That if any shall bring into this State any slave or slaves, *with the intent that they may thereby become free*, or shall be aiding or abetting therein, he or she so offending shall forfeit the sum of $300 for each slave so brought, etc., to be recovered by action of debt. (Rhode Island, 1822.)

CONCLUSION.

In reviewing this rapid comparison of Northern and Southern legislation on the subject of slavery, a few reflections pre sent themselves.

1. To the credit of the North it should be heartily acknowledged that she has long since abolished the institution of slavery.

2. It should be allowed, too, that at the period of her exceptionable legislation and conduct upon this subject, the diffusion of Christian light upon associated topics was far less extensive than at present.

And yet in rigid justice, two things should not be forgotten.

1. It *detracts from the merit of her abolition of the institution* within her borders, that the North never was as extensively involved as was the South; nor was the pecuniary prosperity of the country ever so dependent upon the preservation of the institution as that of the South has been from the day of its introduction. These thoughts should have their weight, and with a good man will not fail of their influence. Had the appeal of slavery to covetousness been as strong and continuous at the North as at the South, had the labor of the slave from the beginning been every way *as profitable* in the Northern as in the Southern field, no man would dare to say that the *liberty-principle of the North* would have been *as prevalent* to-day in this latitude as it is. Had the South no more slaves to dispose of in earlier days than the North had, and no greater compensation for keeping them, no man can reasonably affirm that she would not have been to-day as decidedly Anti-Slavery as he could desire.

2. It detracts from the credit allowed for the comparative darkness of the period in which Northern legislation and agency affronted the spirit of liberty, that while the offenses of the North surpassed the offenses of the South, the *moral intelligence* of the North was equally *superior* to that of the South. I acknowledge myself unprepared to express a *confident judgment* upon the subject. I have no such extensive induction of facts before me as brings assurance to my own mind. From a partial and rapid survey of the field, the truth would seem to lie in the neighborhood of this statement. The transgressions of the South upon the subject of slavery are mainly limited to three points—reception, retention, and defective legislation and management. For aught known to me, the North have been the only, certainly the principal slave *importers* and slave *exporters*, and (from one foreign port to another) slave *transporters;* I may add, the principal, probably the only, *slave-makers*, *statutory justifiers of slave-making*, and practical abettors of

the doctrine of a *chattelism in man impregnable to the claim of government for violation of law.*

Surely a calm, candid comparison of Northern and Southern history and legislation upon the subject of slavery, should temper the Anti-Slavery asperities of the North. If when the North held slaves they felt themselves driven to preserve the peace of society by subjecting their inferiors to the discipline of a severe code of laws, though they had but few to molest them —they should look with more toleration upon their Southern neighbors, who are certainly managing a much larger number of them with a much more benign hand. If so long as slavery opened a door of profit to the North, she found, in conscience, a very feeble barrier against the largest kind of trading, and the severest kind of management, she should sometimes recall this fact when addressing her moral appeals to the South at a time when slaveholding has almost become the life of the land. If it took one Northern State, after the work was commenced, the space of sixty-four years to emancipate 3000 slaves, the North should not demand of the South that she free her 3,000,000 in a day. If the North exercised her own unmolested judgment and will as to the time and method of emancipating her own slaves, in her abundant dealing with the South, some little respect for the independence of her neighbor in the conduct of her own business should hardly be deemed out of place.

E.

Rev. E. J. Pierce, of the Gaboon Mission, in a letter to this country, says of the book entitled, The South-Side View of Slavery:

"Doubtless you hear from many with respect to this book, and from many parts of the country, and it may be from many parts of the world; but I venture to say, not from many parts of Africa. I think at times, my companion (Rev. J. Best) and myself, are ready to exclaim: *Would that all Africa were at the South.* Would that villages and tribes of these poor people could be induced to emigrate to our Southern country, and be placed under the influences *which the slaves enjoy.* My brother thinks that *he would sooner run the risk of a good or bad master, and be a slave at the South*, than to be as one of these heathen people. He refers, when he thus speaks, both to his *temporal* and eternal welfare.

"If the North and the South would only work together in love, and adopt the plan of colonizing this part of the country with free blacks from the North, and freed men from the South, for the colored man at home, how good it would be! *We must change our manner and tone with regard to the South*, and study ways to accomplish it. May the Lord make that book the instrument of doing much to effect this change!"—*New-York Observer*, *Feb.* 21, 1856.

A PRACTICAL TREATISE ON BUSINESS;

OR, HOW TO GET, SAVE, SPEND, GIVE, LEND, AND BEQUEATH MONEY

WITH AN INQUIRY INTO THE CHANCES OF SUCCESS AND CAUSES OF FAILURE IN BUSINESS.

BY EDWIN T. FREEDLY.

Also, Prize Essays, Statistics, Miscellanies, and numerous private letters from successful and distinguished business men.

12mo., cloth. Price One Dollar.

The object of this treatise is fourfold. First, the elevation of the business character, and to define clearly the limits within which it is not only proper but obligatory to get money. Secondly, to lay down the principles which must be observed to insure success, and what must be avoided to escape failure. Thirdly, to give the mode of management in certain prominent pursuits adopted by the most successful, from which men in all kinds of business may derive profitable hints. Fourthly, to afford a work of solid interest to those who read without expectation of pecuniary benefit.

TRUTHS ILLUSTRATED by GREAT AUTHORS.

A DICTIONARY OF OVER FOUR THOUSAND AIDS TO REFLECTION —QUOTATIONS OF MAXIMS, METAPHORS, COUNSELS, CAUTIONS, APHORISMS, PROVERBS, &c. &c., IN PROSE AND VERSE;

COMPILED FROM SHAKSPEARE, AND OTHER GREAT WRITERS, FROM THE EARLIEST AGES TO THE PRESENT TIME.

A new edition, with American additions and revisions.

ONE VOLUME, CROWN OCTAVO, VARIOUS BINDINGS.

The Footpath and Highway;

OR,

WANDERINGS OF AN AMERICAN IN GT. BRITAIN,

IN 1851 AND '52.

BY BENJAMIN MORAN.

This volume embodies the observations of the author, made during eight months' wanderings, as a correspondent for American Journals; and as he travelled much on foot, differs essentially from those on the same countries, by other writers. The habits, manners, customs, and condition of the people have been carefully noted, and his views of them are given in clear, bold language. His remarks take a wide range, and as he visited every county in England but three, there will be much in the work of a novel and instructive character.

One vol. 12mo. Price $1 25.

LIPPINCOTT'S
PRONOUNCING
GAZETTEER OF THE WORLD,
OR,
GEOGRAPHICAL DICTIONARY,

Comprising nearly **2200 Pages,** *including a greater amount of matter than any other single volume in the English Language; giving a description of nearly* **One Hundred Thousand Places,** *with the correct* **Pronunciation of their Names,** *being above 20,000 more Geographical Notices than are found in any other Gazetteer of the World.*

EDITED BY J. THOMAS, M. D., and T. BALDWIN,

Assisted by several other Gentlemen.

TESTIMONIALS.

From the Hon. Edward Everett.

"This work has been evidently prepared with great labor, and as far as I can judge, from the best materials and sources of information. . . . The principles adopted in ascertaining the pronunciation of proper names (as stated in the Introduction) appear to me correct. This is a matter attended with some difficulty and uncertainty, but it is treated with great ability, and in a very satisfactory manner, in your Introduction. I have no doubt your Gazetteer will be found an extremely useful work, well calculated to supply a want which must have been severely felt by almost every class of readers."

From J. E. Worcester, L.L.D., Author of Worcester's Critical Dictionary.

"Having made some examination of 'Lippincott's Pronouncing Gazetteer,' more particularly in relation to Pronunciation, I take pleasure in expressing a concurrence, generally, in what is said by the Hon. Edward Everett, of the value and excellence of the work. The difficult subject of the pronunciation of geographical names appears to me to have been attended to with great care, good taste, and sound judgment; and this feature of the Gazetteer must add greatly to its value."

From the Hon. Robert C. Winthrop.

"I know of no Gazetteer so complete and comprehensive. . . . I entirely concur with Mr. Everett in the opinion he has pronounced of the work, and sincerely hope that it may receive an amount of public patronage in some degree commensurate with the magnitude and costliness of the undertaking."

From Washington Irving.

"I fully concur with the opinions given by Mr. Everett and Mr. Winthrop of its merits, and with their wishes for its wide circulation."

From Prof. C. A. Goodrich, of Yale College, Editor of 'Revised Edition' of Webster's Dictionary.

"Your Pronouncing Gazetteer of the World appears, from the examination I have given it, to be a work of immense labor, very wisely directed. I consider it as of great importance to Teachers."

From the Hon. George Bancroft.

"I have formed a very high opinion of the merits of your Complete Pronouncing Gazetteer; especially for its comprehensiveness, compactness, and general accuracy. I wish you the success which you so richly deserve."

www.ingramcontent.com/pod-product-compliance
Lightning Source LLC
LaVergne TN
LVHW020234110826
845151LV00003B/919

9781425529765